The Rough G

The
Lake District

There are more than one hundred and fifty Rough Guide titles
covering destinations from Amsterdam to Zimbabwe

Forthcoming titles include
Argentina • Croatia • Ecuador • Southeast Asia

Rough Guide Reference Series
Classical Music • Country Music • Drum 'n' Bass • English Football
European Football • House • The Internet • Jazz • Music USA • Opera
Reggae • Rock Music • Techno • Unexplained Phenomena • World Music

Rough Guide Phrasebooks
Czech • Dutch • Egyptian Arabic • European Languages • French
German • Greek • Hindi & Urdu • Hungarian • Indonesian • Italian
Mandarin Chinese • Mexican Spanish • Polish • Portuguese • Russian
Spanish • Swahili • Thai • Turkish • Vietnamese

Rough Guides on the Internet
www.roughguides.com

Rough Guide Credits

Text Editor:	Judith Bamber
Series Editor:	Mark Ellingham
Editorial:	Martin Dunford, Jonathan Buckley, Jo Mead, Kate Berens, Ann-Marie Shaw, Paul Gray, Helena Smith, Orla Duane, Olivia Eccleshall, Ruth Blackmore, Sophie Martin, Geoff Howard, Claire Saunders, Gavin Thomas, Alexander Mark Rogers, Polly Thomas, Joe Staines, Lisa Nellis, Andrew Tomičić, Richard Lim, Claire Fogg, Duncan Clark, Peter Buckley (UK); Andrew Rosenberg, Mary Beth Maioli, Don Bapst, Stephen Timblin (US)
Online Editors:	Kelly Cross (US)
Production:	Susanne Hillen, Andy Hilliard, Link Hall, Helen Ostick, Julia Bovis, Michelle Draycott, Katie Pringle, Robert Evers, Niamh Hatton, Mike Hancock
Cartography:	Melissa Baker, Maxine Repath, Nichola Goodliffe, Ed Wright
Picture Research:	Louise Boulton, Sharon Martins
Finance:	John Fisher, Gary Singh, Edward Downey, Mark Hall, Tim Bill
Marketing & Publicity:	Richard Trillo, Niki Smith, David Wearn, Jemima Broadbridge, Chloë Roberts (UK); Jean-Marie Kelly, Myra Campolo, Simon Carloss (US)
Administration:	Tania Hummel, Charlotte Marriott, Demelza Dallow

To the memory of Dr Frederick A. Stephenson (1937–1998).

Acknowledgements

Jules Brown would like to thank the following for invaluable information, advice and assistance: Mark Murray for his essay on rock climbing; Allan King at the Cumbria Tourist Board, Emma Moody at Cumbria County Council, Mandy Monk and the Youth Hostels Association, Emma Dewhurst and Mike Ashton of the Lake District National Park Authority, Peter and Marian Elkington at Rydal Mount, Dave Yard at Dove Cottage, Vicky Slowe and Mike Humphreys at the Ruskin Museum, Tony Walker and the West Cumbria Tourism Initiative, Judy Johnson and the Furness Tourism Partnership.

Heartfelt thanks are also due to: Mark and Alison for sharing their knowledge about the Lakes and for getting me (eventually) across Striding Edge; mum and dad for road-testing and research; Greg who kept me company and showed me where the wild mouflon lie; Ian for coming walking when Burnley weren't playing; the patient staff at the various Lake District information offices; and Judith for her careful editing. Above all, this book couldn't have been finished without the love, support and dogged research skills of Katie.

The editor would like to thank Katie Pringle for typesetting and all the production team for keeping this project on track, Carole Mansur for proofreading, Melissa Baker and the Map Studio (Romsey, Hants) for cartography, and Jules for producing some great text and remaining dedicated to the project, even after moving halfway across the globe.

This first edition published May 2000 by Rough Guides Ltd, 62–70 Shorts Gardens, London WC2H 9AB.

Distributed by the Penguin Group:
Penguin Books Ltd, 27 Wrights Lane, London W8 5TZ.
Penguin Putnam Inc, 375 Hudson Street, New York, NY 10014, USA.
Penguin Books Australia Ltd, 487 Maroondah Highway, PO Box 257, Ringwood, Victoria 3134, Australia.
Penguin Books Canada Ltd, 10 Alcorn Avenue, Toronto, Ontario M4V 1E4, Canada.
Penguin Books (NZ) Ltd, 182–190 Wairau Road, Auckland 10, New Zealand.
Printed in England by Clays Ltd, St Ives PLC
Typography and original design by Jonathan Dear and The Crowd Roars.
Illustrations throughout by Edward Briant.

ISBN 1-85828-533-X

The Rough Guide to

The
Lake District

Written and researched by
Jules Brown

With additional contributions by
Kate Stephenson, Mark Murray and Jean Brown

ROUGH
GUIDES

Help us update

We've gone to a lot of trouble to ensure that this first edition of *The Rough Guide to The Lake District* is accurate and up-to-date. However, things inevitably change, and if you feel we've got it wrong or left something out, we'd like to know: any suggestions, comments or corrections would be much appreciated. We'll credit all contributions and send a copy of the next edition – or any other Rough Guide if you prefer – for the best correspondence.

Please mark letters "Rough Guide to Lake District update" and send to:
Rough Guides, 62–70 Shorts Gardens, London WC2H 9AB or
Rough Guides, 4th Floor, 345 Hudson St, New York, NY 10014.

Email should be sent to:
mail@roughguides.co.uk

Online updates about Rough Guide titles can be found on our Web site at *www.roughguides.com*

The Author

Jules Brown first visited the Lake District with his parents when he was nine years old; all he can remember is that it was raining. When he was fifteen he slept out in the fields and spent the youth hostel money his mum gave him on beer. And when he was 36 he got stuck up Jack's Rake. In between these memorable lakeland milestones, he has also written and researched Rough Guides to Scandinavia, Sicily, Hong Kong, Barcelona, Washington DC and England, and contributed as researcher and editor to many others.

Rough Guides

Travel Guides • Phrasebooks • Music and Reference Guides

We set out to do something different when the first Rough Guide was published in 1982. Mark Ellingham, just out of University, was travelling in Greece. He brought along the popular guides of the day, but found they were all lacking in some way. They were either strong on ruins and museums but went on for pages without mentioning a beach or taverna. Or they were so conscious of the need to save money that they lost sight of Greece's cultural and historical significance. Also, none of the books told him anything about Greece's contemporary life – its politics, its culture, its people, and how they lived.

So with no job in prospect, Mark decided to write his own guidebook, one which aimed to provide practical information that was second to none, detailing the best beaches and the hottest clubs and restaurants, while also giving hard-hitting accounts of every sight, both famous and obscure, and providing up-to-the-minute information on contemporary culture. It was a guide that encouraged independent travellers to find the best of Greece, and was a great success, getting shortlisted for the Thomas Cook travel guide award, and encouraging Mark, along with three friends, to expand the series.

The Rough Guide list grew rapidly and the letters flooded in, indicating a much broader readership than had been anticipated, but one which uniformly appreciated the Rough Guides' mix of practical detail and humour, irreverence and enthusiasm. Things haven't changed. The same four friends who began the series are still the caretakers of the Rough Guide mission today: to provide the most reliable, up-to-date and entertaining information to independent-minded travellers of all ages, on all budgets.

We now publish 150 titles and have offices in London and New York. The travel guides are written and researched by a dedicated team of more than 100 authors, based in Britain, Europe, the USA and Australia. We have also created a unique series of phrasebooks to accompany the travel series, along with the acclaimed series of music guides, and a best-selling pocket guide to the Internet and World Wide Web. We also publish comprehensive travel information on our Web site: *www.roughguides.com*

Contents

List of maps

MAP SYMBOLS

– – –	Chapter division boundary	▲	Mountain peak
▬▬	Motorway	⋏⋏	Hills/mountains
═══	Major road	⚓	Viewpoint
───	Minor road	⚲	Waterfall
- - - -	Path	⚘	Gardens
▬▬▬	Railway	★	Bus stop
— —	Ferry route	**P**	Parking
─────	Waterway	◉	Accommodation
⏝	Bridge	Ⓧ	Campsite
◆	General point of interest	ⓘ	Tourist office
♖	Castle	⊠	Post office
◓	Cave	▮	Building
♒	Stately home	⊞	Church
⚲	Church (regional maps)	†₊†	Cemetery
⌂	Abbey	░	National park
∴	Ruin		

Maps based upon Ordnance Survey mapping with the permission of The Controller of Her Majesty's Stationery Office, © Crown copyright, Licence No. 43361U

Introduction

The **Lake District** is England's most celebrated, most visited and most hyped scenic area. Tucked into a bulge between the industrial cities of northwest England and the Scottish borders, the small region is literally irresistible to the sixteen million visitors a year who pour in to experience its famous lakes, picturesque villages and alpine landscape. To many, the lure is of a misty-eyed English past – quiet country lanes, ivy-clad inns, agricultural shows and sheep-dog trials – while others seek to tick off English superlatives, including the country's largest and deepest lakes (Windermere and Wast Water respectively). As the Lake District also contains England's highest mountain (Scafell Pike), it should come as no surprise to find that the central lakeland crags – the birthplace of British rock climbing – lure climbers from far and wide. Meanwhile, keen hikers and Sunday strollers flow in year-round to conquer another peak or to follow in the footsteps of chroniclers from Wordsworth to Wainwright. Indeed, the sundry pastoral images could hardly be better known, whether bolstered by the siren words of the Lake Poets or embedded in the minds of the nation's children who grow up with the lakeland tales of Beatrix Potter, Arthur Ransome and John Cunliffe's *Postman Pat*.

There's no shortage, then, of attractions: sixteen major lakes, hundreds of steeply pitched mountains, scores of waterfalls and valleys, and a dozen major literary sites. Indeed, it's hard to think of a region in Britain with a similar breadth of scenery (wild fells to walled grazing land, glacial lakes to forested valleys) in such a small area. And although the Lake District might appear too popular for its own good, tourist numbers are concentrated in fairly specific areas. Even on the busiest of summer days, it's relatively easy to escape the crowds by climbing to the higher fells and more remote valleys. There are parts of the region, particularly in the north and west, where tourism is still decidedly low-key. Choose to come instead in the late autumn or winter – when magical crisp, clear days often enhance the natural backdrop – and even the most beaten paths and over-visited sights can be refreshingly uncluttered.

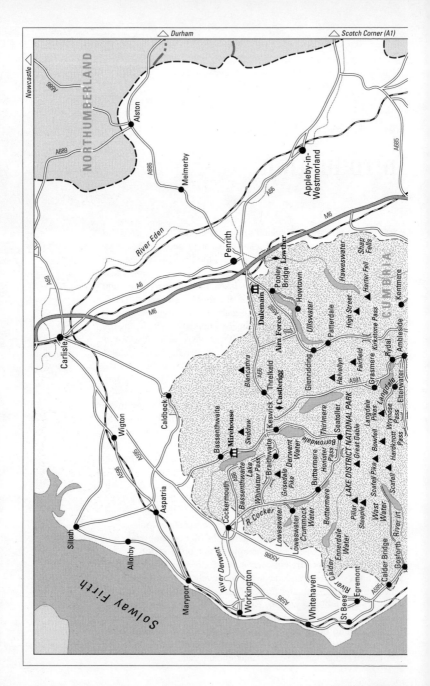

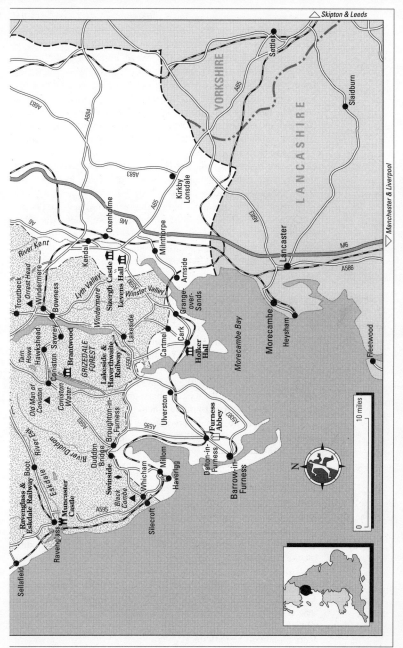

© Crown copyright

Not everyone sees the region through the same rose-tinted, lake-reflected, spectacles. The small-scale, parochial Englishness that attracts so many has repelled others. Aldous Huxley thought it to be "on the pettiest scale, miserably small and hole-and-cornery" (*Eyeless in Gaza*; 1936) and it's true that, on the world stage, the Lake District barely registers as a natural attraction (though it has been nominated as a World Heritage Site). Others berate the slavish attention many visitors give to knocking off compendious lists of lakeland peaks and routes with "every last insignificant feature labelled and smugly celebrated" (Ian McEwan, *Amsterdam*; 1988). There's an element of truth in this, though it's hardly a novel point of view – two centuries ago, Wordsworth was already making fun of those following the early guidebooks without actually looking at the scenery they were reading about.

Perhaps more to the point is that the reality of Lake District life and experience often falls short of the idealized image. The sheer number of visitors overwhelms the 40,000 or so locals and makes some of the most popular villages even busier than the cities the tourists have come from. Between Easter and the end of the summer school holidays, you can expect crowded streets, circling traffic looking for parking space, and bumper-to-bumper queues on country lanes that were never designed for motorized vehicles. Accommodation is often over-subscribed, while the most popular hiking trails have been turned into virtual motorways of hillside erosion. Locals, meanwhile, are confronted with a collapse of traditional industries, from mining to farming, which the relatively short tourist season goes only some way to replacing; while the demand for holiday homes deprives the region's future generations of affordable accommodation. It's a circle that's unlikely to be squared given the manifest attractions of the region to outsiders.

A word about the area covered by this book. Most of what people usually refer to as the Lake District – or simply the Lakes – lies within the **Lake District National Park**, established in 1951. At 880 square miles, it's England's largest national park, yet at a mere 30 miles across and easily reached off the M6 motorway it's hardly inaccessible – which partly explains its popularity. The National Park, in turn, falls entirely within the county of **Cumbria**, formed in 1974 from the historic counties of Cumberland and Westmorland, and the northern part of Lancashire. This book concentrates on the natural attractions, towns and villages **within the National Park**, including all the mountains and lakes and a short stretch of the Cumbrian coastline. Several important local towns – Kendal, Penrith, Cockermouth and Ulverston – and the religious foundations at Cartmel and Furness Abbey lie just outside the National Park boundary, and these are covered in a final chapter, recognizing that people's itineraries and interests don't just follow the somewhat arbitrary outline of the Park itself.

Where to go

Given its relatively small size, it's easy to see a great deal of the Lake District in just a few days, even if you are travelling by public transport or getting around on foot. The southern and central lakes and valleys get the most attention, as well as northern destinations such as Keswick, Derwent Water and Ullswater. Less visited (because they take more effort to reach) are the western lakes and valleys and the far northern reaches beyond Keswick. But determined hikers will be able to find quiet spots almost anywhere in the National Park. If you're pushed for time, you could tour around most of what's detailed below in a week, but you'd be doing precious little walking or relaxing. It's far better to pick a base and see what you can from there, hiking rather than driving between villages, and building in time for doing nothing more strenuous on occasion than taking out a rowboat or picnicking in a meadow.

Windermere is the largest lake with the most boating opportunities and features the National Park headquarters on its shores at **Brockhole**. The lake's towns – Windermere, Bowness and, especially, **Ambleside** – are among the region's busiest settlements and, given their choice of accommodation, cafés, restaurants and pubs, they make obvious bases. Even if they don't plan to stay there, most people at least pass by Windermere on the way to **Grasmere** and the famous Wordsworth houses of **Rydal Mount** and **Dove Cottage**, or to pretty **Hawkshead** and Beatrix Potter's house at **Hill Top**. Nearby **Coniston** is perhaps the least attractive of all the lakeland villages,

---

Lakeland Names and Terms

Many lakeland place-names, geographical features and dialect words have origins which go back to Norse, Saxon or even Celtic times. The list below should help you figure out exactly what you're looking at.

Beck	Stream	Mere	Lake
Blea	Cold blue colour	Nab	Promontory, projection
Cairn	Pile of stones	Pike	Peak
Dodd	Rounded foothill	Pitch	Steep ascent
Dub	River pool	Raise	Summit of a ridge, pile of stones
Fell	Hill, mountain, high common land		
		Rake	Natural rock passsage, a reach
Force	Waterfall		
Garth	Enclosed land or field	Rigg	Ridge
Ghyll, Gill	Narrow ravine, mountain stream	Scar, Scarth	Rock face, crag
		Scree	Bank or slope of loose stones
Hause	Summit of a pass		
Holme	Island	Spout	Waterfall
How, Howe	Rounded hill	Stickle	Sharp peak
Keld	Spring, well	Tarn	Small mountain lake
Knott	Rocky projection	Thwaite	Clearing
Lath	Barn	Wyke	Bay

---

but it sits at the head of engaging Coniston Water which boasts the big draw of **Brantwood**, home of the critic and essayist John Ruskin, and of **Grizedale Forest**. Away from the main settlements and literary trail, there are renowned hikes, peaks and tarns in central **Langdale**, or calm rural pockets in the gentler hills and dales south of Windermere and Coniston.

On the whole, the scenery is more dramatic in the north, where four peaks – **Scafell Pike**, **Scafell**, **Helvellyn** and **Skiddaw** – top out at over 3000 feet, and several other equally famous mountains (including **Great Gable** and **Blencathra**) don't lag far behind. There are, of course, literally hundreds of other mountains, crags and fells to roam, while the quite different lakes of **Derwent Water** and **Ullswater** provide superb backdrops for a day's cruising and walking. **Keswick**, the main town in the north, is the one major lakeland settlement with real year-round character, and it makes a handy base for exploring: south through the precipitous delights of **Borrowdale**, a valley for which the word picturesque might have been invented; west over the forested Whinlatter Pass; or north around the little-visted region known as **Back o' Skiddaw**.

The summer crowds tend to thin out in the western side of the Park. Although **Buttermere** and **Crummock Water** see a fair amount of traffic, **Wast Water**, **Ennerdale Water** and **Loweswater** lie further off the beaten track. The only part of the Cumbrian coastline that lies within the National Park stretches twenty miles south from **Ravenglass**, an undistinguished village, but one which provides a bucolic route into the heart of dramatic **Eskdale** by either road or rail. Outside the National Park, most visitors make time for **Kendal** and its excellent museums, and the historic market towns of **Ulverston**, **Penrith** and **Cockermouth**, the last also famous as the birthplace of Wordsworth. For a glimpse of the erstwhile religious influence on the Lakes, **Furness Abbey** and the priory church in the attractive village of **Cartmel**, both on the southern flanks of the National Park, also demand attention.

Those are the lakeland highlights, though each chapter introduction does a more detailed job of picking out local attractions and offbeat destinations. If hiking and the great outdoors isn't your bag, it's tempting to say that you're on the wrong holiday, though the Lake District does have a fair amount to satisfy other interests. The region's **literary connections** are justly famous, though you may be surprised to find that it's not all Wordsworth, Coleridge and De Quincey: writers and poets as diverse as Sir Hugh Walpole, Norman Nicholson and John Ruskin have left their mark on the Lakes. There's an **industrial history**, too, which manifests itself in scattered mining works, scarred quarry sites, surviving mills (one still working at Stott Park) and a couple of old railway lines – Ravenglass to Eskdale, and Lakeside to Haverthwaite – now converted to tourist use. The Lake District also has one of the country's highest concentrations of classic rural **pubs and inns,** many of them former coaching inns dating back several hundred years. Finally, in summer, the region hosts many of its annual **sports, festivals and events,** many recently revived in the face of tourist interest, but nonetheless providing a fascinating snapshot of traditional rural life.

When to go

High **summer** may be the warmest season – usually – but it isn't the ideal time to visit the Lakes. July and August can see accommodation (and the roads) stretched to capacity as the bulk of the annual visitors descend. Other busy periods include **Easter week** and the few days around **New Year,** when holiday cottage rentals can be hard to come by. April, May and October are better months to visit as the crowds are thinner, the main sights are still open and the high walks unlikely to be snowbound. Moreover, it generally rains less in May and June than other months, and stays light for up to an hour longer than in London in summer. If you're thinking of swimming in the lakes, it's worth knowing that late August and September see the waters at their warmest, as they've had time to soak up the summer sun. To be honest, though, you'll barely notice the difference: the inland waters are pretty cold, at best, year-round.

Spring usually arrives a little later than in the south of England, though in mild seasons you sometimes get the famous daffodils flowering as early as February. Mostly, though, before May you might get bright, blue days, but you can also expect chilly mornings, overnight frosts and cold conditions. The first serious frosts are back by October, though it's always worth coming in early **autumn** to catch the changing colours. December has the shortest and rainiest days; November and January aren't much better. Yet while **winter** as a whole can be cold and dark (and very windy in exposed spots), the temperature often stays well above freezing in the sheltered valleys. And you also get some stunning, clear-blue winter skies, when it can be a real joy to be on the fells.

Considerably fewer people visit the Lakes in the **late autumn, winter** and **early spring,** so if you're looking for relative peace and quiet, these are the seasons to choose. However, be prepared for

AVERAGE DAILY TEMPERATURES IN THE LAKE DISTRICT												
	Jan	**Feb**	**Mar**	**Apr**	**May**	**June**	**July**	**Aug**	**Sept**	**Oct**	**Nov**	**Dec**
°F	38	42	45	50	58	62	65	63	60	52	44	42
°C	4	5	7	10	14	17	19	18	15	11	7	6
AVERAGE DAILY RAINFALL IN THE LAKE DISTRICT												
	Jan	**Feb**	**Mar**	**Apr**	**May**	**June**	**July**	**Aug**	**Sept**	**Oct**	**Nov**	**Dec**
inches	2	1.75	1.75	1.75	1.9	1.8	2.2	2.2	2	2.1	2.3	1.9
mm	50	44	44	44	48	45	55	55	50	53	58	48

many of the indoor sights and attractions to be closed, for public transport services to be limited, and for some hotels, guest houses and campsites to be shut (though those that do stay open tend to offer reduced rates). You're unlikely to regret coming out of season though: there's still plenty to see and do, and a day on an empty fell or around a deserted lake or tarn lingers long in the memory.

Part 1

The Basics

Getting there

The Lake District is in the county of Cumbria, in the northwest of England, 80 miles north of Manchester and 270 miles from London. The M6 motorway gets you within a few miles' drive of the eastern side of the region, while public transport links are good, with trains and buses providing reasonably direct access from most major British cities (and from Manchester Airport). The major points of access are Lancaster, Kendal or Windermere to the south, and Penrith or Carlisle to the north.

By bus

National Express buses **from London's Victoria Coach Station** run twice daily to Windermere, a seven-hour ride (£31 return; £26 if booked seven days in advance). This service continues

from Windermere on to Ambleside (15min), Grasmere (30min) and Keswick (45min). From **Manchester's Chorlton Street Coach Station** there's one National Express service bus a day to Windermere, which takes three hours (£16.50 return) and which also stops in Ambleside, Grasmere and Keswick. This service starts its route at **Manchester Airport**, providing a useful connection for recent arrivals. **From Birmingham**, there are two daily services to Windermere, taking under five hours (£27 return; £22.50 if booked seven days in advance). National Express services **from York, Newcastle and Scotland** all route via Manchester to the Lakes; **from the south, east and west** you'll have to change in London or Birmingham. A £3–5 supplement is charged on all National Express routes for travelling on a Friday. Make bookings with your local travel agent, via the National Express Enquiry line or on the Internet (see box on p.4).

From York (Leeman Rd) Stagecoach Cumberland (service #X9) runs once daily (except Sunday) from late April to late August, through the Yorkshire Dales to Kendal, Windermere and Ambleside (3hr to Windermere; £12.25 return). It also stops at Grasmere and Keswick on Saturdays. In addition, Stagecoach Cumberland has a direct service (#555/556) **from Carlisle** (three daily) to Keswick and points beyond, or **from Lancaster** (hourly) to Kendal, Windermere, Ambleside, Grasmere and Keswick. For these

---

Getting There for Overseas Visitors

Overseas visitors heading straight for the Lake District should consider taking a connecting flight from London, or flying directly to **Manchester Airport**, northern England's major airport, from where there are direct train services to Oxenholme, the station for the Lakes.

Travelling **from Ireland** by ferry, the most logical port to use is Liverpool (sailings from Belfast or Dublin), from where it's an easy train ride to Manchester and on to Oxenholme.

Using the Belfast service to Stranraer in Scotland, you'll need to travel first by train to Glasgow and on from there; arriving in Holyhead from Dublin, take the train via Crewe to Oxenholme. From the rest of Europe, using the **North Sea crossings** makes most sense. Docking at either Hull (from Rotterdam and Zeebrugge) or Newcastle (Hamburg, Amsterdam, Norway and Sweden), take the train to York and change for Manchester and the west-coast main line.

journeys it's cheapest to buy an **Explorer Ticket** (see "Getting around: by bus", on p.5).

Stray Travel's back-packer bus between London and Scotland stops at Ambleside youth hostel on Thursday, Saturday and Tuesday: you can stop off in the Lakes for as long as you like within the confines of the "All-Britain Pass" (£129), valid for a minimum of six days and a maximum of four months.

By train

To reach the Lake District by train, take Virgin Trains' west-coast main line service between London and Glasgow and change at Oxenholme for the First North Western branch line service to Kendal (3min) and Windermere (20min). The only other places in the region directly accessible by train are Penrith (also on the west-coast main line) and Carlisle (west-coast main line, plus connections from Newcastle-upon-Tyne); and the towns along the Cumbrian coast (connections from Lancaster).

From London's Euston Station, there are up to ten departures a day for **Kendal** and **Windermere** (changing at Oxenholme), a four- to five-hour trip. Prices vary wildly, depending on when you book your ticket, but booking between three and seven days in advance can bring the return fare down to £27 or £38. If you buy your ticket on the day, expect to pay more like £56 return, or as much as £62 if you travel on a Friday. To reach Keswick and the northern Lakes, either take the train to Windermere and continue from there by bus or stay on the main line service to Penrith or Carlisle, from where buses also run to Keswick.

From Manchester's Oxford Road station, there are five direct trains daily to Windermere, the quickest of which takes 1hr 45min (£19.50–22.50 return). This service starts its route at **Manchester Airport**, from where there are also direct services to Penrith.

Coming **from Yorkshire**, a longer, more scenic approach is provided by the famous **Settle to Carlisle Railway** (connections from Leeds and Bradford), which runs through stunning Yorkshire Dales countryside. At Carlisle, you'll have to switch to local buses to get you to Keswick, Penrith or Cockermouth.

Finally, the **Furness and Cumbrian Coast** branch line from Lancaster (connections from Manchester, Manchester Airport, Preston and Leeds) runs via Ulverston, Barrow-in-Furness, Ravenglass and the Cumbrian coastal towns to Carlisle. This route provides a leisurely approach to the south and western Lakes. There's no service on Sundays.

Anyone seeing the Lakes as part of a wider northern England trip might consider buying a **North West Rover** ticket (seven days £49; any three days in seven £38), valid for unlimited rail travel in a region which stretches between Carlisle, the Cumbrian coast and Lancaster east into Yorkshire.

From Scotland, trains from Glasgow Central (7 daily; 2hr 30min–3hr 30min) or Edinburgh (6 daily; 3hr 10min–3hr 30min) run to Windermere (changing at Oxenholme), with stops en route at Carlisle and Penrith. Return fares to Windermere from either city start at as little as £17, though you'll need to book several weeks in advance for these. On the day, expect to pay £28–33 return, £33–39 if you travel on a Friday.

By car

The Lake District lies to the west of the **M6 motorway**, which – as it approaches the hills and troughs of the Lakes and the Eden Valley – displays one of the best feats of road engineering in the country: the section between Kendal and Penrith is as impressive as major highways get in England. Where you come off the motorway depends on your ultimate destination – for Keswick and Penrith, take junction 40; for Kendal and Windermere, take junction 38 (north) or 36 (south); for Cartmel and Ulverston, take junction 36.

Count on the drive taking five hours from London and the southeast, an hour and a half from Manchester or Newcastle, two and half

---

TRAVEL INFORMATION

First North Western ☎ 0870/606 6007;
www.firstnorthwest.co.uk
National Express ☎ 08705/808080;
www.nationalexpress.co.uk
National Rail Enquiries ☎ 08457/484950;
www.railtrack.co.uk
Stagecoach Cumberland ☎ 01946/63222.
Stray Travel ☎ 020/7373 7737;
www.straytravel.com
Virgin Trains ☎ 08457/222333;
www.thetrainline.co.uk

DISTANCES IN MILES FROM MAJOR CITIES		
	Windermere	**Keswick**
London	270	305
Birmingham	150	190
Manchester	80	115
York	100	115
Newcastle-upon-Tyne	90	80
Edinburgh	145	135
Glasgow	140	135

hours from York or Birmingham, and three hours from Glasgow or Edinburgh. Once you leave the

motorway, the nature of the roads and the summer traffic can slow you right down, so allow plenty of time if you're aiming for the central fells, Borrowdale or the western lakes. Local radio stations (see p.9) carry regular traffic and weather reports. Both the AA (*www.theaa.co.uk*) and RAC (*www.rac.co.uk*) have useful **route-planning services**. For information, brochures, maps and leaflets en route, there are three useful tourist information offices on the M6: **Cumbria Gateway** (☎01524/792181) at Lancaster Services (formerly Forton Services), between junctions 32 and 33, six miles south of Lancaster; **Killington Lake Services** (☎015396/20138), one mile south of junction 37 (southbound side only) and seven miles east of Kendal; and **Southwaite Services** (☎016974/73445), between junctions 41 and 42, twelve miles north of Penrith.

Getting around

Too many people bring cars to the Lake District and, as a consequence, once-quiet valleys and unspoiled villages have disappeared under the weight of traffic. However, over the last few years – recognizing the damage that's being done to the environment – the local authorities have made great improvements to the public transport network within the National Park to encourage people to leave their cars at home. In summer especially, when services are at their peak, there's no longer any real excuse not to use public transport for at least some journeys. Even isolated beauty spots like Tarn Hows and Watendlath can be reached by bus.

The southern, central and northern band – from Windermere and Coniston through Ambleside and Grasmere to Keswick – is the easiest section of the Lakes to tour by public transport. In the western lakes and valleys, and in the far north beyond Keswick, getting around by bus becomes trickier, if not impossible in some places.

Major bus routes and frequencies of the services on them are listed at the end of each chapter in "Travel details". For extensive coverage of all public transport services – bus, rail and ferry – get hold of a copy of the **Getting Around Cumbria and the Lake District Timetable** (50p), available from tourist information centres and National Park offices.

For hiking, cycling and all other forms of transport, see "Outdoor pursuits", on p.19.

By bus

Stagecoach Cumberland is the biggest bus operator in the Lakes, though many of its routes are subsidized by Cumbria County Council or the National Parks Authority to ensure coverage of areas that wouldn't otherwise be economically viable. Dozens of routes connect every major town and village, and although travel frequencies vary you can usually count on being able to reach most places at least once a day throughout the year. The most frequent services on all routes are between Easter and the end of the school holidays in August, though some peak-period timetables continue into September and October (often at weekends only). Local services connect with express routes at Windermere, Ambleside and Keswick, to places outside the National Park, such as Cockermouth, the Cumbrian coast, Carlisle, Penrith, Kendal, Ulverston and Barrow. Other Stagecoach services run from the Lakes to York and Preston, and, from Carlisle, connect to other services to Hexham and Newcastle.

You can buy tickets on the bus as you go, though the best deal is the Stagecoach **Explorer Ticket** (one-day: adults £5.50, child/seniors £4; four-day £13.60/£9.50) which is valid on the entire network. The one-day ticket can be bought on any bus; the four-day ticket is available in tourist offices. Other special Stagecoach tickets offer hop-on-hop-off transport between Bowness and Grasmere, or bus-and-boat combinations for Coniston and Windermere.

Current Stagecoach routes and ticket details are spelt out exhaustively in the invaluable, free, **Lakeland Explorer timetable**, published annually before Easter and available from tourist offices or by post from Stagecoach or

Cumbria County Council (see box left). Most tourist offices also have individual route timetables available.

Other services in the Lakes are operated by the **National Trust**, which runs free summer buses between Coniston, Hawkshead and Tarn Hows (Tarn Hows Tourer) and from Keswick to Watendlath (Watendlath Wanderer). The post office's **post buses** serve a few outlying areas and take fee-paying passengers, though departures are often very early in the morning. Finally, the **YHA** operates a shuttle-bus service between its most popular hostels from Easter to the end of October (£2 a journey); call Ambleside hostel (☎015394/32304) for more details.

By train

After years of service cuts, and the fulsome embrace of the car, the only place in the Lake District National Park you can now reach on a regular train service is **Windermere**, on the branch line from Oxenholme (on the London–Manchester–Glasgow west-coast main line route) via **Kendal** and **Staveley**. Outside the Park, but still a handy approach to the northern Lakes, **Penrith** is also a stop on the west-coast main line route; while the **Furness and Cumbrian Coast** branch line from Lancaster runs via Ulverston, Ravenglass and the Cumbrian coastal towns to Carlisle. All timetable and ticket details from National Rail Enquiries (see box above).

A **Lakes and Furness Day Ranger** ticket (adult £8.90, child £4.45, family £16.65) is valid after 8.30am Monday to Friday, or all day at weekends and on public holidays, on services from Lancaster to the Cumbrian coast, and between Oxenholme and Windermere. There's also a **Lakes Day Tripper** ticket (various prices), valid for return rail-and-bus travel to Grange-over-Sands or Windermere from Manchester and other northwestern towns and cities. The seven-day North West Rover ticket (see "Getting there: by train", on p.4) covers a much wider geographical area and is little use for a tour of the Lakes.

What the Lakes lack in a regular train network is made up for in a couple of private scenic **steam train lines**. Both **Lakeside and Haverthwaite** (southern end of Windermere) and **Ravenglass and Eskdale** (western fells and valleys) lines are covered in the Guide. The former is the more popular (and easiest to access); the latter provides the more enjoyable ride.

By ferry

Of the lakes themselves, Windermere, Coniston Water, Derwent Water and Ullswater have **ferry** or **cruise** services of varying degrees of usefulness, all covered in detail in the text. Windermere and Ullswater are the most popular choices for a round-trip cruise; the service on Derwent Water is extremely useful for hopping around the lake and accessing Borrowdale walks; while the Coniston launches are used mainly as a means of reaching Ruskin's house, Brantwood.

For·steering yourself around lakeland waters, see "Outdoor pursuits", on p.19.

By car

While driving around the Lakes might seem convenient, it soon loses its attraction in July and August when the roads are jammed and it takes ages to get from village to village and you can't find anywhere to park once you arrive. Leave the car at home, or at your hotel or B&B, whenever you can and you'll get more enjoyment out of the region.

Parking is a nightmare throughout the Lakes, especially in the towns and villages. There is free on-street parking in places such as Ambleside, Windermere, Bowness, Coniston, Grasmere and Keswick, but there's not very much of it and it's usually limited to thirty minutes. The best advice, every time, is to follow the signs to the car parks and pay up. All car parks mentioned in the guide – and marked on our maps – are **pay-and-display** unless otherwise stated, so a supply of change is a necessity. Expect to pay £1.50–2 for up to four hours' parking, and up to £5 for a full day, even in car parks on National Trust land in out-of-the-way places. Most hotels and some B&Bs have private parking, mentioned in the reviews where available.

CAR RENTAL COMPANIES

NATIONAL

Avis ☎ 0990/900500
Budget ☎ 0800/181181
Hertz ☎ 0990/996699
Holiday Autos ☎ 0990/300400
Thrifty ☎ 0990/168238

IN THE LAKES

Bowness: Avis ☎ 015394/45910; Cumbria Car Hire ☎ 015394/44408.

Kendal: Avis ☎ 01539/733852; Hargreaves Carriage ☎ 01539/724420; Westmorland Vehicle Hire ☎ 01539/728532/4.

Keswick: Keswick Motor Company ☎ 017687/72064.

Penrith: Enterprise Rent-a-Car ☎ 01768/891333; Ullswater Road Garage ☎ 01768/864546.

Ulverston: Alan Myerscough (Ford) ☎ 01229/581058.

LOCAL TAXI FIRMS

Ambleside: Brown's Taxis ☎ 015394/33263; Kevin's Taxis ☎ 015394/32371; Steve's Taxis ☎ 015934/33544; see also Bowness and Windermere.

Bowness/Windermere: Bowness Taxis ☎ 015394/46535; Cooper's Cabs ☎ 015394/45282; Lakes Taxis ☎ 015394/46777; TC Taxis ☎ 015394/44055; Tarn Taxis ☎ 015394/47070; Windermere Taxis ☎ 015934/42355.

Cockermouth: AJM Taxis ☎ 01900/823671; Cockermouth Taxis ☎ 01900/826649 or 0860/241671; Irving's Taxis ☎ 01900/824034.

Coniston: Alan Dover ☎ 015394/41683.

Grasmere: Grasmere Taxis ☎ 015394/35506.

Kendal: Blue Star Taxis ☎ 01539/723670; Crown Taxis ☎ 01539/732181; Cumbria Cars ☎ 01539/720620; Signal Taxis ☎ 01539/730785.

Keswick: Davies Taxis ☎ 017687/72676; Keswick Taxis ☎ 017687/75585; Skiddaw Taxis ☎ 017687/75347 or 0800/654321.

Penrith: A Taxis ☎ 01768/863354 or 0800/7315818; Lakeland ☎ 01768/865722; Moorside Taxis ☎ 017687/899066 or 0800/3890956.

Most A and B roads are in good condition, though single-track driving is common – don't park in passing places. Surfaces on high ground and off the beaten track tend to deteriorate rapidly, being little more than unmetalled tracks in places: many routes can be adventurous at the best of times and downright treacherous in winter or bad weather. The steepest road gradients and most difficult driving are on the following **lakeland passes**: Blea Tarn Road (between Great and Little Langdale), Hardknott Pass (Eskdale and Duddon Valley), Honister Pass (Buttermere and Borrowdale), Kirkstone Pass (Ullswater and Windermere), The Struggle (Ambleside and Kirkstone Pass), Whinlatter Pass (Braithewaite and Lorton Vale) and Wrynose Pass (Duddon Valley and Little Langdale).

Tours

If you're short on time, or just want to let someone else do the driving, then a **minibus tour** through the Lakes can show you an awful lot quickly. The specialist operators listed in the box below have some interesting itineraries and can arrange pick-ups from most of the major lakeland towns. Prices usually start at around £15 for a half-day to £25 for a full day out on the road. As well as calling the contact numbers given, you can book most tours at local tourist information offices.

Specialist bus tour operators

Fellrunner (☎01768/88232). Community-run minibus service offering bargain-priced summer-holiday (mid-July to mid-Sept) tours of East Cumbria (including Ullswater).

Lakeland Safari Tours (☎015394/33904). Small (maximum six-seater) safaris with an environmental emphasis, featuring out-of-the-way circuits and themed historic tours. There's scope for requesting your own itinerary or special stops.

Lakes Supertours (☎015394/42751 or 88133). Eleven-seater minibus tours – lakes and moun-

tains or literary themes – with some cruises and house entries included.

Mountain Goat (☎015394/45164 or ☎017687/73962; *www.lakes-pages.co.uk*). Minibus tours that get off the beaten track: Duddon Valley and Back o'Skiddaw as well as the usual lakes and passes. Also five- and seven-night touring holidays.

National Trust (☎015394/35599). "Landscape Minibus Tours" covering the western valleys, lakes and gardens, south Lakes or the north Lakes. Discount for NT members.

Information, maps and media

There's plenty of free information available about the Lakes before you go – either from the official information authorities or, using the Internet, from a plethora of useful Web sites. Keen walkers – in fact, anyone intending to do more than just stroll by the lakeside – will need to buy proper maps too; the best are reviewed below.

Visitor information

For information before you go, contact the **Cumbria Tourist Board** or the **Lake District National Park Authority** (NPA), both of which maintain useful Web sites and can send you a variety of brochures. In the Lake District itself, a series of **visitor information offices** provides help on the ground – all are listed in the Guide. The offices are funded and run by the tourist board, the NPA and by local councils: **opening hours** vary, though in the summer most of the main offices are open daily 10am–6pm, some-

---

Visitor Information

Cumbria Tourist Board, Ashleigh, Holly Rd, Windermere, Cumbria LA23 2AQ (☎015394/44444; brochure line: ☎0990/133059; from abroad: 44-(0)1271/336039; *www.golakes.co.uk*).

Lake District National Park Authority, Brockhole, Windermere, Cumbria LA23 1LJ (☎015394/46601; *www.lake-district.gov.uk*).

Local Radio

BBC Radio Cumbria: North Cumbria 95.6 FM/756 AM; West Cumbria 104.1 FM/1458 AM; South Cumbria 96.1 FM/837 AM; Windermere 95.2 FM/104.2 FM.

The Bay: North 96.9 FM; Lakes/South 102.3 FM; Cumbria 103.2 FM.

times an hour or so later. Opening hours are reduced in winter and, in some offices, may be restricted to weekends only 10am–4pm. At each office you'll be able to book accommodation, check on local weather conditions, and buy guides and maps. At some you can also change money (see "Mail and money", on p.11).

Local publications

Local **newspapers** (published weekly) are a good source of information about lakeland events, politics and personalities. Look for the *Westmorland Gazette* (which covers eastern Cumbria and the southern and central Lakes); the *Lake District Herald* (covering Penrith, Keswick and the northern Lakes); the *Keswick Reminder* (covering just Keswick); and the *Cumberland News* (Carlisle, Keswick and Penrith). Two daily evening papers carve up the region between them: the *North West Evening Mail* (southern Cumbria) and the *Evening News and Star* (northern Cumbria).

The small-format monthly **magazine** *Cumbria* and the bigger, glossier, bi-monthly *Cumbria Life* concentrate on the history, culture and social and natural fabric of the Lakes. The quarterly *Lakeland Walker* is a chatty periodical aimed at hikers and lakeland lovers, featuring walks, news, reviews and equipment-testing. *Park Life* is the free newspaper published twice a year by the National Park Authority, containing news and events from around the region. You should also pick up the NPA's annual *Events* guide, listing all the region's festivals, activities and events.

Maps and walking guides

The best general map of the National Park area is the **Ordnance Survey** (OS) inch-to-the-mile

USEFUL WEB SITES

TOURISM

www.lake-district.gov.uk
Official Web site of the National Park Authority – all you need to know about national park work, services and events.

www.golakes.co.uk
Official Web site of the Cumbria Tourist Board, with an interactive map, accommodation databases and a Webcam (showing the view from Windermere's *Miller Howe*).

www.lake-district-peninsulas.co.uk
Official Web site for the Lake District peninsulas region – information, accommodation and events for Broughton-in-Furness, Lakeside and Newby Bridge, Ulverston and Cartmel.

www.north-lakes.com
Send a digital postcard, or access hotel listings and photos at the Lake District Hotel and Caterer's Association Web site.

www.keswick.org
Keswick Tourism Association site – useful for local sights in the north of the region, what's on info and an accommodation database.

www.ambleside.u-k.org
Community Web site for the Ambleside area, featuring comprehensive local tourist and business listings, what's on information and photographs.

www.cumbria1st.com
Specialist guide to Cumbria and the Lakes, which provides a good local history section, plus informed accounts of towns, lakes, mountains and walks.

www.users.globalnet.co.uk/~jplanner
Cumbria County Council and the Countryside Commission's ever-evolving transport-based Web site: on-line timetables for all forms of local transport, plus illustrated walks, tourist info and other useful links.

WALKING AND THE MOUNTAINS

ldnet.users.netlink.co.uk
John Dawson's incredibly detailed Lake District hiking site features over forty classic walks, complete with route descriptions, photos and a distance calculator.

homepages.enterprise.net/ldsamra
Cumbria's Search and Mountain Rescue Association site, packed full of useful advice for

walkers and mountaineers, and a forbidding tally of accident stats.

www.cumbria.com/FRCC
Mountaineers should go straight to the Web site of the Lake District's Fell and Rock Climbing Club (founded 1906): climbs, crag summaries, photos, wanted/for-sale bulletin board and more.

BUSINESSES

www.cumbria.com
Cumbria on the Internet: a useful searchable database of Cumbrian businesses, from fish suppliers to quarry companies.

www.kendal.mintcake.co.uk
All you ever wanted to know about Kendal's famous energy-boosting sweetie, made by Romney's of Kendal, complete with a list of stockists.

(1:63,360) Touring Map and Guide 3, with hill shading and principal footpaths illustrated. For more detail of Cumbria as a whole (including Carlisle and the coast), you'll need the pink (1:50,000) OS Landranger series of maps (nos. 85, 89, 90, 91, 96 and 97).

Essential for **hikers** are the yellow (1:25,000) OS Outdoor Leisure series – four maps (nos. 4,

5, 6 and 7) which cover the whole Lake District National Park. Map no. 33 (same scale) shows the western half of the Coast-to-Coast walk, the part which cuts through the Lakes. Some prefer the Harvey's Superwalker series of waterproof maps (also 1:25,000) covering North, East, Northwest, West, South and Central Lakeland.

Most bookshops, outdoors stores and information offices sell the full range of maps, as well as various **local walk map-leaflets**. Recommended series include the packs of Lakeland Leisure Walks (five assorted walks in each of the major areas), local fell expert Paul Buttle's various walking booklets, and the National Park Authority's Walks in the Countryside leaflets. For **hiking guides** for the Lake District, see "Books" (p.179).

Mail and money

Each town and major village in the Lakes has a single post office, listed below for reference. Banks are rather more plentiful, in the towns at least, and the reciprocal use of cash-dispensers means you are unlikely to be stuck for money, whoever you bank with.

Post offices

Apart from the usual services, you can exchange travellers' cheques and foreign currency at most lakeland post offices. Normal **opening hours** are Monday–Friday 9am–5.30pm, Saturday 9am–12.30pm, though smaller offices may have restricted hours.

Money

Normal **banking hours** are Monday–Friday 9.30am–3.30pm, with some branches in the major towns open on Saturday morning too. All the major British **banks** (Barclays, Halifax, HSBC, Lloyds-TSB and NatWest) have cash-dispensers (ATMs) in Ambleside, Bowness, Cockermouth, Kendal, Keswick, Penrith, Ulverston and Windermere. Outside the banks in these places you'll be able to **exchange travellers' cheques and foreign currency** at major post offices (see above) and at the tourist offices in Ambleside, Bowness, Coniston, Glenridding, Grasmere, Hawkshead, Keswick and Windermere.

Credit cards are widely accepted in shops, hotels, restaurants and service stations, but don't count on being able to use plastic in B&Bs, guest houses, pubs and cafés: we indicate all those that don't accept credit cards in the Guide. Be aware, however – even those that do accept credit cards, often don't accept American Express.

POST OFFICES

Ambleside: Market Place	(☎015394/32267).	**Grasmere:** Red Lion Square	(☎015394/35261).
Bowness:		**Hawkshead:** Main St	(☎015394/36201)
2 St Martin's Parade	(☎015394/46964).	**Kendal:** 75 Stricklandgate	(☎01539/725592).
Broughton-in-Furness:		**Keswick:** 48 Main St	(☎017687/72269).
Princes St	(☎01229/716220).	**Penrith:** Crown Square	(☎01768/863942).
Cockermouth: Main St	(☎01900/822277).	**Windermere:**	
Coniston: Yewdale Rd	(☎015394/41259).	21 Crescent Rd	(☎015394/43245).

Accommodation

The Lake District has no shortage of accommodation, though it sometimes seems like it at peak periods. At New Year, Easter, public holidays and school holidays (particularly the six-week summer break from late July to the end of August) it's always wise to book ahead.

The Cumbria Tourist Board has a **Booking Hotline** (☎0808/100 8848) for short breaks, special offers and late bookings. Otherwise, local information offices can provide assistance: all offer a free **room-booking service** where you'll be charged a deposit (usually ten percent) that's then deducted from your accommodation bill. For full lists of Lake District accommodation you'll need the following three annual **publications**: *Where To Stay in Central and Southern Lakeland*, the *Keswick and the Northern Lakes Visitor Guide* (both £1), and *Where to Stay in Eden* (free; covers Ullswater, Penrith and the Eden Valley), available from information offices.

Hotels and B&Bs

Accommodation **prices** are slightly higher in the Lakes than in other parts of scenic Britain, with simple **bed-and-breakfast** (B&B) starting at around £16 per person per night. Even in the most basic of places, you should get a sink, a TV and a kettle in the room. These days, most B&Bs and guest houses have added en-suite shower and toilet cubicles to their rooms, for which you'll pay £18–20 – don't expect a great deal of space (or indeed a bath) in these "bathrooms". **Hotels** in the Lakes tend to charge what they can get away with and, as location is everything, lakeside or isolated fellside retreats can get away with an awful lot – you can easily spend £150–200 for a room in one of the classic country-house hotels. Prices in all establishments are often higher at weekends, during summer and over public holidays: conversely, it's always worth asking about **off-season discounts**, which might shade a couple of quid off a B&B room, or up to forty off a hotel.

At weekends, many places insist upon two- or (over public holidays) even three-night **minimum stays**. There again, staying more than a couple of nights in many places brings the standard price down a pound or two a night. There aren't a great many **single rooms** available, and solitary hikers or holiday-makers won't often get much knocked off the price of a double room if that's the only option. Finally, many guest houses and hotels offer a discounted **dinner, bed and breakfast** rate which – provided you want to eat there in the first place – is usually a much better deal than the standard B&B rate: the Guide picks out those D, B&B places where the cooking is particularly good. Note, though, that some hotels only offer stays on a D, B&B basis while others are so remote that there's nowhere else to eat anyway.

At all the establishments listed in this guide, **payment by credit card** is accepted unless oth-

---

ACCOMMODATION PRICE CODES

All **hotel** and **B&B** accommodation in the Guide is priced on a scale of ① to ⑨, indicating the **average price** you could expect to pay per night for a **double/twin room** in high season. **Breakfast** is usually included, and rooms are **en-suite**, unless otherwise stated. **Youth hostels** are not given a price cod since they fall within a fairly narrow price band, see p.13.

① under £40	④ £60–70	⑦ £110–150
② £40–50	⑤ £70–90	⑧ £150–200
③ £50–60	⑥ £90–110	⑨ over £200

erwise stated. However, even where credit cards are accepted, American Express cards often aren't – pack another card, just in case.

Youth hostels

There are 25 Youth Hostel Association (YHA) **youth hostels** in the Lake District (plus one in Carlisle, one in Arnside on Morecambe Bay, and a couple of independent back packers' lodges). Several, including those in Ambleside and Grasmere, are amongst the most popular in the country, so advance booking is a good idea at any time of the year. Gone are the days of curfews, tasks and sackcloth comforts: many lakeland hostels have rooms with just three, four or six beds, and are well-equipped with laundry and kitchen facilities; some have licensed cafés, bike rental and Internet access. A YHA shuttle bus runs between the major Lake District hostels (see "Getting around: by bus", p.5, for more) or buy a copy of *The Lake District Youth Hosteller's Walking Guide* by Martin Hanks (Landmark Publishing), which describes walks between every lakeland hostel.

You need to be a hostel member to stay at a YHA hostel: either join your home country's hostelling association before you go (which gives you access to YHA hostels), or simply join on your first night at the hostels themselves. A YHA **reservation service** (daily 9am–6pm; ☎015394/31117) lets you book any hostel in the Lake District up to seven days in advance, free of charge.

Prices start at around £7 per night for a bed at simple, remote establishments like those at Black Sail, Honister Hause or Skiddaw House, rising to £11.90 for the flagship Ambleside hostel. Breakfast costs an extra £3.20, a three-course dinner £4.80, and packed lunches are usually available too. Half a dozen of the major hostels (Ambleside, Borrowdale, Derwentwater, Grasmere Butterlip How, Hawkshead and Windermere) also have **family rooms** available (£32–60, sleeps 4–6). Many hostels have restricted **opening periods** in the winter – call the numbers given in the Guide for specific details.

Holiday property rental

The dream of renting a pretty rural **holiday cottage** in the Lakes is easily accomplished. The hardest thing is deciding what you want, with choices ranging from simple stone cottages to large country houses, by way of barn conversions, former mills, town houses and shooting lodges. There are

---

HOLIDAY PROPERTY AGENCIES

CottageNet.co.uk (*www.cottagenet.co.uk*). Internet-based reservations company for holiday cottages, with a large selection in the Lakes.

Country Holidays (☎01282/445500; *www.country-holidays.co.uk*). National firm with over a hundred properties in the Lakes.

Cumbrian Cottages (☎01228/599960; *www.cumbrian-cottages.co.uk*). A wide range of cottages and apartments in the Lake District.

Goosemire Cottages (☎015394/47477; *www.goosemirecottages.co.uk*). Thirty conversions and traditonal cottages in the Ullswater and Haweswater region.

Heart of the Lakes (☎015394/32321; *www.leisuretime.co.uk*). Excellent choice of over two hundred quality properties all over the Lakes.

Holidays in Lakeland (☎015395/31716; *www.holidays-in-lakeland.co.uk*). Anything from modern studios to traditional cottages in the southeastern area of the Lakes.

Lakeland Cottage Co. (☎015395/30024; *www.lakeland-cottage-company.co.uk*). Southern Lakes specialist – from simple cottages to large country houses.

Lakeland Cottages (☎017687/71071; *www.lakelandcottages.co.uk*). Period cottages and farmhouses in the Keswick and Borrowdale area.

Lakelovers (☎015394/88855; *www.lakelovers.co.uk*). A large range of properties mainly in the western and southern Lakes.

Landmark Trust (☎01628/825925; *www.landmarktrust.co.uk*). The Trust has just one property in the area – expensive Howthwaite (sleeps seven), behind Wordsworth's Dove Cottage in Grasmere, with lovely gardens.

National Trust (☎01225/791199). Thirteen lakeland properties – mainly around Ambleside, Little Langdale, Eskdale and Loweswater.

---

lots of companies out there vying for your custom but all offer the same kind of basic deal. The minimum rental period is usually a week, though outside the summer season and especially in the winter you may be able to negotiate a three-day/long weekend rate – except, that is, at Christmas, New Year and Easter when prices are at their highest and demand at its most intense. All properties come with a fully equipped kitchen, and many (but not all) provide bed-linen and towels. Prices vary dramatically – from £160 to £200 a week for the smallest properties to as much as £1000 for a week in a large, luxury property with admission to the local pool and health club thrown in.

The list of **agencies** (on p.13) should help in finding the property you want, but it's worth scanning accommodation brochures and notices in local shop windows for other choices. Throughout the Guide we've also picked out recommended individual self-catering rental properties.

Campsites and camping barns

The Lake District has scores of **campsites**, though in the Guide we've tended to recommend those that favour tents over the large family-style caravan-RV parks. Many sites close between November and March, while in July and August it's always worth booking a pitch in advance.

Prices vary considerably, from a couple of quid to stick your tent in a farmer's field (and possibly the use of a toilet and cold tap) to £10 a night for the use of all the facilities in one of the supersites, complete with shop, bar and hot showers. The National Trust also maintains three popular campsites – Great Langdale, Low Wray and Wasdale Head (all featured in the Guide) – in fantastic locations and moderately priced at £3.50 a head per night.

The YHA co-ordinates a series of eleven **camping barns** within the National Park: self-catering converted farm buildings with basic, communal facilities. The cost is under £4 per person per night though you'll need a sleeping bag, foam mat and other camping equipment (not all have cooking utensils available). To check availability and make reservations, call the Lakeland Barns Booking Office (☎017687/ 72645).

Food and drink

Few people come to the Lakes purely for the gastronomic experience, but many are pleasantly surprised by the range and quality of food on offer. Pub and café meals have improved immeasurably over the last few years, while in restaurants right across the region there's good lakeland cooking in abundance, using local ingredients – fish, lamb, locally grown veg, home-made bread – and a dash of flair. Those with more cosmopolitan tastes will be relieved that cappuccino machines have continued their steady march north, and though there aren't any sushi bars in the Lakes there are decent pizzerias, Modern-British restaurants, inventive pub menus and gourmet vegetarian places. There just aren't very many of them.

Eating out

Traditionally, **fine dining** in the Lakes – as in the rest of England – was very much a silver-service roast-and-veg affair, or heavily Anglo-French in character, a state of affairs that still survives in many old-fashioned lakeland hotels. But some

---

Restaurant Price Codes

Restaurants listed in this guide have been assigned one of four price categories:

Inexpensive under £10
Moderate £10–20
Expensive £20–30
Very Expensive over £30

This is the price you can expect to pay per person for a three-course meal or equivalent, excluding drinks and service.

---

regional chefs have married contemporary flavours and trends with well-sourced local ingredients to produce something slightly different: if not a specific lakeland style of cuisine then at least a welcome change to old-school menus. At the more adventurous places expect to see plenty of pan-searing and char-grilling of local meat and fish; together with seasonal veg, soups and fruit given ethnic and fusion twists. You're as likely to come across such a meal in a tearoom or café as in a hotel dining room, though the Lake District does offer a dozen of the finest (though stratospherically priced) **country-house dining** experiences in England (including *Sharrow Bay, Miller Howe, Michael's Nook* and *Gilpin Lodge*).

As for **local specialities**, it's pretty much as you would expect in farming and fishing country, with lamb, beef and pork supplemented on menus by local trout (farmed on Ullswater and elsewhere, as well as found wild), Morecambe Bay shrimps and, on occasion, the lake-caught char (see p.37), a fish peculiar to the Lake District. As you go, keep an eye out at roadside stalls, craft outlets and village shops for locally made honey and preserves – the Lyth Valley's damson harvest, for example, ends up in jams and even beer. Locally made chutneys and pickles are often served as part of a ploughman's lunch, and Alston in northern Cumbria provides many outlets with speciality mustards.

In many places, **breakfast** is the best meal of the day – no surprise in England. Even the humble B&B makes an occasional outstanding effort (the best are noted in the Guide), with homemade bread and muesli, yoghurt, muffins, pancakes, rissoles and other delights appearing alongside the ubiquitous fry-up. And on that subject, the Lake District is the best place to try **Cumberland sausage**, a thick, spicy, herby pork

sausage (traditionally made in a spiral shape); the supreme example is that made by Woodall's of Waberthwaite (near Millom), suppliers by Royal Warrant to the Queen, and purveyors too of fine dry-cured hams and bacon.

No rundown of local treats would be complete without **Kendal Mintcake**, a brutal peppermint confection favoured by strong-toothed hikers. There are plaudits too for Cartmel Village Shop's **sticky toffee pudding** and **Penrith fudge and toffee**, while creamy lakeland **ice cream** is increasingly available in local shops and cafés.

All cafés, restaurants and pubs listed in the Guide serve **lunch and dinner** unless otherwise stated. Winter opening hours are notoriously fickle, so a phone call before you set out never does any harm. Listed places all take **credit cards** unless otherwise stated (though this often doesn't include American Express, except in the more expensive hotels and restaurants).

Pubs and beer

There's a fine selection of country **pubs** and former coaching **inns** throughout the region, many dating back several hundred years. Those tied to the major breweries feature the same range of drinks you'll find all over England, but it's worth seeking out those owned by the main regional breweries and other independent (ie, free house) pubs for the best selection of local beer.

Jennings has the main lakeland stranglehold and offers brewery tours (see p.165) at its base in Cockermouth: you'll come across its beers everywhere – a Bitter (alcohol-by-volume strength 3.5 percent), Cumberland Ale (4.0), and the stronger Cocker Hoop (4.6) and Sneck Lifter (5.1) ales.

Several small brewers have just single-pub outlets, or are confined to the pubs in one village or local area. Ones to keep an eye out for include: the **Coniston Brewing Company**, which sells its award-winning Bluebird bitter (3.6 percent), Old Man (4.4) and Opium (4.0) ales at the village's *Black Bull* and around fifteen other local pubs; **Barngates Brewery** at the *Drunken Duck* near Tarn Hows – serving Cracker Ale (3.9 percent), Tag Lag (4.4) and Chester's Strong and Ugly (4.9); and the **Hesket Newmarket Brewery**'s Blencathra Bitter (3.1 percent), Skiddaw Special (3.7), Old Carrock Strong Ale (5.6), Cat Bells Pale Ale (5.1) and Great Cockup Porter (3.0), available at the *Old Crown*, Hesket

Newmarket. In addition, the **Mason's Arms** at Strawberry Bank, Cartmel Fell, produces a very strong home-made (fruit-based) Damson Beer (7.0 percent); and the **Bitter End** pub in Cockermouth bravely brews a small range of beers on Jennings's home soil.

Festivals, shows, sports and annual events

The region maintains its traditions in a unique series of annual festivals, shows and events held throughout the old lands of Cumberland and Westmorland. Some date back centuries, while others are modern revivals of past festivals, but what they all have in common is a shared celebration of rural tradition and activity. Nearly all are held outdoors and, not surprisingly, the summer months (particularly August) host the main events.

The month-by-month calendar opposite picks out the annual highlights: many traditionally take place on fixed days (often fairly convoluted), so for exact annual dates you should contact local information offices, the Cumbria Tourist Board (☎015394/44444) or the National Park Authority (☎015394/46601). In addition to the annual festivals and shows, there are scores of other events held throughout the year in the region – guided walks, exhibitions, lectures, craft demonstrations, re-enactments, concerts and children's entertainments. Many are sponsored by the NPA (which publishes its own *Events* brochure) and held at Brockhole Visitor Centre (p.39); you'll come across others at museums, churches, halls, farms and villages throughout the region.

Festivals and events

The oldest festivals – dating back to medieval times – are the annual **rushbearings**, harking back to the days when church floors were covered in earth rather than stone. The rushes, or reeds, laid on the floors (on which churchgoers knelt or stood) would be renewed once a year. Now the rushes are fashioned into crosses and garlands and carried in symbolic procession around the village and into the church: the most famous rushbearing festivals (with accompanying bands and hymns) are held at Grasmere, Ambleside and Urswick.

Towns such as Kendal, Keswick, Cockermouth and Ulverston host a variety of annual **festivals** concentrating on music, dance, film, drama, processions and other entertainments. And the **Summer Music Festival** brings together an international line-up of talent at venues across the Lake District. In the west, there are a couple of peculiarly Cumbrian affairs. The **Egremont Crab Fair**, held annually since 1267, features such arcane events as greasy-pole-climbing and pipe-smoking competitions and the World Gurning Championship (where contestants stick their head through a horse collar and pull faces). And at a pub in Santon Bridge, Wasdale, the **Biggest Liar in the World Competition** attracts porky-tellers from all over Cumbria to a century-old event. The rules, incidentally, specifically exclude politicians from entering.

Shows, meets and sheepdog trials

As befits a largely rural region, many of Cumbria's annual events take the form of **agricultural**

FESTIVALS AND EVENTS CALENDAR

MARCH

Third week (Sat & Sun): Daffodil and Spring Flower Show, Ambleside.

MAY

Second or third week: Keswick Jazz Festival.

JUNE

First week: Holker Garden Festival, Holker Hall.
First week: Keswick Beer Festival.
Third week (Sat): Cockermouth Carnival.
Fourth week (last Sun): Ullswater Country Fair, Patterdale.

JULY

First week (Sat): Ambleside Rushbearing Festival.
First week (Sat): Ulverston Carnival.
Second or third week (Fri & Sat): Furness Tradition, Ulverston.
Third week (Sat): Cumberland Show, Carlisle.
Fourth week (Thurs before first Mon in Aug): Ambleside Sports.
Fourth week (Sat): Millom and Broughton Agricultural Show, Broughton-in-Furness.
Fourth week (Sun): Coniston Country Fair.

AUGUST

First week (Wed): Cartmel Agricultural Show.
First week (Thurs before first Mon in Aug): Ambleside Sports.
First week (Thurs): Lake District Sheepdog Trials, Ings, Staveley.
First week (Sat): Grasmere Rushbearing.
First week (Fri–Sun): Lowther Horse Trials and Country Fair, Lowther Castle.
First and second weeks: Lake District Summer Music Festival.
Second week (Thurs): Rydal Sheepdog Trials.
Second week (Fri–Sun): Summer Flower Show and Craft Fair, Ambleside.
Third week (Wed): Gosforth Agricultural Show.
Third week (Wed): Threlkeld Sheepdog Trials.
Third week (Sat): Skelton Agricultural Show, Penrith.

Third week (Sun): Langdale Country Fair, Great Langdale.
Third or fourth week (Sun): Grasmere Sports and Show.
Third or fourth week (penultimate Tues of the month): Hawkshead Agricultural Show.
Fourth week (last Wed): Ennerdale and Kinniside Show.
Fourth week (Sat before bank-hol Mon): Patterdale Dog Day.
Bank-holiday Mon: Muncaster Country Fair, Muncaster, Ravenglass.
Bank-holiday Mon: Keswick Agicultural Show and Sports.

SEPTEMBER

First week: Wasdale Head Inn Beer Festival.
Second week (Fri): Kendal Torchlight Procession.
Second week (Thurs): Westmorland County Show, Crooklands, Kendal.
Third week (Thurs): Loweswater Agricultural Show.
Third week (Sat): Egremont Crab Fair and Sports.
Third week (Sun): Borrowdale Shepherds' Meet, Rosthwaite.
Fourth week (last Thurs): Kentmere Sheepdog Trials.
Fourth week (last Sat): Eskdale Show, Brotherilkeld Farm, Hardknott Pass, Boot.
Fourth week (last Sun): Urswick Rushbearing, Ulverston.

OCTOBER

Second week (Sat): Wasdale Head Show and Shepherds' Meet.
Second week (Sat & Sun): Kendal Mountain Film Festival.
Second or third week (Sat): Buttermere Show and Shepherds' Meet.

NOVEMBER

Third week (Thurs): Biggest Liar in the World Competition, Santon Bridge, Wasdale.

DECEMBER

First week (Sun): Keswick Victorian Fair.

shows, featuring farming equipment, trade and craft displays (including dry-stone walling), food stalls, vegetable-growing and sheep-shearing competitions, and prize-winning animals. The separate Cumberland (Carlisle) and Westmorland (Kendal) shows are the largest examples – relics of the days when they were the annual county shows – but the smaller shows in places such as Gosforth, Coniston, Loweswater and Ennerdale are highly enjoyable affairs where it's still very much a case of local communities coming together.

Some very traditional shows (at Buttermere, Borrowdale, Wasdale and Eskdale) are termed **shepherds' meets**, since that's what they once were – opportunities for shepherds to meet once a year, return sheep belonging to their neighbours, catch up on local gossip and engage in competitions, sporting or otherwise. The mainstay of these events are things like sheep- and dog-judging competitions, bouts of hunting-horn blowing and displays of decorated shepherds' crooks. In addition, there are several annual **sheepdog trials**, the main ones at Rydal and Patterdale, where border collies are put through their paces, rounding up sheep into pens at the call and whistle of their owner.

Sports, races and pastimes

Some annual shows specifically announce themselves as **Sports**, such as those at Grasmere and Ambleside, the two most important gatherings. At these (but in practice at all of the agricultural shows and meets too) you'll encounter a whole host of special Cumbrian sports and activities, as well as bicycle and track events, carriage-driving, gymkhanas, ferret- or pigeon-racing and tugs-of-war.

Cumberland and Westmorland wrestling is the best-known of the local sports, probably dating back to Viking times: two men, dressed in embroidered trunks, white tights and vests, grapple like Sumo wrestlers and attempt to unbalance each other – if both men fall, the winner is the one on top. It's hugely technical, yet balletic, and has its own vocabulary of holds and grips, like the "hype", the "hank" and the "cross buttock". The winner is declared "World Champion".

Fell-running is basically cross-country running up and down the fells. It's a notoriously tough business, dominated by local farm workers and shepherds who bound up the fells like gazelles. The famous Joss Naylor of Wasdale, now in his sixties, is typical of the breed: in 1975 he raced over 72 peaks in under 24 hours and in 1986 ran the 214 Wainwright fells in a week. The sports show races are shorter than those, but no less brutal.

The other main event is **hound trailing**, derived from the training of fox-hounds for hunting. A trail is set across several miles of countryside using an aniseed-soaked rag and the dogs are then released, with the owners calling them in across a finish line at the show. Trailing (and the heavy betting that accompanies it) also occurs most weeks during spring and summer outside the shows, followed by the **fox-hunting** season proper throughout the winter – long a Cumbrian pastime (on foot in the Lakes, not on horseback) and which no amount of contemporary social disapproval is likely to curtail.

Outdoor pursuits

The Lake District can be seen as one big outdoor playground, though you'll have to be prepared to get wet to take part in many of the possible activities (walking included, sorry to say). As a rule you can escape the crowds by getting around on foot, though serious fell-side erosion on the most popular routes may suggest otherwise. Splashing about on the water, especially on Windermere in summer, isn't always a lonely occupation either. But by choosing lesser-travelled routes and more remote lakes, or by coming outside the peak summer season, you'll often have the place to yourself.

Walking

An almost unchartable network of paths connects the lakes themselves, tracks the ridges of the fells, or weaves easier courses through the valleys, around the flanks and onto the tops. So whatever your level of fitness or expertise, you can find a Lake District walk to suit – from an hour's stroll up to a local waterfall to an all-day circuit, or "horsehoe" route, around various peaks and valleys.

Of the **long-distance paths**, Wainwright's Coast-to-Coast, which starts in St Bees, near Whitehaven, spends its first few sections in the northern lakes, while the Dales Way finishes in Windermere, but the only true Lake District hike is the seventy-mile **Cumbria Way** between Ulverston and Carlisle, which cuts through the

heart of the region via Coniston and Langdale. The fifty-mile **Allerdale Ramble**, from Seathwaite (Borrowdale) to the Solway Firth, spends around half its time in the National Park area, running up Borrowdale and across Skiddaw.

The **walks detailed in this guide** – often in special feature boxes – aim to provide a cross-section of lakeland experiences, from valley bottom to fell top. Some of the most famous mountain ascents are included, as well as gentle round-lake perambulations. It's vital to note that the brief descriptions in the Guide are not in any sense to be taken as specific route guides, rather as providing start and finish details and other pieces of local information. There are any number of local walking guides on the market: the best are reviewed on p.180.

Experience isn't always necessary but for any walk you should be **properly equipped**. Wear strong-soled, supportive walking shoes or boots – you can turn your ankle on even the easiest of strolls. Colourful, warm, wind-and-waterproof clothing, a watch, water (two litres each on hot days) and something to eat are all essential on longer hikes. If you don't have your own, Summitreks in Coniston (see box on p.22) or George Fisher's in Keswick (p.100) can rent you a pair of boots and some waterproofs.

Bad weather can move in quickly, even in the height of summer, so before starting out on the fells you should check the **weather forecast** – many hotels, all hostels and most outdoor shops post a daily forecast, or call one of the weather forecasting services (see "Introduction: climate chart", p.xv). Above all, **take a map** (see p.9) and, for up on the fells, a compass – they're not fashion accessories, so know how to use them. If you're uncertain or inexperienced, you might want to join a guided walk or attend a map-and-compass course – the National Park Authority runs both in spring and summer.

Cycling

Cycling is becoming increasingly popular in the Lakes, though walkers and environmental organizations are concerned at the detrimental effect

---

Hiking Support Services

The **Sherpa Van** (☎020/8569 4101; *www.sherpavan.com*) carries back packs and baggage for walkers and cyclists between overnight stops on the Coast-to-Coast, Sea-to-Sea, Cumbria Way or Dales Way. Service operates April–Oct daily.

Coast-to-Coast Packhorse (☎017683/71680; *www.cumbria.com/ packhorse*) offers a similar service on the Coast-to-Coast route, and provides left-luggage storage too for overseas visitors. Service operates May–Sept daily.

CYCLING TOUR OPERATORS

Country Lanes (☎01425/655022; *www. countrylanes.co.uk*). Bike-touring specialist offering group tours, day trips and a three-day "Taste of the Lakes" self-guided circuit (from £295).
Discovery Travel (☎01904/766564; *www. discoverytravel.co.uk*). Self-guided cycle tours: three-night breaks in Langdale from £130, or a seven-night Lake District circuit (from £325).

Holiday Lakeland Cycling (☎016973/71871; *www.holiday-lakeland.co.uk*). Five-night cycling tours (including hotel accommodation, baggage transfer): either the "Nine Lakes Tour" (£195) or the "Sea to Sea Adventure" (£225; includes two nights in the Lakes). May–Sept only.

BIKE RENTAL

AMBLESIDE

Biketreks, 9 Compston Rd (☎015394/31505).
Ghyllside Cycles, The Slack (Nov–Easter closed Wed; ☎015394/33592).

CONISTON

Meadowdore, Tilberthwaite Ave (March–Nov only; call for availability winter weekends; ☎015394/41638).
Summitreks, 14 Yewdale Rd (☎015394/41212).

GRIZEDALE

Grizedale Mountain Bikes, Old Hall Car Park, Grizedale Forest Park (☎01229/860369).

HAWKSHEAD

Croft Mountain Bike Hire, Croft Caravan & Campsite, North Lonsdale Rd (☎015394/36374).

KESWICK

Keswick Mountain Bikes, Southey Hill (☎017687/75202); branch also at Lakeland Pedlar, Henderson's Yard, Bell Close Car Park (☎017687/75752).

LANGDALE

Great Langdale Campsite, Great Langdale, B5343 (☎015394/37668).

STAVELEY

Millennium Bike Co., Bankside Barn, Crook Rd (☎01539/821167).

ULLSWATER

Tindals, Glenridding Pier (March–Oct only; ☎017684/82393).

WHINLATTER

Lakeland Mountain Bike Hire, Revelin Moss, Whinlatter Forest Park, Whinlatter Pass (March to mid-Oct only; ☎0780/104 7458).

WINDERMERE

Country Lanes, The Railway Station (Easter–Oct 9am–5pm; Nov–Easter by arrangement; ☎015394/44544; *www.countrylanes.co.uk*).

---

that mountain-biking is having on ancient bridle ways. Provided you exercise caution and respect walkers' rights of way there's a lot of fun to be had, and local **bike rental** outfits (see the list above) can kit you out with all the gear. The going rate is around £15 for a full-day's rental of a mountain bike, with helmets, locks and often route maps usually included in the price. Children's bikes, trailer bikes and tandems are also often available. A limited number of local buses will carry bikes: call the Cumbria County Council Journey Planner (☎01228/606000) for details.

Cycle **touring** in the Lakes per se isn't much fun, given the traffic, the narrow roads and the severe hills (some of the passes are the steepest roads in England), but it's still a popular pastime. Many youth hostels have bike sheds, though you should call ahead to check facilities at B&Bs and hotels. Long-distance tourers have the choice of shadowing walkers on the **Sea-to-Sea (C2C) cycle route**, a 140-mile trip between

Whitehaven/Workington and Sunderland/ Newcastle (information from SUSTRANS: ☎0117/ 926 8893; www.sustrans.org.uk), or using the **Cumbria Cycle Way**, which circles the region. More information, and touring information route sheets (free to members) for Cumbria and the Lakes, from the Cyclists' Touring Club (CTC: ☎01483/417217; www.ctc.org.uk).

Boating and water sports

You can rent a **rowboat** on most of the major lakes – Windermere, Coniston Water, Derwent Water and Ullswater included. The piers are detailed in the Guide and prices start at around £2.50 per person per hour; boats usually aren't available in the winter. Various outlets also rent out **canoes and kayaks** (from around £5 an hour), **sailing-boats** (from £50 half-day, £70 full-day) and small, self-drive **motorboats** and **electric boats** (from £35 half-day, £45 full-day).

There's also **power-boating, water-skiing and jet-skiing** on Windermere. As with mountain-biking, these sports ruffle environmental feathers – and with good reason once you see how busy and noisy the lake becomes on a summer's day. Restrictions are in place on many of the lakes: both Coniston Water and Ullswater have a 10mph speed limit, power boats aren't allowed on Bassenthwaite or Derwent Water, while Windermere has a speed limit of 6mph in certain clearly marked zones – for more information call the Windermere Lake Wardens (☎015394/42753), who enforce the restrictions.

Contact the companies and marinas listed in the box below for rental prices, instruction courses and other details.

On the land

Activity centres throughout Cumbria and the Lakes offer diverse opportunities, from horse riding and pony trekking to gorge-climbing, ghyll-scrambling, go-karting and orienteering. A selection is highlighted in the box below, but check also the noticeboards in local tourist offices. Prices vary wildly, though you can expect to pay around £10–15 per person for a guided walk or pony-trekking session, £15–20 for a gorge-climbing/ghyll-scrambling session, £50 for a full-day's activity and up to £150 for a balloon flight over the Lakes.

BOAT RENTAL AND WATER SPORTS CENTRES

CONISTON WATER

Coniston Boating Centre, Lake Rd, Coniston (March to mid-Oct only; ☎015394/41366). Electric boats, sailing, canoes – rental only, no instruction.

DERWENT WATER

Derwentwater Marina, Portinscale, Keswick (☎017687/72912). Sailing, kayaking, canoeing, windsurfing.

Nichol End Marine, Portinscale, Keswick (☎017687/73082). Windsurfing, sailing, canoeing and motorboats.

Platty Plus, Lodore Boat landings, Borrowdale (March–Oct only; office ☎017687/76572, waterfront ☎017687/77282). Canoeing, kayaking and sailing.

ULLSWATER

Glenridding Sailing School, The Spit, Glenridding (Easter–Oct only: ☎017684/82541). Canoes, kayaks and dinghies.

Tindals, Glenridding Pier (March–Oct only; ☎017684/82393). Rowboats, motorboats and electric boats.

Ullswater Marine, Rampsbeck Boatyard, Watermillock (Easter–Oct only; ☎017684/86415). Motorboat rental.

WINDERMERE

Low Wood, Windermere, a mile south of Ambleside (Easter–Nov only; ☎015394/39441; www.elh.co.uk). Water-skiing, sailing, windsurfing, kayaking, speed boats and power-boat lessons.

Windermere Lake Holidays Afloat, Gilly's Landing, Glebe Rd (☎015394/43415; www.windermere-lake-holidays-afloat.co.uk). Motorboat and canoe rental, plus sailing and water-skiing instruction.

Activity and Equestrian Centres

Armathwaite Hall Equestrian Centre, Coalbeck Farm, Bassenthwaite Lake (☎017687/76949).
Country hikes and pub rides, cross-country instruction, and pony-care days, residential courses and riding holidays.

Holmescales Riding Centre, Holmescales Farm, Old Hutton, near Kendal (☎01539/729388).
Riding instruction, pony trekking and hacking.

Touchstone Keswick ("Keswick Wall"), Southey Hill, Great Bridge, Keswick (☎017687/72000; *www.keswickwall.force9.co.uk*).
Indoor climbing wall, plus canoeing, ghyll-scrambling and abseiling.

Park Foot Trekking, Pooley Bridge, Howtown Rd, Ullswater (March–Oct only; ☎017684/86696).
Pony trekking on the fells.

Pleasure in Leisure, Tirobeck, Keldwyth Park, Windermere (☎015394//42324).
Archery, ballooning, go-karting, climbing and abseiling.

Rookin House Farm, Troutbeck, A5091, Penrith (☎017684/83561; *www.rookinhouse.freeserve.co.uk*).
Horse riding, pony trekking, go-karting, quad-biking, archery and clay-pigeon shooting.

Summitreks, 14 Yewdale Rd, Coniston (☎015394/41212).
Gorge-climbing, abseiling, adventure days and guided hikes.

Directory

Emergencies Dial ☎999 for all emergencies: in relevant circumstances ask for "Mountain Rescue".

English Heritage PO Box 1BB, London W1A 1BB (☎020/7973 3434). Historic properties (free to members) are denoted in the Guide by the suffix "EH".

Friends of the Lake District Campaigning group, established in the 1930s, dedicated to protecting the region: contact Friends of the Lake District, no. 3, Yard 77, Highgate, Kendal, LA9 4ED (☎01539/720788).

Hospitals There are accident and emergency services at the following hospitals: Cumberland Infirmary, Newtown Rd, Carlisle (☎01228/523444); Cockermouth Cottage Hospital, Isel Rd, Cockermouth (☎01900/822226); Westmorland General Hospital, Burton Rd, Kendal (☎01539/732288); Keswick Cottage Hospital, Crosthwaite Rd, Keswick (☎017687/72012); Penrith New Hospital, Bridge Lane, Penrith (☎01768/245300).

Laundry Most youth hostels have washing-and-drying facilities of some sort, and B&B owners can sometimes be persuaded (or offer) to help out. There are self-service laundries in: Ambleside (Laundromat, Kelsick Rd); Keswick (Laundrette, 24 Helvellyn St); and Windermere (Windermere Launderette, 19 Main Rd). There are no laundry services in Grasmere or Coniston.

Markets For local fruit and veg, household goods, cheap clothes and other market staples, check out one of the following Lake District markets: Monday (Cockermouth, Kendal), Tuesday (Broughton-in-Furness, Penrith), Wednesday (Ambleside, Kendal), Thursday (Ulverston), Saturday (Kendal, Keswick, Penrith, Ulverston).

National Trust 36 Queen Anne's Gate, London SW1H 9AS (☎020/7222 9251); Regional Office, The Hollens, Grasmere, Cumbria LA22 9QZ (☎015394/435599). The Lake District's largest landowner maintains a series of gardens and properties (free to members), denoted in the Guide by the suffix "NT".

Opening hours Full opening hours are given in the Guide for sights, attractions and tourist offices. Church opening hours vary considerably, though most of those mentioned in the Guide open daily between 9 or 10am and 4 or 5pm, but you can't count on it. Early closing day (when the shops shut for the afternoon) is still observed in many towns and villages, usually on Thursday in the Lakes.

Pharmacies Those in the main towns and villages (all listed below) are open standard shop hours, though local newspapers list pharmacies which stay open later (usually on a rota basis). Ambleside: Thomas Bell, Lake Rd (☎015394/ 33345); Boots, 8–9 Market Cross (☎015394/ 33355). Bowness: Lakeland Pharmacy, 5 Grosvenor Terrace, Lake Rd (☎015394/43139). Cockermouth: Allison, 31 Main St (☎01900/

822292); Boots, 56–58 Main St (☎01900/ 823160). Hawkshead: Collins & Butterworth, Post Office Pharmacy, Main St (☎015394/36201). Kendal: Boots, 10 Elephant Yard (☎01539/ 720180); Lloyd's, Station Yd (☎01539/723988). Keswick: Boots, 31 Main St (☎017687/72108); Lightfoot's, 25 Main St (☎01768/72108). Penrith: Boots, Grahams Lane (☎01768/862735); Lightfoot's, Middlegate (☎01768/862695). Windermere: Boots, 10–12 Crescent Rd (☎015394/43093); David Carter, 16 Crescent Rd (☎015394/43417).

Police There's 24-hour cover at the following regional police stations: Kendal (☎01539/ 722611) for Kendal, Windermere, Ambleside and Hawkshead; Penrith (☎01768/864355) for Penrith and Ullswater; Workington (☎01900/ 602422) for Keswick and Cockermouth; and Barrow (☎01229/824532) for Coniston and Ulverston. Call ☎999 in an emergency.

Shopping and souvenirs Various interesting craft outlets, galleries and museum shops are detailed throughout the Guide, while for specifically lakeland gift ideas consider buying: carved walking sticks; items (house numbers and the like) made from locally quarried slate; emroidered lace (first pioneered by Ruskin); locally produced foodstuffs (see "Food and drink", p.14); or Herdwick woolly jumpers. Hiking, camping and climbing equipment is no cheaper in the Lakes than anywhere else, but there is a wider selection available – Ambleside and Keswick are the best places to shop for outdoors gear. Bookshops, for Wordsworthian miscellanea, lakeland tracts, maps and first editions, are listed on p.179.

Swimming The lakes can be very cold for swimming, while steeply shelving sides, water craft and power boats (on Windermere) put some areas off-limits for bathers. We point out the best places for a dip in the Guide, but you might want to stick to local swimming pools instead: Cockermouth Sports Centre, Castlegate Drive (☎01900/823596); Kendal Leisure Centre, Burton Rd (☎01539/729777); Keswick Leisure Pool, Station Rd (☎017687/72760); Penrith Leisure Centre, Southend Rd (☎01768/863450); Troutbeck Bridge Swimming Pool, Troutbeck Bridge, near Windermere (☎015394/43243).

Public and Bank Holidays in the UK

January 1
Good Friday (late March or early April)
Easter Monday (as above)
First Monday in May
Last Monday in May
Last Monday in August
December 25
December 26
Note that if January 1, or December 25 or 26 falls on a Saturday or Sunday, the next weekday becomes a public holiday.

Part 2

The Guide

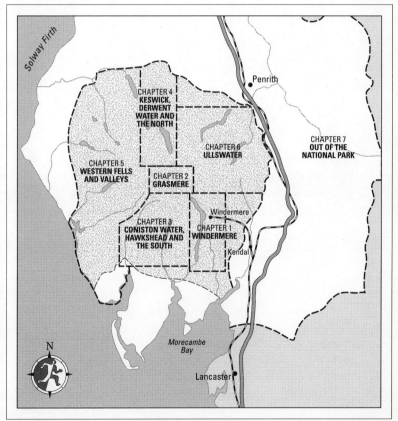

© Crown copyright

Chapter 1

Windermere

The elongated comma that is **Windermere**, England's largest and most famous lake, rarely fails to impress. Its rocky inlets, secluded bays, grassy banks and wooded heights form the very core of most people's image of the Lake District. And on bitingly cold winter days, or in the dappled spring and autumn sun, there are few finer places in England to soak up the scenery. Hardly surprisingly, its manifest attractions make it far too popular for its own good. In the summer, especially during school and public holidays, the roads in its vicinity become traffic bottlenecks, there's more chance of winning the lottery than finding parking space, and accommodation is packed to the gills. You're unlikely to find real solitude, though the remarkably underdeveloped southern and western reaches of the lake provide more possibilities than the

---

ACCOMMODATION PRICE CODES

Hotel and **B&B** accommodation is priced on a scale of ① to ⑨ (see below), indicating the **average price** you could expect to pay per night for a **double or twin room** in high season. **Youth hostels** are not given a price code since they fall within a fairly narrow price band. For more accommodation details, see Basics, p.12.

① under £40	④ £60–70	⑦ £110–150
② £40–50	⑤ £70–90	⑧ £150–200
③ £50–60	⑥ £90–110	⑨ over £200

CAFÉ AND RESTAURANT PRICE CODES

Cafés and restaurants listed in this guide have been assigned one of four price categories:

Inexpensive under £10
Moderate £10–20
Expensive £20–30
Very expensive over £30

This is the price you can expect to pay per person for a three-course meal or equivalent, excluding drinks and service.

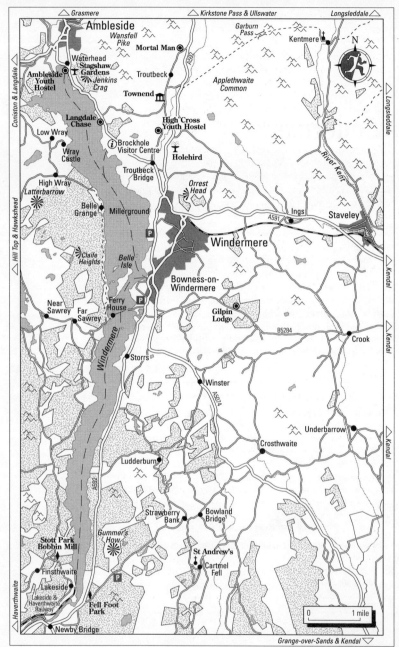

Ambleside
Wansfell Pike
Mortal Man ◉

Waterhead
Stagshaw Gardens
Ambleside Youth Hostel
Jenkins Crag
Troutbeck

Garburn Pass
Kentmere †

N

Langdale Chase ◉
Low Wray
Wray Castle
High Wray
Latterbarrow

Townend 🏛

High Cross Youth Hostel

Applethwaite Common

ⓘ **Brockhole Visitor Centre**
Holehird ⚘
Troutbeck Bridge

Belle Grange
Millerground

Orrest Head

Ings

Staveley

River Kent

A591

Claife Heights
Belle Isle

P

Windermere

Near Sawrey
Far Sawrey
Ferry House
P

Bowness-on-Windermere

Gilpin Lodge ◉

B5284

Crook

Storrs

Winster

A5074

Underbarrow

Crosthwaite

Ludderburn

Strawberry Bank
Bowland Bridge

Stott Park Bobbin Mill |
Gummer's How ⚘
Finsthwaite
Lakeside
Lakeside & Haverthwaite Railway
P
Fell Foot Park
Newby Bridge

St Andrew's
Cartmel Fell

0   1 mile

Coniston & Langdale ◁
Hill Top & Hawkshead ◁
Windermere
Haverthwaite ◁
Longsleddale ▷
Kendal ▷
Kendal ▷

dubious delights of the over-touristed settlements on its eastern shore.

Windermere town itself (a mile inland of the lake) has been the largest engine of change – literally so, since it was the coming of the railway in the mid-nineteenth century that brought the first mass influx of tourists. Even today, most people approaching the central lakes and fells from the south at least funnel through the town, getting their first glimpse of the lake at nearby **Bowness** – formerly a medieval lakeside village, though now the National Park's largest resort and boating centre.

Wordsworth himself thought that "None of the other Lakes unfold so many fresh beauties" and it makes sense to get out on the water as soon as possible. The cruise-boat ride south provides access to **Lakeside** and its aquarium, and to the picnic lawns of **Fell Foot Park**, while combined boat-and-train tickets are available for trips on the popular **Lakeside and Haverthwaite Railway**. Heading north from Bowness there are landings at **Brockhole** – whose magnificent gardens form the backdrop for the Lake District National Park headquarters and visitor centre – and at Waterhead for nearby **Ambleside**. This is the northernmost settlement on Windermere, and suffers from the same seasonal overcrowding that bedevils Bowness, but many use it as a handily sited hiking and touring base.

Away from the lake, the quiet hamlet of **Troutbeck** is strung along a gentle valley between Windermere and Ambleside. There's good walking from here, as there is from the neighbouring **Kentmere** valley, where the River Kent tumbles down through the old mill village of **Staveley** – only four miles east of the hubbub at Windermere but refreshingly unvisited.

Windermere town

The completion of the railway from Kendal in 1847 changed the face of Windermere for ever, providing direct access to the lake for Victorian day-trippers and holiday-makers. The hillside hamlet of Birthwaite, lying a good mile fom the water, was entirely subsumed within a newly created town, soon named **WINDERMERE** to emphasize the link with the lake itself. Not everyone welcomed the development. William Wordsworth, ever more conservative in his old age, feared the effects of the railway (while conveniently forgetting that his own *Guide to the Lakes* had done much to popularize the district in the first place). The poet attempted to keep out the hordes by means of a sonnet – "Is then no nook of English ground secure from rash assault?" – and by penning rambling broadsides which must have sorely tested the patience of their recipient, the editor of the *Morning Post*. Wordsworth's defence of the "picturesque" had reason behind it, and he can hardly be said to have been wrong in fearing the "railway inundations [of an] Advance of the Ten Thousand". But (like most

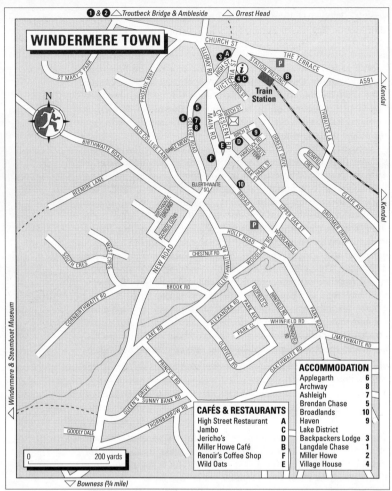

WINDERMERE TOWN

❶ & ❷ △ Troutbeck Bridge & Ambleside   △ Orrest Head

CHURCH ST
ST MARY'S PARK
PHOENIX WAY
ELLERAY RD
HIGH ST
VICTORIA ST
STATION RD
THE TERRACE
A591
Kendal
❸ Ⓐ
ⓘ
❹ Ⓒ
Ⓑ
STATION PRECINCT
P
Train Station
❺
❻
CRESCENT RD
BEECH ST
BIRCH ST
❾ Ⓓ
OLD COLLEGE LANE
GABLE MEWS
COLLEGE ROAD
MAIN RD
BIRTHWAITE ROAD
HANROCK RD
DROOST DRIVE
THWAITES LA
BOWEL CRES
Ⓔ Ⓓ
Ⓕ
OAK ST
HAZEL ST
CLAIFE AVE
Kendal
BEEMIRE LANE
ELLERTHWAITE SQ
❿
BROAD ST
UPPER OAK ST
DROOMER DRIVE
WEST CRES
BIRTHWAITE GROUND
PATHS & GDNS
NEW ROAD
HOLLY ROAD
WOODLAND RD
WOODLAND CT
SOUTH CRES
CHESTNUT RD
ELLERTHWAITE RD
PARK ROAD
LIMETHWAITE RD
CORNBIRTHWAITE RD
BROOK RD
ALEXANDRA RD
OLDFIELD RD
PARK AV
BIRKFIELD RD
WHINFIELD RD
SPRINGFIELD RD
P
Windermere & Steamboat Museum
LAKE RD
PARK CL
OAKTHWAITE RD
PRINCE'S RD
QUEEN'S DRIVE
SUNNY BANK RD
THORNBARROW RD
GOODLY DALE

N

0 _____ 200 yards

CAFÉS & RESTAURANTS
High Street Restaurant	A
Jambo	C
Jericho's	D
Miller Howe Café	B
Renoir's Coffee Shop	F
Wild Oats	E

ACCOMMODATION
Applegarth	6
Archway	8
Ashleigh	7
Brendan Chase	5
Broadlands	10
Haven	9
Lake District Backpackers Lodge	3
Langdale Chase	1
Miller Howe	2
Village House	4

▽ Bowness (¾ mile)

© Crown Copyright

gentlemen of his day) his real fear was that of the great unwashed, the "imperfectly educated", sullying his back yard with their "wrestling matches, horse and boat races ... pot houses and beer shops".

Most of the villas and guest houses built for the Victorians still stand, and Windermere town remains the transport hub for the southern and central lakes, but there's precious little else to keep you in the slate-grey streets. Instead, all the traffic pours a mile downhill to its older twin town, lakeside Bowness, and the only reason for not doing the same is to take time to climb the heights of **Orrest Head** (784ft), just to the north of Windermere town. The bare summit gives a famous 360° panorama, sweeping from the Yorkshire fells to Morecambe Bay, the Langdale Pikes to Troutbeck valley. This was the very first lakeland climb made by a young Alfred Wainwright (see p.158), on his earliest visit to the Lake District in 1930 – one that, in his own words, cast a spell that changed his life. It's an easy twenty-minute stroll up through shaded Elleray Wood: the signposted path begins just to the left of the large *Windermere Hotel* on the A591, across from the train station.

Windermere town

Arrival and information

The A591 between Kendal and Ambleside runs across the northern side of town, past the **train station**. Windermere is a major **bus terminus**, with National Express and all local services stopping outside the station – useful routes include the #555/556 or #599 (to Bowness, Kendal, Ambleside, Grasmere and Keswick), the #505/506 (Ambleside and Hawkshead), and #530/531 (Lakeside and Cartmel). There are **car parks** inside the train station yard and on Broad Street; on-street parking is limited to thirty minutes. A few yards away from the station, in the wooden chalet, opposite NatWest bank, stands the **tourist information centre** at the top of Victoria Street (daily: July & Aug 9am–7.30pm; rest of the year 9am–6pm; ☎015394/46499).

Windermere services:

bike rental p.20;

laundry p.22;

pharmacy p.23;

post office p.11;

swimming pool p.23;

taxis p.7.

Accommodation

Windermere doesn't have the waterside advantages of Bowness, but it does have a lot more **accommodation**. Good first places to look for B&Bs are on High Street and neighbouring Victoria Street, with other concentrations on College Road, Oak and Broad streets. At the bottom of town, halfway to Bowness, Lake Road has a line of mid-range guest houses and hotels, but these are a long walk (or bus ride) from either Bowness or Windermere. The nearest YHA **youth hostel** is at Troutbeck (though there is a back packers' in Windermere itself), while for **camping** you'll have to head down to Bowness.

Hotels, guest houses and B&Bs

Applegarth Hotel, College Rd (☎015394/43206). Detached hotel that retains its ornate Victorian interior (including a panelled lounge and bar, and stained-glass windows) and terraced garden. The eighteen rooms are well-proportioned – best (fell) views are at the back, at the top. Parking. ④.

Archway, 13 College Rd (☎015394/45613, *archway@btinternet.com*). Known for its breakfasts (home-made granola, yoghurt, fresh and dried fruit, American-style pancakes, or traditional full English breakfast), served communally in a pine breakfast room. Trim rooms, with the best light and views at the front. ③.

Ashleigh, 11 College Rd (☎015394/42292). Smart, non-smoking house whose four tasteful rooms have been furnished in welcoming country pine. Breakfast includes home-made preserves. No credit cards. ②.

Windermere Town

Brendan Chase, 1–3 College Rd (☎015394/45638). Popular place with a good-humoured owner who keeps the house spick-and-span. Rooms (half with en-suite facilities) are very reasonably priced, especially the family/group rooms which sleep three or four. ①.

Broadlands, 19 Broad St (☎015394/46532, *broadlands@clara.co.uk*). In a line of stone-terraced guest houses, Broadlands stands out: a cheerily run family home with four rooms (the top one lovely and light), whose owners, the Pearsons, can provide walk leaflets and bike rental. ②.

Haven, 10 Birch St (☎015394/44017). Non-smoking corner house whose big windows let the light into its three comfortably appointed rooms. Only one (with a nice brass bedstead) has its own en-suite shower; otherwise you share a smart bathroom. No credit cards. ①.

Langdale Chase, A591, three miles north of town, just past Brockhole (☎015394/32201, *sales@langdalechase.co.uk*). Lounge on the magnificent lakeside terrace or swoon at the style in this lavish country-house hotel with its stupendous carved-oak interior (including a transplanted seventeenth-century fireplace), fine restaurant, tennis courts and croquet lawn. Ask about the Boat House room, right on the water. Parking. Minimum two-night stay at weekends. ⑦, ⑧ with dinner.

Miller Howe, Rayrigg Rd (A592), half-mile west of town (☎015394/42536, *lakeview@millerhowe.com*). The best hotel in Windermere – and a candidate for best in the Lakes. The antique- and art-filled rooms (the finest with lake views) come with supremely theatrical dinners and breakfasts. Lounges, conservatory, terrace and landscaped gardens provide relaxation. Parking. Closed Jan. ⑨.

Village House, 5 Victoria St (☎015394/46041). Three small rooms available (one with a double and single bed) in a cosy, non-smoking, family house, very near the train station. No credit cards. ①.

Youth hostel

Lake District Backpackers Lodge, High St (☎015394/46374). Musty hostel (opposite the *Lakes Hotel*) with the cheapest beds in town, where international travellers fill the cramped dorms (there's one private room which sleeps up to three people; ①) and catch up on their laundry. No credit cards.

Cafés and restaurants

High Street Restaurant, 4 High St (☎015394/44954). Reliable Anglo-French restaurant – goat's cheese crostini, followed by rack of lamb, with crème brûlée to finish is a typical dinner – with a good-value *table d'hôte* menu. Dinner only, closed Sun. Expensive.

Jambo, Victoria St (☎015394/43429). Boasting a fashion-conscious menu, loaded with Mediterranean flavours, this is a good spot for fish and vegetarian eaters. Moderate.

Jericho's, Birch St (☎015394/42522). With years of *Miller Howe* experience behind them, *Jericho's* owners provide rich, seasonally changing, menus for discerning town diners – five choices, starters and mains, always including a vegetarian option. Dinner only, closed Mon. Expensive.

Miller Howe Café, inside Lakeland Ltd, behind the train station (☎015394/46732). Occupying a corner of the kitchen/home-furnishings store, this superior caff's snacks, lunches and high teas attract peak-period queues. Sensational honey-baked ham baguette sandwiches, gravadlax, devilled mushrooms, feta cheese and olives, and other delights. Daytime only. Inexpensive.

Renoir's Coffee Shop, Main Rd (☎015394/44863). Sandwiches, croissants, cakes and frothy coffees – if the sun's out, eat at the couple of tables outside. Daytime only. Inexpensive.

Wild Oats, Main Rd (☎015394/43583). Wholefood café that's not afraid to put meat on the menu, so alongside the veggie breakfasts and sandwiches are stew and chilli. Daytime only. Inexpensive.

Bowness and the lake

BOWNESS-ON-WINDERMERE – to give it its full title – is undoubtedly the more attractive of the two Windermere settlements, spilling back from its lakeside piers in a series of terraces lined with guest houses and hotels. Set back from the thumb-print indent of Bowness Bay, there's been a village here since at least the fifteenth century, and a ferry service across the lake for almost as long. On a busy summer's day, crowds swirl around the trinket shops, cafés, ice cream stalls and lakeside seats but, assuming you don't take one look at the congestion and turn tail, there are more than enough scattered attractions to fill your day. And come the evening, when the human tide has subsided and the light fades over the wooden jetties and stone buildings, a promenade around Bowness Bay conjures visions of the Italian lakes.

Arrival and information

Bus #599 leaves Windermere train station (Easter–Oct daily every 20min; rest of year Mon–Sat hourly) for the ten-minute run down Lake Road to Bowness. The bus stops at the piers, which is also the terminus for local services to Ambleside, Hawkshead and Coniston (#505/506) and to Lakeside (#530/531). **The Bowness Bay Information Centre** is by the piers on Glebe Road (Easter–Oct Mon–Thurs & Sun 9.30am–6pm, Fri & Sat 9.30am–6.30pm; Nov–Easter Fri–Sun 9.30am–5pm ☎015394/42895). Parking anywhere in Bowness is a nightmare: there's free two-hour parking on Glebe Road, but otherwise you're going to have to put up with the car park charges.

*Bowness
services:
car rental p.7;
pharmacy
p.23;
post office p.11;
taxis p.7.*

Accommodation

Budget accommodation in Bowness is in short supply, so if you want to spend a night by the lake you should book ahead. And be warned that a lake view itself doesn't come cheap. Apart from the places recommended below, Kendal Road has a line of other possibilities. The two nearest campsites (listed below) are both within half a mile of Bowness centre, and are very popular – book at least a few days ahead in summer.

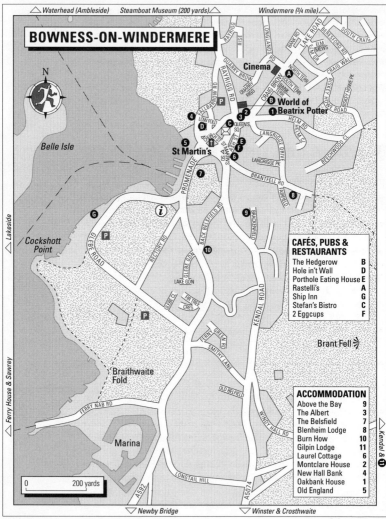

BOWNESS-ON-WINDERMERE

△ Waterhead (Ambleside)   Steamboat Museum (200 yards) △   Windermere (¾ mile) △

N

Cinema

World of Beatrix Potter

St Martin's

Belle Isle

Lakeside

Cockshott Point

i

Braithwaite Fold

Marina

Brant Fell ⇒

△ Ferry House & Sawrey

△ Kendal & ⑪

0   200 yards

▽ Newby Bridge   ▽ Winster & Crosthwaite

© Crown Copyright

CAFÉS, PUBS & RESTAURANTS

The Hedgerow	B
Hole in't Wall	D
Porthole Eating House	E
Rastelli's	A
Ship Inn	G
Stefan's Bistro	C
2 Eggcups	F

ACCOMMODATION

Above the Bay	9
The Albert	3
The Belsfield	7
Blenheim Lodge	8
Burn How	10
Gilpin Lodge	11
Laurel Cottage	6
Montclare House	2
New Hall Bank	4
Oakbank House	1
Old England	5

Hotels and B&Bs

Above The Bay, 5 Brackenfield (☎015394/88658, *ysx97@dial.pipex.com*). An elevated house in a residential area, just off Kendal Road, five minutes' from the water. Three spacious rooms (with generously sized bathrooms) open out onto a private terrace with huge lake views. Free entry to local leisure club. Parking. No credit cards. ②.

The Albert, Queen's Square (☎015394/43241). Smart accommodation in a central pub – king-sized beds give a bit more room for manoeuvre. ④.

The Belsfield, Kendal Rd (☎015394/42448 or ☎0345/334400). Stunning old mansion (once home of a Barrow steel magnate) with a large covered pool and lake-view lawns. But some of the standard rooms – heavy on Victorian furniture – are undersized, and there's a two-night minimum stay. Parking. ⑦.

Blenheim Lodge, Brantfell Rd (☎015394/43440). The steep climb from town is rewarded by great lake views (only one room doesn't overlook Windermere) and no-smoking rooms which vary in style from country-pine to Victorian-repro. Parking, restaurant and laundry facilities. ④.

Burn How, Back Belsfield Rd (☎015394/46226, *burnhowhotel@btinternet. com*). Upscale chalet units – all family-sized – with sheltered private patios, or smart doubles (some with four-posters) in the main lodge. Breakfast is served in the restaurant, or you can have continental served in your room. Parking. ⑥.

Gilpin Lodge, Crook Rd (☎015394/88818 or ☎0800/269460, *hotel@ gilpin-lodge.demon.co.uk*). A country-house retreat, a couple of miles east on the B5284 (Kendal road), opposite the golf course. The fourteen elegant rooms are individually styled, some with four-posters, others with whirlpool baths or private patios. And it's renowned by foodies for its serious Anglo-French cuisine. Minimum two-night stay at weekends. Parking. ⑦–⑧.

Laurel Cottage, St Martin's Square (☎015394/45594). Three pretty doubles with low ceilings in the seventeenth-century, oak-beamed cottage or more space, for a few extra pounds, in the adjacent Victorian building. Good beds and a public bathroom (the bedrooms have only showers) make this a boon for walkers. Parking. No credit cards. ③.

Montclare House, Crag Brow (☎015394/42723). For simple B&B accommodation, these plainly furnished rooms (three with shower) above a café are the best-value in Bowness. No credit cards. ①.

New Hall Bank, Fallbarrow Rd (☎015394/43558). Detached Victorian house with a lake view and a central location (a few yards from the *Hole in't Wall* pub). The en-suite facilities may be tiny, and the rooms themselves not much bigger, but they're all freshly decorated, decked out in pine, with better views the higher you go. Good breakfast too, and parking. ③.

Oakbank House, Helm Rd (☎015394/43386). Rugs and flowers, scatter cushions and co-ordinated furniture, and a welcoming sherry decanter single out the splendid *Oakbank*, some of whose rooms have lake views – all have TV and video. Parking, packed lunches and good winter discounts available. Closed Jan. ④.

The Old England, Church St (☎015394/42444 or ☎0870/400 1830). This lakeside grande-dame with a Georgian kernel sports a small, heated outdoor pool and superb terrace. Lake-view rooms attract a small premium, though prices drop significantly between Nov and March. Parking. ⑦.

Campsites

Braithwaite Fold, near the ferry to Sawrey (☎015394/42177). Closed Nov–Easter.

Falbarrow Park, by the lakeside, off Rayrigg Rd (☎015394/44428, *info@ falbarrow.co.uk*). Caravans and RVs only. Closed Nov–Easter.

The town

What's left of the oldest part of Bowness survives in the few narrow lanes around **St Martin's Church**, consecrated in 1483. The church is notable for its stained glass, particularly that in the east window, now very difficult to make out but sporting the fifteenth-century arms of John Washington, a distant ancestor of first American president George Washington. Outside in the churchyard is the grave of one Rasselas Belfield (died 1822), "a native of Abyssinia" who was born a slave – and found himself shipped to Cumbria – but as a free man became servant to the Windermere gentry.

Most tourists, though, bypass the church and everything else in Bowness bar the lake for the chance to visit **The World of Beatrix Potter**, in the Old Laundry on Crag Brow (daily: Easter–Sept 10am–5.30pm; Oct–Easter 10am–4pm; £3.25; ☎015394/88444). It's unfair to be judgmental – you either like Beatrix Potter or you don't – but it is safe to say that the displays here (including lakeland scenes complete with Peter Rabbit and pals), gift shop and themed café find more favour with children than the more formal Potter attractions at Hill Top (see p.89) and Hawkshead (see p.85).

A better all-round bet is a visit to the **Windermere Steamboat Museum**, on Rayrigg Road (Easter–Oct daily 10am–5pm; £3.25; ☎015394/45565), which displays a variety of water-craft in its wet and dry docks. The oldest exhibit is a fragment of an eighteenth-century yacht, the most curious the duck-punt with its mounted blunderbuss, and the most prized the 1850 *Dolly*, claimed to be the world's oldest mechanically driven boat, and extremely well preserved after spending 65 years in the mud at the bottom of Ullswater. An Arthur Ransome exhibition reveals the inspiration behind the boats *Swallow* and *Amazon*, and you're allowed a peek at Captain Flint's houseboat, *Esperance*, as well as a closer look at Ransome's own boat, *Coch-y-Bondhu*, which became the boat *Scarab* in *The Picts and the Martyrs*. There are also knot-tying and Morse-code-sending games, as well as steam-launch cruises on some of the museum's gleaming specimens (call for times; £4.75). The museum is a fifteen-minute walk north of Bowness centre: bus #505/506 runs past the entrance every hour.

For more on Arthur Ransome, and Swallows and Amazons, *see p.90.*

Out on the lake

All the attractions in Bowness come second-best to a trip on **Windermere** itself – the heavyweight of Lake District lakes, at ten-and-a-half miles long, a mile wide in parts and a shade over two-hundred feet deep. As so often in these parts, the name derives from the Norse ("Vinandr's Lake") and since "mere" means lake, references to "Lake Windermere" are tautologous. The only settlements are at Bowness and Ambleside, which means that the views from the water tend towards the magnificent: north to the central fells, or south along a wooded shoreline that is mostly under the protection of the National Trust. The seasons are reflected in the changing colours and tree cover around the lake. Autumn can be a real treat, though global warming has put paid to the spectacular freezing winters of yesteryear – in the 1890s, excursion trains brought astonished sightseers to skate on the lake and marvel at the icicles hanging from the trees. Many of the private lakeside mansions built for Victorian Lancashire mill owners are now hotels, though **Belle Isle** – the largest of eighteen islets in the lake – is still privately owned: for over two hundred years (until the 1990s), its guardians were various members of the Curwen family who built the island's eye-catching Georgian round house, visible through the trees if you get close enough on a boat.

Bowness is a major **boating** centre and there are more opportunities here than on any other lake just to turn up and pootle about on the water. And although it's freezing cold, people do jump in at various spots; indeed, every September there are a couple of **Windermere swims**. The first Thursday of the month sees a cross-lake swim between Wray Castle and Ambleside (which takes between 30 and 45 minutes), while on the first Saturday is the ten-mile endurance route up the lake from Fell Foot Park to Ambleside, which has a nine-hour limit imposed upon it – the record is under four hours. Many people come here for the fishing, hooking perch, pike, roach and brown trout. You can also catch **char**, a reddish lake trout related to the Arctic char and landlocked in the Lakes after the last Ice Age. It thrives in the deep, cold waters of Windermere (and is usually on local menus between May and October). Daniel Defoe recommended potting this "curious fish" and sending it to your best friend.

Rowboats and motorboats are available at **Bowness piers**, with more boating and water-sport outlets further around the bay by the Glebe Road marina. There's no speed limit on the lake except in the more congested areas where navigation can be hazardous (including Waterhead, and the Bowness Bay and Fell Foot Park areas). In these zones – clearly signposted – Lake Wardens enforce a speed-limit of 6mph.

For more on water sports, see p.21.

The traditional **ferry service** is the chain-guided contraption which chugs across the water from Ferry Nab on the Bowness side to Ferry House, Sawrey (Mon–Sat 7am–10pm, Sun 9am–10pm, departures every 20min; 40p, cars £2). It's a useful service, providing access to Beatrix Potter's former home at Hill Top and to Hawkshead beyond, but as it can take only around eighteen cars at a time queues soon build up in summer. The Ferry Nab pier is a ten-minute walk south of the cruise piers, through the parkland of Cockshott Point (or follow the road signs from the promenade).

Cruises

The main operator on the lake is **Windermere Lake Cruises** (☎015394/43360) which operates modern cruisers and vintage steamers from Bowness to Brockhole (£4.30 return), as well as to Lakeside at the southern tip (£5.90 return) and Waterhead (for

Ambleside) at the northern end (£5.70 return). There's also a shuttle service between Bowness piers and Ferry House, Sawrey (£2 return), saving pedestrians the walk down to the car ferry. A 24-hour **Freedom-of-the-Lake ticket**, valid on all routes, costs £9.50. Services on all routes are very frequent between Easter and October (every 30min to 1hr at peak times and weekends), but much reduced during the winter. As well as these routes, from mid-May to mid-August the company operates an enjoyable 45-minute circular **cruise** around the islands (£4.40) and an evening wine cruise (£5.70) – more information from Bowness's pier-side ticket office.

Walks and picnics

While Bowness itself gets very busy in summer, there are plenty of other quieter lakeside spots in the vicinity. The grassy slopes of **Cockshott Point** are a popular picnic spot, as is the National Trust shoreline north of Bowness at **Millerground** (where there's also parking). The Victorians liked to cross the lake to take tea on the shore below the woods on the west side and, if you're up for an afternoon's walk away from the crowds, this still makes the best sense. Crossing to Ferry House at Sawrey, a gentle path runs two miles north along the shore to Belle Grange, from where you can climb up to Latterbarrow for lake views before returning along the paths of **Claife Heights** and back to Sawrey. The steep descent through the woods from Far Sawrey to the ferry pier passes the ruins of **The Station**, a castellated viewing platform from which eighteenth-century tourists would view the lake and mountains through a "claude-glass", a convex mirror used to "frame" their view. These viewing-stations were very popular until well into the nineteenth century and formed part of any tour of picturesque lakeland, but the views from this one have been lost to the over-arching trees.

Eating, drinking and entertainment

There are several places in Bowness to get a pizza or a budget café meal, while a couple of highly rated **restaurants** as well as the dining rooms of the major hotels serve fancier food. The best **pub** by far is the *Hole in't Wall*, though the *Ship Inn*, round by the marina, has lakeside seats and views of the boats, while for morning coffee or sunset drinks, you can't beat the terraces of *The Old England* or the *Belsfield*, both open to non-residents. *The Royalty* on Lake Rd (☎015394/43364) boasts the Lake District's biggest **cinema** screen; and the *Old Laundry Theatre* on Crag Brow (☎015394/88444) hosts an annual six-week **Autumn Festival** of theatre, music and the performing arts.

2 **Eggcups**, 6a Ash St (☎015394/45979). The best sandwich in Bowness – check the board for specials – plus nachos, enchiladas and veggie bakes in this cute and amiable caff. A couple of outdoor tables catch the sun. Daytime only, though open early evenings in summer. No credit cards. Inexpensive.

The Hedgerow, Crag Brow, Lake Rd (☎015394/45002). Serves an all-day breakfast, a better-than-usual variety of tea shop standards and a good range of teas and fruit infusions. Daytime only. Inexpensive.

The Hole in't Wall, Fallbarrow Rd (☎015394/43488). The town's oldest hostelry, behind Bowness church (and officially the *New Hall Inn*), is named after the hole through which ostlers once had their beer passed to them. Enjoy the stone-flagged floors, open fires, real ales, outdoor tables and popular bar meals. Inexpensive.

Porthole Eating House, 3 Ash St (☎015394/42793). The Porthole serves quality regional Anglo-Italian cuisine in a converted seventeenth-century cottage. Great home-made bread, antipasto, seasonal meat and fish, operatic warbling, open fires in winter, and a terrific wine list. Closed Sat lunch, Tues, and mid-Dec to mid-Feb. Expensive.

Rastelli's, Lake Rd (☎015394/44227). Long a local favourite for pasta and pizza (the calzone comes smothered with bolognese sauce), so expect to have to wait for a table in summer. Dinner only. Closed Wed. Moderate.

Stefan's Bistro, Queen's Square (☎015394/43535). Bistro favourites, from salmon and trout to chicken, steak and pasta. Dinner only Mon–Fri, Sat & Sun open lunch & dinner. Moderate.

Brockhole Visitor Centre

Brockhole, A591, three miles northwest of Windermere ☎015394/46601. Open Easter–Oct daily 10am–5pm; grounds and gardens open all year. Admission free, though there's a charge for parking. Buses #555/556 and #599 stop outside, or take the launch from Waterhead, Ambleside.

The Lake District National Park has its headquarters and main information point at **Brockhole Visitor Centre**, a late-Victorian mansion set in lush grounds on the shores of Windermere, to the north of Bowness. Besides the permanent natural history and geological displays, the centre hosts a full programme of guided walks, children's activities (including a popular adventure playground), garden tours, special exhibitions, lectures and film shows – the centre, and any local tourist office, can provide a schedule. On a warm day, the gardens are a treat, with their little arbours, lakeside paths, grassy lawns and picnic areas. The landscaping is among the finest in the Lakes, the work of the celebrated Lancastrian garden architect Thomas Mawson (1861–1933), who also designed the grounds for other Victorian piles at Holehird, Langdale Chase, Holker Hall and Rydal Hall. Inside the former mansion (built originally for a Manchester silk merchant), there's a bookshop – one of the best in the region for local guides and maps – and a café whose outdoor terrace looks down to the lake.

From Brockhole, clearly marked bridle paths (starting across the A591) run up to Townend and Troutbeck, providing a good walk if you're parked at the centre for the day.

Any **bus** between Windermere and Ambleside stops at the visitor centre, though for a much more enjoyable ride come by **Windermere Lake Cruises** launch from Waterhead, Ambleside (Easter & May–Sept hourly 10.45am–4.45pm; £4.30 return). The launch docks at the foot of the gardens.

Lakeside and Newby Bridge

From Bowness, boats head five miles down the lake to the piers at
LAKESIDE, where gentle wooded hills frame Windermere's serene
southern reaches. This is the quayside terminus of the **Lakeside and
Haverthwaite Railway** (Easter–Oct 6–7 services daily; £3.50 return;
☎015395/31594), whose steam-powered engines puff along four
miles of track through the woods of Backbarrow Gorge, the only surviving remnant of a line which used to stretch all the way to
Ulverston and Barrow. There's parking and a station tearoom at
Haverthwaite (closed Jan & Feb) and a chance to look around the
engine-shed, where (when it's not out on duty) Britain's oldest working standard-gauge loco, built in Manchester in 1863, is kept. Boat
arrivals at Lakeside connect with train departures throughout the
day and there's a joint boat-and-train ticket (£8.80 return) available
from Bowness piers. Haverthwaite station itself is on the A590,
across the busy main road from the actual village of Haverthwaite –
take bus #518 between Windermere, Bowness or Ulverston.

Also on the quay at Lakeside is the **Aquarium of the Lakes** (daily
9am–5.30pm; £4.95; ☎015395/30153), an entertaining natural history attraction centred on the fish and animals found in and along a
lakeland river. There's a pair of captive otters (Filly and Smudge)
and a walk-through tunnel aquarium (with char, perch and diving
ducks), while educational exhibits give the low-down on everything
from cockles to pike and leeches to lobsters; kids will love it.
Afterwards you can grab a drink in the lake-view café and peruse the
comings and goings of the boats. There's a joint ticket available with
the boat ride from Bowness (£9.10 return, includes aquarium entry,
available at Bowness piers).

Top **accommodation** choice is the *Lakeside Hotel*
(☎015395/31207, *lshotel@aol.com*; ⑦), across from the quayside
and aquarium, with waterside conservatory, restaurant and gardens.
Or there's B&B at *Landing Cottage*, a hundred yards back from the
lake (☎015395/31719; no credit cards; ②), a couple of whose
rooms have en-suite facilities. **NEWBY BRIDGE**, a winding mile or
so to the south, has a few more options, including the *Swan Hotel*
(☎015395/31681; ⑥), a classic old inn with riverside tables by the
handsome five-arched bridge.

Fell Foot Park and the Winster Valley

Fell Foot Park, on Windermere's southeastern reach (daily
9am–7pm or dusk; free; car park charge; NT; ☎015395/31273),
makes a relaxed picnic spot, where you can lounge on the Victorian
landscaped lawns and explore the rhododendron gardens and oak

and pine plantations. There was once a private mansion here, to go with the grounds, though that's long gone. But the mock-Gothic boathouse still stands and offers rowboat rental, while doubling as a rather superior tearoom – from the tables outside you can watch the Lakeside and Haverthwaite trains chuff into the station just across the lake. Launches run across to the park from Lakeside (Easter–Oct daily 11am–5pm; 75p each way), usually every twenty minutes depending on demand and the weather. By car, access is from the A592 (Bowness road), a mile north of Newby Bridge; bus #518 from Ulverston and Newby Bridge to Bowness passes close by.

Fell Foot Park and the Winster Valley

An ancient packhorse route from Newby Bridge to Kendal, now a steep and winding minor road, passes to the northeast behind Fell Foot. A mile up, there's free parking by the start of the footpath to **Gummer's How**, the gorse-topped fell which peers over the southern half of Windermere. It's an easy walk up to the little stone trig-point on the summit – it'll take an hour there and back, including a rest at the top to gaze down at the Fell Foot marina and the snaking River Leven.

Two miles further along the road, the *Mason's Arms* at **STRAW-BERRY BANK** is impeccably sited overlooking the low stony out-crops and tidy plantations of the **Winster Valley**. The pub's terrace is a great place for a beer – there are hundreds on offer, from all cor-ners of the globe, including a damson beer made on the premises – and the food is good too (especially for vegetarians), though the stone-flagged bar gets packed at weekends when half of Cumbria seems to decide what it needs is a Belgian fruit beer brewed by Trappist monks. If you fancy the look of the surroundings, it's worth knowing that the *Mason's Arms* has a couple of **holiday cottages** and apartments available (☎015395/68486 for details).

Arthur Ransome moved to the Winster Valley in 1925 and it was here that he wrote *Swallows and Amazons*. His house, known as **Low Ludderburn** (not open to the public), can be seen if you take the tortuous bracken- and bramble-lined road north from the pub for a couple of miles. To the south, exactly a mile from the *Mason's Arms* (follow the signposts), **St Andrew's Church** lies tucked into a hollow on the side of Cartmel Fell. The church dates from 1504 – it was built as an isolated, outlying chapel of Cartmel priory – and despite some brutal modern exterior cladding preserves a character-ful seventeenth-century interior: exposed rafters, a triple-decker pul-pit and twin "box" pews once reserved for the local gentry.

From Strawberry Bank, the road drops a mile to **BOWLAND BRIDGE**, whose *Hare & Hounds* (☎015395/68333; ③) – right by the bridge – is another nice old inn, this time with rooms and a shel-tered beer garden. It's run by former soccer player Peter Thompson, once of Liverpool and England. Beyond Bowland Bridge, a minor road makes its way north along the upper Winster Valley as far as **WINSTER** itself (on the A5074), where the *Brown Horse* pub is another pleasant stop for a drink. For food and rooms, though, you're better off a couple of miles south, down and off the A5074 at **CROSTHWAITE**, where the sixteenth-century *Punch Bowl Inn* (☎015395/68237; ③), next to the church, serves lakeland produce adorned with Modern-British trickery at fairly reasonable prices.

There is a **bus** (#541) from Kendal to Windermere, via Crosthwaite, every couple of hours (not Sun), but no public transport through the Winster Valley.

Finsthwaite and Stott Park Bobbin Mill

Half a mile up the hill from Lakeside, below Finsthwaite Heights, stands one of England's few working mills, **Stott Park Bobbin Mill** (Easter–Sept daily 10am–6pm; Oct 10am–5pm; last tour 1hr before closing; £3; EH; ☎015395/31087). It was founded in 1835 to supply the British textile industry with bobbins – rollers or spools for holding thread – and, as elsewhere when the cotton industry declined, the mill later diversified to manufacture pulleys, hammers, mallets, spade handles, yo-yos and even duffel-coat toggles. Commercial production finally ceased in 1971, at a time when plastic had replaced wood for most bobbins. Former workers guide visitors on a 45-minute tour through the processes of cutting, roughing, drying, finishing and polishing on machinery that hasn't changed since it was introduced in the mid-nineteenth century. Note that the steam engine driving the waterwheel operates only on Tuesdays, Wednesdays and Thursdays.

From a car park above the mill (follow the road to Finsthwaite) there's a pleasant walk up to **High Dam**, the reservoir whose water used to drive the mill machinery – allow an hour or so to circle the

---

Bobbins and coppicing

For a time in the nineteenth century the south Lakes' bobbin mills formed an important part of the national economy, supplying up to half of all the bobbins required by the booming British textile mills. There were two reasons for the industry's strength in the Lakes: the fast running water from lakeland rivers to drive the mills and the seemingly inexhaustible supply of wood. To make bobbins and other items, "coppiced" wood was required, from trees cut to stumps to encourage the quick growth of long poles, which were then harvested for use. It's a technique that's been used for over five thousand years, and in more recent times in the southern Lakes, including the area around Stott Park, ash, beech, birch, chestnut, hazel and oak were all grown in this way. The bark was peeled off and used in the tanneries, while coppiced wood was also used widely in charcoal-making (another key local industry), thatching and the production of tent pegs, cask bindings, fencing, agricultural implements (such as rakes) and so-called "swill" baskets (cradle-shaped Cumbrian panniers).

---

water and return. Alternatively, if you head for Finsthwaite hamlet itself, half a mile above the mill, you can clamber up through the woods of **Finsthwaite Heights** to the naval commemorative tower and viewpoint over Windermere.

Both the bobbin mill and Finsthwaite can be reached by #534 bus (June to mid-July Sat & Sun; mid-July to Aug daily), but it takes a bit of working out (the best connections are from Grange-over-Sands and Newby Bridge) and anyway, the walk up from Lakeside is nice enough.

Ambleside

AMBLESIDE, five miles northwest of Windermere, at the head of the lake, lies at the hub of the central and southern Lakes region. It's a popular, if commercial, base for walkers and tourers, but has lost most of its traditional market-town attributes. The original market square and associated buildings were swept away in a typically vigorous piece of Victorian redevelopment (though the market cross still stands) and today's thriving centre – more a retail experience than a lakeland town – consists of a cluster of grey-green stone houses, shops, pubs and B&Bs hugging a circular one-way system, which loops round just south of the narrow gully of Stock Ghyll.

Arrival and information

Buses (including National Express) all stop on Kelsick Road, opposite the library, with regular local services to and from Windermere, Grasmere and Keswick, plus seasonal services to Hawkshead and Coniston (#505/506), Elterwater and Langdale (#516), and Grizedale and Ulverston (#515). Walking up to town from the ferry piers at Waterhead takes about fifteen minutes, though a horse-and (motorized)-carriage service runs from the piers to the *White Horse* pub on Market Place (Easter–Oct daily 11am–5pm; £1.50). The A591 runs right through town and drivers are best advised to make straight for the signposted **car parks**, though be warned that these fill quickly in summer – you may not find a space on your first pass through. The **tourist office** is in the centre of town in the Central Buildings on Market Cross (daily 9am–5.30pm; ☎015394/32582).

Ambleside services: bike rental p.20; laundry p.22; pharmacy p.23; post office p.11; taxis p.7.

Ambleside is rife with **outdoors stores**, which makes it a good place to pick up walking and climbing gear and camping equipment at reasonable prices. Classic old stores such as F.W. Tyson (Market Place) or Wilf Nicholson (Market Cross) complement specialists such as The Climber's Shop (Compston Corner; walking boot rental available) and large retailers including the YHA Adventure Shop or Gaynor Sports (these last two part of the Market Cross shopping centre).

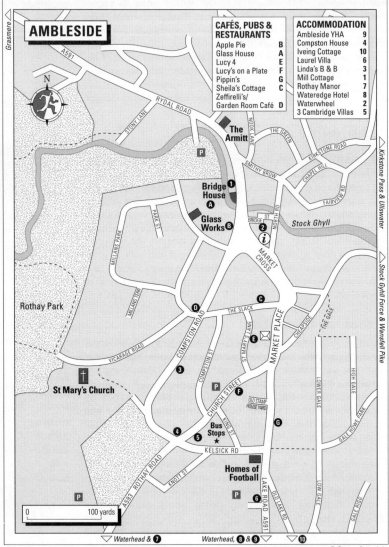

CAFÉS, PUBS & RESTAURANTS

Apple Pie	B
Glass House	A
Lucy 4	E
Lucy's on a Plate	F
Pippin's	G
Sheila's Cottage	C
Zeffirelli's/	
Garden Room Café	D

ACCOMMODATION

Ambleside YHA	9
Compston House	4
Iveing Cottage	10
Laurel Villa	6
Linda's B & B	3
Mill Cottage	1
Rothay Manor	7
Wateredge Hotel	8
Waterwheel	2
3 Cambridge Villas	5

© Crown Copyright

Accommodation

Lake Road, running between Waterhead and Ambleside, is lined with **B&Bs**, and there are other concentrations on Church Street and Compston Road. Ambleside's **youth hostel** is not in town but by the lake at Waterhead and is one of the most popular in the country – advance reservations are essential during most of the year. The nearest **campsite** is three miles south, too far out without your own transport to be used as a base for Ambleside itself.

Hotels and B&Bs

3 Cambridge Villas, Church St (☎015394/32307). The pick of the bunch on Church Street, the well-kept house hides a variety of agreeably furnished rooms, including one single. No credit cards. ②.

Compston House Hotel, Compston Rd (☎015394/32305, *compston@ globalnet.co.uk*). Inside this traditional lakeland house the American owners have cleverly created one of the Lakes' most individual B&Bs – Art Deco lounge, iconic American prints, lovely light (non-smoking) rooms themed after various US states, snazzy small bathrooms, and (if you wish) pancakes and maple syrup for breakfast. ③.

Iveing Cottage, Old Lake Rd (☎015394/32340). Rambling assortment of frayed-at-the-edges dorms, doubles and family rooms, sharing shower rooms, a couple of lounges and laundry facilities. It's a cheap base for groups/back-packers, with an acre of gardens and just ten minutes from lake or town. Parking. No credit cards. ①.

Laurel Villa, Lake Rd (☎015394/33240). Superbly restored villa with a rich William Morris interior, and fine original fittings, from the tiled entrance hall to the panelling and fireplaces. Rooms vary in size and decor, some with four-posters. Parking. ④–⑤.

Linda's B&B, *Shirland*, Compston Rd (☎015394/32999). The cheery spirit never flags and the bargain prices – the lowest in Ambleside – go some way to compensating for the weary decor and simple facilities. Guests can use the kitchen, while two of the four rooms (all of which share a bathroom) can sleep three or four. No credit cards. ①.

Mill Cottage, Rydal Rd (☎015394/34830). Long on atmosphere, but with rooms short on space, this converted sixteenth-century fulling mill (next to Bridge House) has its moments – particularly when you can while away time in the downstairs riverside café-restaurant. Two-night minimum at week-ends. ②.

Rothay Manor, Rothay Bridge (☎015394/33605, *hotel@rothaymanor. co.uk*). The most sought-after rooms in this Regency-style mansion are those at the front with their own private balcony. Plenty of interior space (including good-sized bathrooms, with baths), stylish decor, appealing grounds, and good food. Parking. ⑦, ⑨ with dinner.

Wateredge Hotel, Waterhead (☎015394/32332). Waterhead's top choice, a secluded retreat with rooms in the main hotel or garden-suites with balcony or patio. The continental/Cumbrian food wins plaudits, and off-season discounts are considerable (though require a two-night minimum stay). Parking. ⑧, includes dinner.

Waterwheel Guesthouse, Bridge St (☎015394/33286). The very picture of an old-fashioned Lake District cottage, with its climbing rose and a waterwheel outside. The three rooms fill quickly; there's one shared bathroom. The cottage is up the cobbled alley off Rydal Road, by the bridge across Stock Ghyll. No credit cards. ①.

Youth hostel and campsite

Ambleside YHA, Waterhead, A591 (☎015394/32304). Impressive lakeside affair with small dorms, doubles and family rooms, licensed café, bike rental, Internet and laundry facilities, and its own jetty (for jumping off). The drawbacks are that it's a fifteen-minute walk from Ambleside itself and usually packed with school parties.

Low Wray Campsite, off B5286, 3 miles south of Ambleside (☎015394/32810). National Trust site on the western shore of the lake, where there's a small shop, and canoe and bike rental; bus #505/506 (to Coniston) passes within a mile. Closed Nov–Easter.

The town and Waterhead

Stock Ghyll powered Ambleside's old fulling and bobbin mills whose buildings survive intact on either side of Bridge Street, as do a couple of restored waterwheels. Straddling Stock Ghyll is the town's favourite building, tiny **Bridge House** (Easter–Oct daily 10am–5pm; free; ☎015394/35599), a topsy-turvy, two-storey, two-roomed, slate-roofed house, now a National Trust information centre. Scurrilous legend has it that a Scotsman built the house to evade land taxes, but its true origins are as a covered bridge-cum-summer house used by a local family to access their orchards across the stream. It's had many other uses over the years, mainly for storage, though records show that in the nineteenth century it was briefly home to a family of eight. Behind the house is **Adrian Sankey's Glass Works** (daily 9am–5.30pm; 30p; ☎015394/33039), where you can watch glass being blown, then splash out on one of the finished products. The adjacent restaurant (see below), with its turning wheel, occupies restored fifteenth-century mill premises.

For more on Ambleside's history, stroll a couple of minutes' along Rydal Road to **The Armitt** (daily 10am–5pm; £2.50; ☎015394/31212), the latest and most splendid incarnation of the town's literary museum and library. First founded in 1909 (by local society intellectual Mary Louisa Armitt), the collection catalogues the very distinct contribution to lakeland society made by writers and artists from John Ruskin to Beatrix Potter: others, like the writer Harriet Martineau (author of her own *Guide to the Lakes*) and educationalist Charlotte Mason, made their home in the town, and The Armitt contains cases full of personal memorabilia – from a life-mask of Martineau to a lock of Ruskin's hair. There's plenty, too, on the remarkable Collingwood family (see p.83), plus displays related to the life and work of Herbert Bell (1856–1946), pharmacist of Ambleside turned pioneering lakeland photographer. And anyone driven to distraction by the bunny-and-hedgehog side of Beatrix Potter should be prepared to revise their opinion on viewing The Armitt's changing selection of her early scientific watercolour studies of fungi and mosses – a beautifully painted sequence donated to The Armitt by Potter herself.

Walks from Ambleside

Ambleside is impressively framed – Loughrigg Fell to the west, the distinctive line of the Fairfield Horseshoe to the north and Wansfell to the east – and even inexperienced walkers have plenty of choice.

Stock Ghyll

The traditional stroll is up Stock Ghyll Lane (which starts behind *The Salutation* hotel) and through the leafy woods of Stock Ghyll Park (with wonderful daffs in spring) to the tumbling waterfall of **Stock Ghyll Force**, which drops 60ft through a narrow defile. Allow an hour there and back if you linger on the viewing platform and rest on the benches.

Wansfell

Those with loftier ambitions can regain the lane by Stock Ghyll Park and, a little way further up, look for the signposted path (over a wall-ladder) up Wansfell to **Wansfell Pike** (1581ft). A stone path has been laid all the way to the top, so bad was the previous fell-side erosion, but it's still a punishingly steep walk – an hour all told to the top, for superb views of Windermere and the surrounding fells. Circular hikers either cut due south from the summit to Skelghyll and return via Jenkins Crag (2hr), or head east across a clearly defined path to Troutbeck and Townend before cutting back (4hr).

Jenkins Crag and Stagshaw Gardens

The viewpoint of **Jenkins Crag**, a mile from Waterhead, gives a glimpse of the lake as well as the central peaks of the Langdales and the Old Man of Coniston. From Ambleside, walk down Lake Road (though there's a handy car park near Hayes Garden World) and follow the signs up Skelghyll Lane, a thirty-minute walk. On the way back you can detour to the National Trust's woodland **Stagshaw Gardens** (Easter–June daily 10am–6.30pm; £1.50), at their best in spring for the shows of rhododendrons, camellias and azaleas.

See Basics, p.19, for general walking advice in the Lakes; recommended maps are detailed on p.9.

Spare time, too, for **St Mary's Church**, off Compston Road, whose rocket-shaped spire is visible from all over town. Completed in 1854, it was designed by George Gilbert Scott – the architect responsible for London's Albert Memorial and St Pancras station – and contains a mural of the town's annual rush-bearing ceremony, its figures resplendent in their 1940s' finery. The ceremony itself dates from medieval times and derives from the custom of replacing the worn rushes (or reeds) on unflagged church floors. In Ambleside, the event takes places on a Saturday in the first two weeks of July, with a procession through town of decorated rushes and the church congregation singing the specially commissioned Ambleside Rushbearers' Hymn. Behind the church, the green pastures of **Rothay Park** stretch down to the River Rothay.

The Lake District's most famous annual rushbearing ceremony takes place in Grasmere; see p.60.

Final port-of-call is soccer photographer Stuart Clarke's terrific gallery, **The Homes of Football**, at 100 Lake Rd (daily: July & Aug 10am–10pm; rest of year 10am–6pm; £1; ☎015394/34440). What started as a peripatetic exhibition, recording games and grounds from the Premier League down to the smallest amateur teams, has blossomed into a permanent archive of over 60,000 images, the massive selection on show all framed and available for sale. It's irresistible for soccer fans, who just might be persuaded to part with £200–300 for a unique memento of their team – though your entrance fee gets you a free soccer-ground photo-postcard.

Waterhead

The rest of town lies a mile south at **Waterhead**, a harbour on the shores of Windermere that's filled with ducks, swans and rowboats and overlooked by the grass banks of **Borrans Park**. Waterhead was the earliest settled part of Ambleside, known as Galava to the Romans, who built a turf-and-timber fort on the lake-edge in 90 AD, later superseded by a larger stone structure housing five-hundred auxiliary soldiers, which was finally abandoned at the end of the fourth century. The Roman scholar Robin Collingwood first excavated the two forts in separate digs between 1913 and 1920 (The Armitt holds many of the objects recovered), though there's little left to see *in situ* as the foundations of various buildings, including a large granary with hypocaust, are now largely grass-covered. But it's an emotive spot, backed by glowering fells and with views across the rippling Windermere waters – the perfect place for sunset-watching or star-gazing.

Eating, drinking and entertainment

There's more choice in Ambleside for **eating** than just about anywhere else in the Lakes, from cafés and takeaways to gourmet restaurants, which is one of the reasons the town makes such a good base. It's not served so well by its **pubs**, which, although plentiful, are for the most part fairly forgettable save for their outdoor terraces which come into their own in summer – popular spots are the *White Horse* (Market Place), the *Royal Oak* (Church Street) and the garden of the *Waterhead Hotel*, at Waterhead (which also has a full-on Irish theme bar, *McGinty's*). Cosiest spot on a cold night is the *Golden Rule* (Smithy Brow), the long-standing beer-lovers' and climbers' favourite, while *The Unicorn* (North Road) is an enjoyable old inn with real ales. Finally, there's a **cinema** at *Zeffirelli's* (see below; programme information on ☎015394/31771).

For details of Ambleside's famous annual traditional sports festival, see p.18.

Apple Pie, Rydal Rd (☎015394/33679). Busy café with patio garden seating and a range of dishes from BLTs and baked potatoes to quiche, soups and great home-made pies. Daytime only. Inexpensive.

The Glass House, Rydal Rd (☎015394/32137). Easily the best restaurant in town, housed in a renovated fulling mill with waterwheel – accomplished

Mediterranean/Modern-British cooking, whose £5 lunches and £10 early-bird dinners are a bargain, or you can just sit in the sunny courtyard and sip a cappuccino. Dinner reservations advised. Closed Mon Nov–Easter. Expensive.

Lucy 4, 2 St Mary's Lane (☎015394/34666). Tapas and good-time offshoot of *Lucy's On A Plate*, with an authentic menu, decent wines by the glass and salsa dancing nights. Dinner only. Closed Sun. Inexpensive to Moderate.

Lucy's On A Plate, Church St (☎015394/31191). Slightly scatty, stripped-pine bistro offering an inventive, seasonally changing menu (try the char when it's on) and a varied wine list. There's a good associated deli next door. Moderate.

Pippins, 10 Lake Rd (☎015394/31338). Grab a booth seat in this easy-going joint and you're set for all-day breakfasts (including continental), burgers and filled baguettes, with pizzas served in the evening. Inexpensive.

Sheila's Cottage, The Slack (☎015394/33079). The only in-town foodie rival to the *Glass House* serves lunch and dinner in country-cottage style surroundings, mixing local flavours and ingredients with the exotic. Plus a tearoom menu during the day. Expensive.

Zeffirelli's, Compston Rd (☎015394/33845). *Zeff's* is a star – crisp (wholemeal-base) pizzas, inventive veggie pastas (such as paoloroti, pasta quills with roasted red pepper, tomato and mascarpone sauce), a funky dining room, and a dinner-and-cinema special. Closed lunch Mon–Fri, though the downstairs *Garden Room Café* (daily until 5pm; ☎015394/31612), and its terrace and conservatory, takes up the slack during the day. Moderate.

Troutbeck

Troutbeck Bridge, three miles southeast of Ambleside along the A591 (and just a mile or so from Windermere town), heralds the start of the gentle **Troutbeck valley** below Wansfell, accessed by two roads, one either side of the valley's namesake beck. The main A592 to Patterdale runs north into the valley, passing the Lakeland Horticultural Society's splendid gardens at **Holehird** (daily dawn–dusk; free, though small donation requested; ☎015394/46008), whose four acres encompass various different habitats from rock and alpine gardens to rose gardens and shrubberies. The better route, though, is up a minor road (Bridge Lane) running high above the west side of Trout Beck. A mile along here is a **youth hostel**, *High Cross* (☎015394/43543), built originally as a private mansion and, although now deprived of its turrets, ballroom and boating lake, still with magnificent lake views.

Less than a mile further up the road from the hostel, **Townend** (Easter–Oct Tues–Fri & Sun 1–5pm, last admission 4.30pm; £3; NT; ☎015394/32628) is a seventeenth-century house, built in 1626 for George Browne, a wealthy yeoman farmer, one of that breed of independent farmers known in these parts as "statesmen", after the estates they tended. Remarkably, the house remained in the hands of eleven generations of the Browne family, for more than three hundred years, until 1943 when the National

Trust took it over. It's an extraordinary relic of seventeenth-century vernacular architecture, with its round chimneys (of the sort admired by Wordsworth) surmounting a higgledy-piggledy collection of small rooms, some added as late as the nineteenth century. The house is well-known for its woodcarvings and panelling, and lavishly embellished beds, fireplaces, chests, chairs and grandfather clocks are scattered around the various rooms. You'll also see the surviving laundry room (complete with mangle), dairy, library and parlour.

Townend is at the southern end of **TROUTBECK** village, really just a straggling, though striking, hamlet with a post office (which sells cups of tea and ice cream). Several hikes pass through village and valley, with the peaks of Yoke, Ill Bell (the highest at 2476ft) and Froswick on the east side forming the barrier between Troutbeck and Kentmere (see p.51). The most direct route into Kentmere is the track over the Garburn Pass, while many use Troutbeck as the starting point for the energetic five-hour walk along **High Street**, a nine-mile range running north to Brougham near Penrith. The course of a Roman road follows the ridge, probably once linking the forts at Brougham and Galava in Waterhead.

Troutbeck's famous **inn**, the *Mortal Man* (☎015394/33193, *The-Mortalman@btinternet.com*; ⑥, ⑦ with dinner; closed mid-Nov to mid-Feb) – at the northern end of the village – lords it over the valley. For non-residents, coffee and biscuits or a bar meal in the garden is a great way to soak up the seventeenth-century atmosphere. Its name, incidentally, derives from the doggerel written on the inn sign: "O Mortal Man, that lives by bread, What is it makes thy nose so red? Thou silly fool, that look'st so pale, Tis drinking Sally Birkett's ale". There are cheaper **B&Bs** in the village, like *High Fold Farm*, near the post office (☎015394/32200; no credit cards; ②), and *High Green Lodge*, nearer the inn (☎015394/33005; no credit cards; ②–③); while Troutbeck's other traditional inn, the *Queen's Head*, down on the main A592 (☎015394/32174; ④; two-night minimum stay at weekends) serves good food.

North of Troutbeck, the A592 makes a gradual ascent to **Kirkstone Pass**, four miles from the village, at the head of which there's a superbly sited pub, whose picnic tables (across the road) offer terrific views. A minor road from here cuts down directly to Ambleside – so precipitous that it's known as "The Struggle" – while the A592 continues over the pass and down the valley to Ullswater.

Public transport to Troutbeck is limited. For the hostel, a YHA shuttle-bus service operates from Windermere train station (meeting arriving trains) and from Ambleside youth hostel, while bus #517 runs up the A592 and over the pass three times a day (May to mid-July Sat & Sun; mid-July to Aug daily).

Staveley

Four miles east of Windermere, the pretty little village of **STAVELEY** lies tucked away on the banks of the River Kent. It's bypassed by the A591, which keeps the streets fairly quiet, and you can get here on the train line from Kendal and on the #555/556 bus. The river has powered mills in Staveley for over seven hundred years and in the eighteenth and nineteenth centuries there was prosperity of sorts as first cotton was produced and then wooden bobbins were manufactured here in sizeable quantities. These wood-turning skills have survived into modern times, with Staveley woodwork still a thing of beauty. **Peter Hall & Son** (Mon–Fri 9am–5pm, Sat 10am–4pm; ☎01539/821633), a mile out on the Windermere road, produces renowned handcrafted furniture and household goods, while other cottage industries occupy the old mill buildings themselves in Mill Yard, off Main Street.

An easy half-hour stroll around the village starts by the restored tower of **St Margaret's** on Main Street, all that survives of Staveley's original fourteenth-century church. Follow the path at the side of the church tower down to the river, turn left and walk along the riverside path and road to the old bridge, from where you return through the village, passing the replacement nineteenth-century church of **St James** – inside which is a superb Burne-Jones-designed stained-glass window depicting a star-clustered heavenly choir surmounting the crucifixion.

Back at Mill Yard, pop into *Wilf's Café* (closes at 5pm; ☎01539/822239), housed in an old wood mill, where breakfasts, rarebits, chillis, filled baked potatoes and cappuccinos are served at locally made tables; an upstairs deck overlooks the river and weir. The bread, incidentally, comes from Pain de Paris, another of Mill Yard's businesses, handy for picnic fixings. Staveley's *Eagle & Child* is the nicest local **pub**, though many drive the mile or so west to the *Watermill Inn* at Ings (☎01539/821309, *all@watermill-inn.demon.co.uk*; ②), a real-ale pub with a huge choice of beers, a garden and popular bar food.

Kentmere and Longsleddale

North of Staveley a narrow road runs its dappled way alongside the river, widening out after three miles into the splendid broad valley of **Kentmere**, with its isolated chapel perched on a bluff in the distance. This marks the start of the **Kentmere Horseshoe** (12 miles; 7hr), a reasonably strenuous hike along ridges and saddles on either side of Kentmere Reservoir. The walk starts by the chapel, where there's extremely limited parking, so get there early. You can walk up from Staveley, following Bowfoot Lane and then a river path, via Kentmere

Tarn, or on summer weekends (mid-July to Aug) take the #519 Kentmere Rambler **bus** from Staveley, whose return service is scheduled to allow an all-day hike.

Both Kentmere and **Longsleddale**, to the east (linked by bridleway), provide the deeply rural environs which inspired the "Greendale" of John Cunliffe's *Postman Pat* stories. There's no lake of course in either valley, so Cunliffe used Grasmere as his model for "Berkmere". Longsleddale is perhaps less visited than Kentmere, due in part to its harsher upper reaches, but there's a similar parking shortage at graceful Sadgill Bridge, which is as far as you can go by car. Beyond here, hikers make their way up to the abandoned Wrengill Quarry and its waterfall and then up the old packhorse trail over Gatesgarth Pass to Haweswater.

Travel details

From Ambleside

See Windermere below for main routes (#555/556 and #559).

Bus #515 (3 daily) to: Hawkshead (20min), Grizedale Forest (40min), Newby Bridge (1hr) and Ulverston (1hr 30min). Service operates mid-July to Aug Mon–Sat; May to mid-July, Sept & Oct Sat only.

Bus #516 (5–6 daily) to: Skelwith Bridge (10min), Elterwater (17min), Chapel Stile (20min), Old Dungeon Ghyll (30min). Service operates April–Oct daily; rest of year Mon–Sat only.

From Bowness

Bus #505/506 (hourly) to: Brockhole (7min), Waterhead (10min), Ambleside (15min) and Coniston (45min–1hr). Service operates April–Oct only.

From Windermere

Bus #530/531 (up to 3 daily) to: Bowness (10min), Newby Bridge (30min) and Grange-over-Sands (1hr 20min).

Bus #555/556 (hourly, every 2hr on Sun) to: Troutbeck Bridge (5min), Brockhole (7min), Waterhead (12min), Ambleside (15min), Grasmere (30min) and Keswick (50min); also to Staveley (12min) and Kendal (25min).

Bus #599 (every 20–30min) to: Bowness (10min); also to Troutbeck Bridge (5min), Brockhole (7min), Waterhead (12min), Ambleside (15min) and Grasmere (30min).

Chapter 2

Grasmere and the central fells

Grasmere – lake and village – is the traditional dividing line between the north and south Lakes; between the heavily touristed Windermere region and the more rugged fells on either side of Keswick. It lies on the only north–south road through the Lakes (the A591), which cuts through the pass of **Dunmail Raise** (782ft), three miles north of Grasmere – remembered (though with precious little evidence) as the site of the decisive battle in 945 between Dunmail, last independent king of Cumbria, and the Saxon king Edmund (who, in victory, handed Cumbria to Malcolm of Scotland).

Rather than for its own charms (which are considerable), Grasmere owes its wild popularity to its most famous former resi-

---

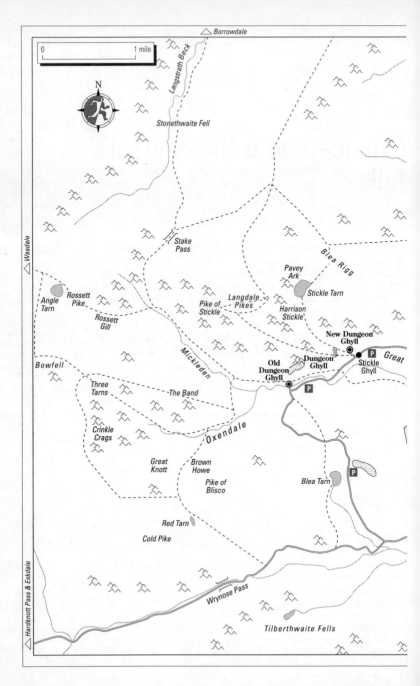

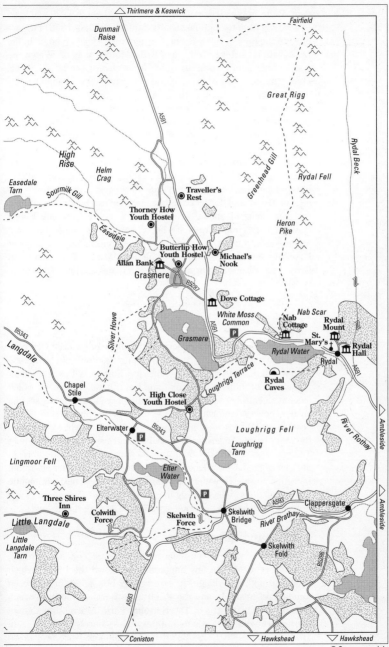

© Crown copyright

dent, **William Wordsworth**, who first moved here in 1799 and lived in a variety of houses in the vicinity until his death in 1850. Two are open to the public: **Dove Cottage**, where he first set up home in the Lakes with his sister Dorothy; and **Rydal Mount**, on Rydal Water, the comfortable family home to which he moved at the height of his fame. The influence of other literary lakeland names hangs heavily on Grasmere, too, notably those of Thomas De Quincey, who lived here for more than twenty years and married a local girl; and of the dissolute Coleridges – father Samuel Taylor and son Hartley, whose separate periods of residence often tried the Wordsworths' patience to breaking point.

The region's other attraction is the proximity of the **central fells**, including some of the Lake District's most famous peaks and valleys. Routes from Grasmere and Ambleside forge west into the superb valleys of Great and Little **Langdale**, overlooked by the prominent rocky summits of hikers' favourites such as the **Langdale Pikes**, **Bowfell** and **Crinkle Crags**. It's not all hard going though: there are easier walks to tarns and viewpoints in the bucolic surroundings of **Easedale** and Little Langdale, while hamlets such as **Skelwith Bridge** and **Elterwater** provide classic inns and country B&Bs for an isolated night's stay.

Grasmere

Four miles northwest of Ambleside, the village of **GRASMERE** consists of an intimate cluster of grey-stone houses on an old packhorse road which runs beside the babbling River Rothay. With a permanent population of under a thousand, and just a handful of roads which meet at a central green, it's an eminently pleasing ensemble, set in a shallow bowl of land which reaches down to an alluring lake. Thirty years before Wordsworth put down roots here, the "white village" on the water in this "unsuspected paradise" had also entranced the poet Thomas Gray (of "Elegy" fame) whose journal of his ground-breaking tour of the Lakes did much to bring the region to wider attention. Indeed, if you see Grasmere as being in the "very eye of the Romantic storm" (as does Melvyn Bragg in his *The Maid of Buttermere*) you have some idea of its enduring significance as a tourist magnet.

Arrival and information

Grasmere lies west of the main A591 (Ambleside–Keswick road), with the centre just a few hundred yards down the B5287 which winds through the village. It is served by **bus** #555/556 between Kendal and Keswick, and the #599 from Bowness, both of which stop on the village green. The **National Park Information Centre** (April–Oct daily 9.30am–5.30pm; Nov–March Sat & Sun 10am–3.30pm; ☎ 015394/35245) is five minutes' walk away down

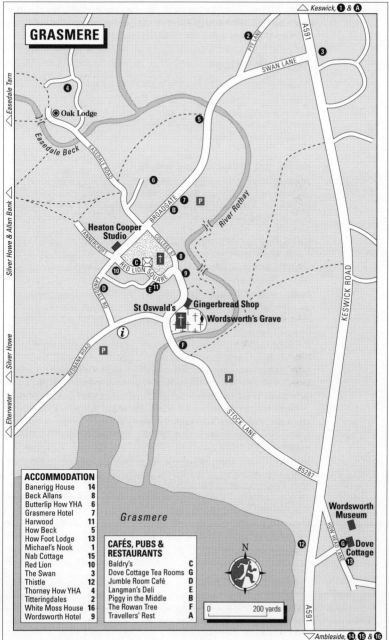

GRASMERE

Keswick, **1** & **A**

2
3

PIE LANE

SWAN LANE

A591

4

Oak Lodge

Easedale Tarn

Easedale Beck

Silver Howe & Allan Bank

5

6

EASEDALE ROAD

BROADGATE

River Rothay

7 P

8

Heaton Cooper Studio

TANNERCROFT

COLLEGE ST

10 RED LION SQUARE

D

LANGDALE RD

E 11

8

9

St Oswald's

Gingerbread Shop

Wordsworth's Grave

i

REDBANK ROAD

P

F

KESWICK ROAD

P

STOCK LANE

B5287

Silver Howe

Elterwater

Grasmere

Wordsworth Museum

G Dove Cottage

HOW HEAD LANE

12

13

A591

N

0   200 yards

ACCOMMODATION	
Banerigg House	14
Beck Allans	8
Butterlip How YHA	6
Grasmere Hotel	7
Harwood	11
How Beck	5
How Foot Lodge	13
Michael's Nook	1
Nab Cottage	15
Red Lion	10
The Swan	3
Thistle	12
Thorney How YHA	4
Titteringdales	2
White Moss House	16
Wordsworth Hotel	9

CAFÉS, PUBS & RESTAURANTS	
Baldry's	C
Dove Cottage Tea Rooms	G
Jumble Room Café	D
Langman's Deli	E
Piggy in the Middle	B
The Rowan Tree	F
Travellers' Rest	A

Ambleside, **14**, **15** & **16**

© Crown Copyright

Langdale Road, next to the main **car park** on Redbank Road at the southern end of the village. There's a second car park on Stock Lane, on the east side as you come in from Dove Cottage.

Accommodation

Accommodation can be hard to come by in summer and you should book well in advance, especially for the two popular **youth hostels**. If both are full, *Langdale High Close* (see "Elterwater", p.69) is the nearest alternative, though it's a good two miles south of the village. Grasmere has no campsite.

B&Bs, guest houses and hotels

Banerigg House, 1 mile south on A591 (☎015394/35204). A detached (non-smoking) lakeside property fifteen-minutes' walk from the village, past Dove Cottage. Six doubles and one single – mostly en-suite with lake views – plus parking, drying facilities, good breakfasts, and the use of a boat. No credit cards. ②.

Beck Allans, College St (☎015394/35563). Quality B&B in a new but traditionally built house in the centre – the more you pay, the larger the room but all are smartly furnished and well-equipped and boast baths. Riverside gardens, parking and self-catering apartments available too. No credit cards. ④.

Grasmere Hotel, Broadgate (☎015394/35277). If you like floral flounce, velvet and rooms named after famous writers, this is the lakeland villa for you. Three of the bigger rooms have four-posters and baths (as well as showers). Parking. Closed Jan. ⑤–⑦.

Harwood, Red Lion Square (☎015394/35248, *harwoodlan@aol.com*). Eight smallish, simply furnished rooms in a genial, non-smoking, family-run hotel. Walkers will appreciate that rooms have baths, not showers; a couple have lace-trimmed four-posters. Low-season rates drop a category. ③.

How Beck, Broadgate (☎015394/35732). Just one double room available in this agreeable family house on the outskirts of the village, but it's a great choice for vegetarians: full veggie breakfast, fruit in the room, as well as a corner bath and use of the sun lounge. Also two cottages for rent in Grasmere. ②.

How Foot Lodge, Town End (☎015394/35366). The position – a few yards from Dove Cottage – couldn't be better for Wordsworth groupies. The spacious Victorian villa is owned by the National Trust, and the spacious non-smoking rooms (one with its own sun lounge), grand lounge and gardens are kept with care. Closed Jan. Parking. ③.

Michael's Nook, half-mile north off A591 (☎015394/35496). Superior Victorian country house, stuffed with period features and antiques. It's all a bit grand, but no one faults the food – a French-inspired five-course dinner is included in the price. The best rooms have balconies, and there's parking. ⑧–⑨, includes dinner.

Nab Cottage, Rydal (☎015394/35311, *ell@nab.dial.lakesnet.co.uk*). Both De Quincey and Hartley Coleridge lived in this gorgeous seventeenth-century oak-beamed farmhouse, two miles southeast of Grasmere (on the A591). It's now a language centre, but offers B&B in seven rooms (three en-suite) when space is available – call to check. ②.

Red Lion, Red Lion Square (☎015394/35456). Central, sympathetically styled eighteenth-century coaching inn, with village and fell views. Most rooms have jacuzzi-baths, and there's a steam, sauna and spa room, as well as parking. The public bar here is the best choice in Grasmere for a drink, and packed to the rafters at weekends. ⑥.

The Swan, end of Swan Lane on A591 (☎015394/35551). On the main road just outside Grasmere, this former coaching inn rated a mention in Wordsworth's *The Waggoner* and remodelling hasn't robbed the public rooms at least of their essential eighteenth-century character. Nice restaurant (serving lakeland specialities) and a bar too. Parking. ⑦, ⑧ at weekends.

Thistle (☎015394/35666 or ☎1-800/181716). Edwardian pile (formerly the *Prince of Wales*) providing large-hotel comfort and facilities, though at a price and with supplements charged for lake-view rooms or breakfast taken in the lovely lakeside gardens. The price drops a category if you book two consecutive nights. Parking. ⑦.

Titteringdales, Pye Lane (☎015394/35439, *Titteringdales@grasmere. net*). Cosy, spick-and-span detached house five minutes' walk from the centre, with fell views from the dining room and a ground-floor room with its own patio. Parking. No single-night advance reservations. Closed Jan. No credit cards. ②.

White Moss House, Rydal Water (☎015394/35295, *dixon@whitemoss. demon.co.uk*). Easy-to-miss early eighteenth-century, ivy-clad house – look for the sign at the northern end of Rydal Water. Five individually styled, antique-filled rooms in the main house (two share a lounge and terrace) and two more in a cottage-suite. The five-course dinner (not Sun) starts with drinks on the terrace, followed by well-regarded regional and English dishes. Parking. Closed Dec–Feb. ⑨, includes dinner.

Wordsworth Hotel, College St (☎015394/35592). The plum choice in the village itself – relaxed, attractive and comfortable, with a heated pool, gorgeous conservatory and terrace, and Wordsworthian-styled bar (the *Dove & Olive Branch*). Parking. ⑦–⑧.

Youth hostels

Butterlip How, Easedale Rd (☎015394/35316, *grasmerebh@yha.org.uk*). Closest of the hostels to the centre, this converted Victorian house is just five minutes north of the green. Modern bedrooms, plentiful showers, carpeting and decent furniture throughout, and a dining room overlooking grassy gardens.

Thorney How (☎015394/35591). Grasmere's smaller hostel is further out, a characterful (ie, unmodernized) former farmhouse just under a mile along the road past *Butterlip How*: look for the signposted right turn. The road's unlit so bring a torch.

The village

For the most part, Grasmere's assorted gift shops, galleries, cafés and hotels occupy nineteenth-century buildings and houses, though the village is much older than that. St Oswald is reputed to have preached here in the seventh century, while the present church bearing his name dates from the thirteenth – you can still follow the medieval "**Coffin Trail**" from Rydal over White Moss Common, along which coffin bearers struggled with their load on their way to the church. Moreover, the village's famous rushbearing ceremony (see p.16) and traditional sports festival (p.18) both date from medieval times.

The main point of pilgrimage is the **churchyard of St Oswald's**, around which the river makes a sinuous curl. Here, beneath the yews, Wordsworth is buried alongside his wife Mary and sister Dorothy, together with his beloved daughter Dora (buried in her married name Quillinan) and two much younger children, Catherine and Thomas, whose deaths marred the Wordsworths' early years in Grasmere. A worn Celtic cross behind the Wordsworth plots marks the grave of Hartley Coleridge, Samuel Taylor's son. Like his father, Hartley possessed an addictive personality though – unlike his father – his lapses never produced a formal break with the Wordsworths, with whom Hartley remained a family favourite. Inside, the church's unique twin naves are split by an arched, whitewashed wall. Wordsworth descibed its "naked rafters intricately crossed" in *The Excursion*; while Thomas De Quincey married the farmer's daughter Margaret Simpson here (a match disapproved of by the snobbish Wordsworths). Associations aside, it's a rather plain church, though there is a memorial plaque to Wordsworth ("a true philosopher and poet") on the wall to the left of the altar, as well as his prayer book on display in a small case in the nave.

At the rear entrance to the churchyard stands **Sarah Nelson's Gingerbread Shop** (Mon–Sat 9.30am–5.30pm, Sun 12.30–5.30pm), formerly the village schoolhouse (where Wordsworth taught for a time in 1812). Grasmere gingerbread has been made on the premises since the mid-nineteenth century and the recipe is a closely guarded secret.

Wordsworth spent most of his Grasmere years living in houses outside the village – Dove Cottage and Rydal Mount – but the five years in between these major residences (1808–1813) saw the extended Wordsworth family and visiting friends occupying two houses in the village itself. Both are closed to the public, though there's nothing to stop you walking past the **Old Rectory** (opposite St Oswald's) and the more imposing **Allan Bank** – the latter reached up a signposted path to Silver Howe (for which, see box opposite). Coleridge was a permanent guest here for almost two years, producing his literary and political periodical, *The Friend*, from a room in the house while sinking ever further into drug-induced decline. Later, Canon Rawnsley of the National Trust (see p.110) owned the house; he left it to the Trust on his death.

There's a biography of Wordsworth on p.187; for more on De Quincey, see p.65; for Coleridge, p.105.

The only other place to visit in Grasmere is the **Heaton Cooper Studio**, opposite the green (Mon–Sat 9am–6pm, Sun noon–6pm; winter closes at 5pm; ☎015394/35280). It's a showcase for the works of one of the Lakes' most durable and talented artistic families, headed by the landscapes and village scenes of Alfred Heaton

Walks from Grasmere

Grasmere makes a good base for a wide selection of walks, from lazy round-the-lake rambles to full-on day hikes requiring a bit of experience. A decent cross-section is detailed below; and also see "The lake and surrounding fells" section on p.62 for a few more ideas.

Around Grasmere and Rydal Water

This is an easy circuit (4 miles; 2hr) which skirts the lake and Loughrigg Fell. From Loughrigg Terrace, the route heads east above **Rydal Water**, passing the dripping maw of **Rydal Caves**, a disused slate quarry (seen in Ken Russell's *The Lair of the White Worm*), before crossing the A591 to Rydal Mount. Above the house the **"Coffin Trail" bridle way** runs back high above the northern shore of Rydal Water, via **White Moss Tarn** (look out for butterflies), emerging at Dove Cottage.

Loughrigg Fell

There are all sorts of possible ascents of **Loughrigg Fell** (1101ft) – and it's also easily climbed from Ambleside – but the simplest ascent is straight up the hillside from Loughrigg Terrace: the views are fantastic. A six-mile circuit from the terrace, over the top to Ambleside and back takes three to four hours.

Silver Howe

Best direct climb from the village is up to the top of **Silver Howe** (1292ft), above the west side of the lake, from where the views take in the Langdales, Helvellyn and High Street. It's a two-hour climb there and back: the footpath is signposted off the lakeside Redbank Road. Another route up from the village passes Allan Bank – coming this way and circling round via Dow Bank and down to the lakeside road is a five-mile (three-hour) walk.

The Fairfield Horeshoe

The classic hiker's circuit from the Grasmere area is the **Fairfield Horeshoe**, an eleven-mile (seven-hour) walk encompassing eight different peaks, starting from behind Rydal Mount, heading north along the ridges to Fairfield itself (2864ft) and then turning to descend to Ambleside via the attractive High Sweden Bridge.

See Basics, p.19, for general walking advice in the Lakes; recommended maps are detailed on p.9.

Cooper (1864–1929). Cooper became a well-known illustrator of guidebooks, especially in the first two decades of the twentieth century, and was succeeded in this by his son William Heaton Cooper (1903–1995), who climbed with the pioneering lakeland mountaineers. William produced paintings and sketches for four topographical Lake District guidebooks and then virtually ensured a dynastic succession by marrying the sculptress Ophelia Gordon Bell. Examples of all their work are on show in the gallery, together with

those of a rake of contemporary Heaton Coopers – grandson Julian
Cooper is the most notable, a climber-artist who produces huge oil
paintings of the world's more remote locations.

The lake and surrounding fells

It's ten minutes' walk from the centre down Redbank Road to the
western side of fell-fringed **Grasmere** itself. You can rent a rowboat
at the landing stage – and take a picnic out to the wooded islet in the
middle of the lake – or continue walking the mile to the southern
reaches where **Loughrigg Terrace** sits under the crags of Loughrigg
Fell (look for a track off the road through Redbank Woods, signposted "Loughrigg Terrace and YHA"). From the terrace there are
tremendous views back up the lake and across the broad valley, culminating in the pass of Dunmail Raise.

Wordsworth composed most of his poetry during long rambles
around the lake and up in the surrounding fells, and – clutching a volume of his collected verse – it's still possible to track down the
sources of his inspiration. Behind *Michael's Nook* hotel (on the east
side of the A591) a path rises to the "tumultuous brook" of
Greenhead Gill, whose surroundings formed the backdrop to the
masterful early lyric poem *Michael* (1800), a moving tale of a shepherd abandoned by his wayward son.

Easedale and its tarn (northwest of the village) conjures the most
resonant images. The first version of Wordsworth's autobiographical
work, *The Prelude*, was partly composed after long hours tramping
up and down the valley, while the tragic deaths of George and Sarah
Green of Easedale – who died in a blizzard, leaving behind six children – prompted a memorial poem ("Who weeps for strangers? /
Many wept for George and Sarah Green; / Wept for that pair's unhap-
py fate, / Whose graves may here be seen"). The Wordsworths even
took into care one of the orphans, a story exhaustively chronicled by
De Quincey (in *Recollections of the Lakes and the Lake Poets*). A
brisk hike (follow Easedale Road, past the youth hostels), up the tumbling, fern-clad, Sourmilk Gill to the tarn and back, takes around two
hours; and there's lakeland ice cream from the *Oak Lodge* teashop,
opposite the bridge across Easedale Beck at the start of the path. You
also come this way, up Easedale Road, to climb Grasmere's most celebrated peak, **Helm Crag** (1299ft) – keep on (past the bridge and
Easedale path) to the end of the road and follow the sign (2hr, there
and back). Its distinctive summit crags are known as "The Lion and
the Lamb" and have thrilled visitors since Wordsworth's day.

Cafés, pubs and restaurants

Baldry's, Red Lion Square (☎015394/35301). Tearooms decked out in
Provençal colours, serving filled baguettes, home-made cakes, scones, tarts
and quiche. Daytime only (Mon & Fri–Sun only in winter). Inexpensive.

Dove Cottage Tea Rooms & Restaurant, Town End (☎015394/35268). Trendy spot – hardwood floors, terracotta walls – serving tearoom favourites during the day and a fashionable dinner menu (Wed–Sat only, 7–9pm) combining Asian and Med influences. A few outdoor tables catch the sun; dinner reservations recommended. Moderate.

Jumble Room Café, Langdale Rd (☎015394/35188). Funky daytime café with the organic touch to its ethnically diverse menu. Open Fri & Sat evenings in summer, weekend (days) only in winter. Moderate.

Langman's Deli & Bakery, Red Lion Square (☎015394/35248). Stuffed sandwiches, baguettes and ciabatta, deli supplies, and a tearoom; it's under the *Harwood*. Daytime only. Inexpensive.

Piggy in the Middle, Broadgate (☎015394/35009). All-day big breakfasts, including a veggie option, plus pizzas until 8.30pm. Inexpensive.

The Rowan Tree, Church Bridge, Stock Lane (☎015394/35528). Mainstream vegetarian dining (the menu talks better than it walks), enhanced by its gorgeous position on a lazy bend in the river, opposite the church. An outdoor terrace for sunny evenings; and takeaway business from adjacent *RT2Go* during the day. Moderate.

Traveller's Rest, half-mile north on the A591 (☎015394/35604). A popular place for bar meals though the thundering main road does the pub's outdoor tables no favours. Inexpensive.

Dove Cottage

Dove Cottage, Town End, A591 ☎015394/35544. Open daily 9.30am–5.30pm; closed mid-Jan to mid-Feb. Admission £4.80. Buses #555/556 & #599 stop outside.

On the southeastern outskirts of Grasmere village, in the former hamlet of Town End, stands **Dove Cottage**, home to William and Dorothy Wordsworth from 1799 to 1808 and where Wordsworth wrote some of his best poetry. He first saw the house in November 1799 while on a walking tour with his friend Samuel Taylor Coleridge, with whom he had published *Lyrical Ballads* the previous year. Keen for a base in the Lakes, Wordsworth negotiated a rent of £8 a year for what had originally been an inn called the *Dove & Olive-Bough*; he and his sister moved in just before Christmas of that year. It was a simple stone house with a slate roof – Wordsworth at this time was far from financially secure – where the poet could live by his guiding principle of "plain living but high thinking". But its main recommendation as far as Wordsworth was concerned was one that is no longer obvious: the views he had enjoyed to the lake and fells were lost when new housing was erected in front of Dove Cottage in the 1860s. When the Wordsworths left in 1808, their friend Thomas De Quincey took over the lease and Dove Cottage is as much a monument to his happiest days in Grasmere (he married from here) as it is to Wordsworth's plain living; the house has been open to the public since 1917.

Dove Cottage

The **cottage** forms part of a complex administered by the Wordsworth Trust, whose guides, bursting with anecdotes, lead you around the rooms, little changed now but for the addition of electricity and internal plumbing. There's precious little space and – downstairs, at least – very little natural light: belching tallow candles would have provided the only illumination. William, not wanting to be bothered by questions of a domestic nature, kept to the lighter, upper rooms or disappeared off on long walks to compose his poetry. De Quincey later reckoned that Wordsworth had walked 175,000 to 180,000 miles in the course of his poetry writing – "a mode of exertion which, to him, stood in the stead of wine, spirits, and all other stimulants whatsoever to the animal spirits".

For more on the poet's life, loves and work, see p.187.

Wordsworth married in 1802 and his new wife, Mary Hutchinson, came to live here, necessitating a change of bedrooms for everyone; three of their five children were later born in the cottage (John in 1803, Dora in 1804 and Thomas in 1806). Sister Dorothy kept a detailed journal of daily life and the endless comings and goings of visitors, notably Coleridge and his brother-in-law Southey, but also Walter Scott, William Hazlitt and, once he'd plucked up the nerve to introduce himself, Thomas De Quincey (see box opposite). The garden behind the cottage was tamed, while William chopped wood for the fire, planted runner beans, built a summerhouse and hid the disliked cottage whitewash behind a train of roses and honeysuckle. And with all this going on, Wordsworth produced a series of odes, lyric poems and sonnets that he would never better, relying on Dorothy and Mary to make copies in their painstaking handwriting. After eight years at Dove Cottage it became clear that the Wordsworths had outgrown their home and, reluctantly, the family moved to a larger, new house in Grasmere called Allan Bank – Wordsworth had watched it being built and referred to it as a "temple of abomination". They were never as happy here, or in the Old Rectory to which they later relocated, and it wasn't until 1813 and the move to Rydal Mount that the Wordsworths regained the sense of peace they had felt at Dove Cottage.

Most of the furniture in the cottage belonged to the Wordsworths, while in the **upper rooms** are displayed a battered suitcase, a pair of William's ice-skates and Dorothy's sewing box among other possessions. There are surprisingly few reminders of De Quincey's long tenancy, save a pair of opium scales, yet he lived here far longer than did the Wordsworths. If you visit the cottage, you've already paid for the adjacent **museum** in which you can learn as much or as little as you like about Wordsworth's life and times. It's full of paintings, portraits, original manuscripts (including that of *Daffodils*), pages from Dorothy's journals and more memorabilia, most poignantly Mary's wedding ring. In good weather, the **garden** is open for visits as well. Dove Cottage is the headquarters of the

Thomas De Quincey in the Lakes

"The direct object of my own residence at the lakes was the society of Mr Wordsworth."

Thomas De Quincey,
Recollections of the Lakes and the Lake Poets.

The young **Thomas De Quincey** (1785–1859) was one of the first to fully appreciate the revolutionary nature of Wordsworth's and Coleridge's collaborative *Lyrical Ballads*, and as a student at Oxford in 1803 he had already written to Wordsworth praising his "genius" and hoping for his friendship. In reply, Wordsworth politely invited him to visit if he was ever in the area. It took De Quincey four years (and two abortive visits, abandoned out of shyness) to contrive a meeting, eventually through the auspices of Coleridge, a mutual friend.

De Quincey first came to Dove Cottage in November 1807 to meet his hero, trembling at the thought: the meeting is recorded in one of the more self-effacing chapters of his *Recollections*. When the Wordsworths moved to Allan Bank the following year, De Quincey – by now a favourite with the Wordsworth children – went too, staying several months. His small private income enabled him to take over Dove Cottage in February 1809, which he filled full of books (in contrast to Wordsworth, who had very few). He also demolished the summerhouse and made other changes in the garden which annoyed the Wordsworths, while the relationship further cooled after 1812 following the deaths of young Catherine and Thomas Wordsworth. De Quincey was particularly badly affected by the loss of Catherine, his "sole companion", and for two months after her death passed each night stretched out on her grave in Grasmere churchyard.

The truth is, De Quincey wasn't a well man. Since his university days, he had been in the habit of taking opium in the form of laudanum (ie, dissolved in alcohol), and at Dove Cottage he was taking huge, addictive doses – the amount of alcohol alone would have been debilitating enough. He closeted himself away in the cottage for days at a time, complaining that Wordsworth was spoiling the books he borrowed from him, and began an affair with Margaret (Peggy) Simpson of nearby Nab Cottage, a local farmer's daughter who bore him an illegitimate child. The drug-taking was bad enough for the upright, snobbish Wordsworths, but when De Quincey married Peggy in 1817 (at St Oswald's Church, Grasmere) any intimate relationship was at an end.

His inheritance gone, De Quincey needed employment and following a disastrous stint as editor of the *Westmorland Gazette* he became a critic and essayist for various literary periodicals. His *Confessions of an English Opium-Eater* (1821) first appeared in the *London Magazine* and made his name, and he had sufficient resources to take on another house (Fox Ghyll, south of Rydal) for his growing family (he eventually had eight children), retaining Dove Cottage as a library. Growing success meant De Quincey spent less and less time in the Lakes, giving up Fox Ghyll in 1825 and finally abandoning Dove Cottage in 1830 to move to Edinburgh, where he lived for the rest of his life. It was only between 1834 and 1839 – long after he'd left the area – that De Quincey started writing his Lake "recollections", offending Wordsworth all over again.

Centre for British Romanticism, which together with the Wordsworth Trust sponsors special exhibitions, residential conferences and summer poetry readings attracting some top names – call for details.

Rydal Mount and around

Rydal Mount, Rydal, A591 ☎015394/33002. Open March–Oct daily 9.30am–5pm; Nov–Feb Wed–Mon 10am–4pm. Admission £3.50. Buses #555/556 and #599 stop at Rydal Church, 200 yards from the house.

Following the deaths of their young children Catherine and Thomas in 1812, the Wordsworths couldn't bear to continue living in Grasmere's Old Rectory. In May 1813 they moved a couple of miles southeast of the village to the hamlet of **Rydal** (see below), little more than a couple of isolated cottages and farms set back from the eastern end of Rydal Water. Here William rented Rydal Mount from the Flemings of nearby Rydal Hall, where he remained here until his death in 1850.

Rydal Mount is a fair-sized family home, a much-improved-upon Tudor cottage set in its own grounds, and reflects Wordsworth's change in circumstances. At Dove Cottage he'd been a largely unknown poet of straitened means, but by 1813 he'd written several of his greatest works (though not all had yet been published) and was already being visited by literary acolytes. More importantly, he'd been appointed Westmorland's Distributor of Stamps, a salaried position which allowed him to take up the rent of a comfortable family house. Wordsworth, Mary, the three surviving children (John, aged 10; Dora, 9; and William, 3) and Dorothy arrived, plus his wife's sister Sara Hutchinson, by now living with the family. Later the household also contained a clerk, a couple of maids and a gardener. Dances and dinners were held, the widowed Queen Adelaide visited, and carriage-loads of friends and sightseers came to call – a far cry from the "plain living" back at Dove Cottage.

Wordsworth only ever rented the property, but the house is now owned by descendants of the poet, who have opened it to visitors since 1970. It's a much less claustrophobic experience than visiting Dove Cottage and you're free to wander around what is still essentially a family home – summer concerts feature poetry readings by Wordsworth family members, and there are recent family pictures on the sideboard alongside more familiar portraits of the poet and his circle. In the light-filled **drawing room** and **library** (two rooms in Wordsworth's day) you'll find the only known portrait of Dorothy, as an old lady of 62, and also Mary's favourite portrait of Wordsworth, completed in 1844 by the American portraitist Henry Inman. Memorabilia abound: Wordsworth's black leather sofa, his ink-stand and despatch box, a brooch of Dorothy's and, upstairs in the attic, their beloved brother John's sword (recovered from the shipwreck he drowned in) and the poet's own encyclopedia and prayer book. **William and Mary's bedroom** has a lovely view, with Windermere a splash in the distance; in daughter **Dora's room** hangs a portrait of Edward Quillinan, her Irish dragoon, whom she married in 1841, much against Wordsworth's will. The couple spent their honeymoon at Rydal Mount, while the delicate Dora – often ill and eventually a victim of influenza – later came home to die in the house in 1847. The other bedroom was Dorothy's, to which she was virtually confined for the last two decades of her life, suffering greatly from what was thought to be a debilitating mental illness – an underactive thyroid is the current opinion. She died at Rydal Mount in 1855; Mary died there in 1859.

Many people's favourite part of Rydal Mount is the four-and-a-half-acre **garden**, largely shaped by Wordsworth who fancied himself as a gardener. He planted the flowering shrubs, put in the terraces (where he used to declaim his poetry) and erected a little rustic summer house (for jotting down lyrics) with its views of Rydal Water. Lining the lawns and surrounding the rock pools are rhododendrons and azaleas, maple, beech and pine. If you're looking for an unusual souvenir, head for the Rydal Mount **shop**, which sells fell-walking sticks fashioned from the wood found in the garden.

Rydal and Rydal Water

RYDAL itself, as the name suggests (ie, Rydale), sits at the foot of its own valley, whose beck empties into the River Rothay. As a hamlet, it's hardly any bigger than it was in Wordsworth's day; though, having seen Rydal Mount, you may as well wander back down the road for the other local sights – namely Rydal's lake, church and hall and, under a mile west, Nab Cottage, the former home of Hartley Coleridge.

There was no local church in Rydal until **St Mary's** (at the foot of Rydal Mount on the main A591) was built in 1824 – Wordsworth was church-warden here for a year in the 1830s. A swing-gate by the church entrance leads into **Dora's Field** (always open; NT), a plot of land bought by Wordsworth when he thought he might have to leave Rydal Mount because the owners, the Flemings, wanted it back. Wordsworth planned to build a house here instead, but when the Flemings changed their minds, he gave the land to his daughter. On Dora's death in 1847, the heartbroken Wordsworths planted the hillsides with daffodils.

Across from the church, a driveway leads to **Rydal Hall**, erstwhile home of the Flemings. The hall has a sixteenth-century kernel but was considerably renovated during Victorian times; it's now a residential conference centre. The formal gardens to the front (open dawn to dusk; donation requested) were laid out by Thomas Mawson on classical lines in 1909 and there are captivating views of Rydal Water from the terrace. Around the back of the hall, a summer **tea-**

room (daily 11am–5.30pm) has picnic tables from where you can watch Rydal Beck tumble under a moss-covered packhorse bridge. There's a series of small falls a few hundred yards up Rydal Beck.

Few people bother much with **Rydal Water**, one of the region's smallest lakes at under three-quarters of a mile long and only fifty feet deep in parts. It's handsome enough – though it was considerably quieter before the A591 traced its northern shore – and there's a nice walk along the southern shore, back to Grasmere past Rydal Caves. For the best views of the water itself, follow the original route to Grasmere, along the "**Coffin Trail**", which starts directly behind Rydal Mount and runs west under Nab Scar (see "Walks from Grasmere", p.61). Medieval coffin bearers en route to St Oswald's would haul their melancholy load along this trail, stopping to rest at intervals on the convenient flat stones.

Nab Cottage, less than a mile west of Rydal on the A591, overlooks Rydal Water. This was the family home of Margaret Simpson before she married Thomas De Quincey; and it was rented much later by the sometime journalist and poet Hartley Coleridge, a Wordsworth family favourite ("O blessed vision! happy child!") despite his trying ways. Abandoned by his father and effectively brought up in Robert Southey's Keswick household (see p.106), Hartley was a frail, precocious child who took to the demon drink and failed to live up to his early promise. But Wordsworth always retained a soft spot for him and when Hartley died in Nab Cottage in 1849 Wordsworth picked out a plot for him in Grasmere churchyard.

Nab Cottage offers B&B throughout the year; see p.58 for details.

Skelwith Bridge and Little Langdale

Langdale is a byword for some of the region's most stunning peaks, views and hikes, and the route there starts at **SKELWITH BRIDGE**, around three miles south of Grasmere and the same distance west of Ambleside. Here, a cluster of buildings huddles by the bridge over the River Brathay, prime among them **Kirkstone Galleries** (daily: April–Oct 10am–6pm; Nov–March 10am–5pm), an ornamental stonemasons' showroom specializing in Westmorland green slate, with a souvenir store and terrace seating outside *Chesters* coffee shop. The *Skelwith Bridge Hotel*, on the main road (☎015394/ 32115, *skelwithbr@aol.com*; ⑤), has rooms, food and a public bar (the *Talbot*). **Bus** #505/506 from Ambleside or Coniston stops at Skelwith Bridge, as does the #516 between Ambleside and the Old Dungeon Ghyll Hotel in Great Langdale.

From the bridge, there's a riverside stroll along a signposted footpath to Elterwater, a mile away, passing the fairly unimpressive gush that is **Skelwith Force**. For a finer waterfall altogether follow the hilly footpath west of Skelwith Bridge (it starts on the south side of

the river) the mile or so to **Colwith Force**, hidden in the woods off
the minor road to Elterwater. A circuit taking in both falls and
Elterwater won't take more than a couple of hours. There's another
local walk from Skelwith, north through Neaum Woods to pretty
Loughrigg Tarn, where there's basic **camping** (toilets and a cold
tap) at *Tarn Foot Farm* on the south side.

Heading west, a very narrow minor road off the A593 twists into
Little Langdale, a bucolic counterweight to the dramatics of Great
Langdale to the north. The *Three Shires Inn* (☎015394/37215; ⑤,
⑥ with dinner), about a mile west of Colwith Force, is the traditional starting point for local walks, notably the stroll down to the old
packhorse crossing of Slater Bridge and to Little Langdale Tarn. A
longer route – shadowed by a very minor road – runs north over
Lingmoor Fell (1530ft) via **Blea Tarn** (where there's parking) into
Great Langdale – the eight-mile circuit, returning to the *Three
Shires Inn* via Elterwater, takes around four hours. The name of the
inn, incidentally, is a reference to the fact that it stands near the
meeting-point of the old counties of Cumberland, Westmorland and
Lancashire. West from Little Langdale, the ever-narrower, ever-
hairier road climbs to the dramatic **Wrynose Pass** (1270 ft), before
dropping down to Cockley Beck for the Duddon Valley or on to the
Hardknott Pass.

Elterwater

ELTERWATER village lies half a mile northwest of its water, the
latter named by the Norse for the swans which still glide upon its
surface. It's one of the more idyllic lakeland beauty spots, with its
riverside setting, aged inn, spreading maple tree, and aimless sheep
getting among the sunbathers on the pocket-sized green.
Historically, the village made its living from farming, quarrying and
lace-making, though these days it's almost entirely devoted to the
passing tourist trade: only around a quarter of the houses here are
lived in, the rest are used as holiday cottages.

The #516 **bus** stops by the village green. Elterwater sees its fair
share of Langdale-bound hikers, not least because of the two local
youth hostels. *Elterwater Langdale* (☎015394/37245) is the most
convenient, a simple converted farmhouse and barn, just across the
bridge from the green; *Langdale High Close*, a mile northeast of
Elterwater (☎015394/37313), has a more spectacular setting, high
on the road over Red Bank to Grasmere. There's traditional hospi-
tality at the *Britannia Inn* (☎015394/37210, *britinn@edi.co.uk*;
④), the solid old lakeland **pub** on the green, with comfortable rooms
(some in an annex over the road) and tasty food in the bar, including
home-made pies and often such exotica as tuna or swordfish steaks.
The *Eltermere Country Hotel* (☎015394/37207; ⑤) is an imposing
retreat just a little way past the Elterwater Langdale hostel, with

grounds stretching down to the lake. For **cottage rental**, contact Wheelwright's (☎015394/37635, *Enquiries@Wheelwrights.com*) who should be able to fix you up with something in the vicinity. The **village shop**, Maple Tree Corner (open daily), opposite the pub, has basic grocery supplies and can sell you a newspaper or a map.

It's an easy half-mile stroll northwest up the river to **Chapel Stile**, where a simple quarrymen's chapel sits beneath the crags. *Wainwright's Inn* has drinks and meals; the Langdale Cooperative, in business since 1884, has everything else – from cornflakes to hiking boots.

Great Langdale

Beyond Chapel Stile you emerge into the wide curve of **Great Langdale**, flanked by some of the Lake District's most famous peaks – Crinkle Crags, Bowfell and the Langdale Pikes. It's a dramatic, yet sobering, valley, one of the few in the Lakes where you get a real sense of scale from the lie of the land. It's also one of the oldest occupied parts of the region, the evidence in the shape of Stone Age axes found in "factory" sites in the upper valley. A footpath from Elterwater (signposted as the Cumbria Way) runs up the valley to its head – eight miles from Ambleside – from where there are popular onward hiking routes over the passes to Wasdale or Borrowdale. Parking by the side of the B5343 road is discouraged, and drivers should make for either of the valley's main (signposted) car parks, depending on their target for the day.

From the car park at **Stickle Ghyll**, where the Langdale Pikes and Pavey Ark form a dramatic backdrop, most recreational walkers aim no further than **Stickle Tarn**, an hour's climb up Stickle Ghyll itself, following a wide stone-stepped path that's been put in place to prevent further erosion of the hillside. Another easy target is the dramatic sixty-foot waterfall of **Dungeon Ghyll**, less than half an hour away – the "dungeon" in question is a natural cave. The other car park, a mile further west up the road near the **Old Dungeon Ghyll Hotel**, is the starting-point for a series of more hardcore hikes (see box opposite), though there's the option of an easier walk south over Lingmoor Fell (see "Little Langdale" on p.69).

Practicalities

The #516 **bus** from Ambleside runs via Skelwith Bridge, Elterwater and Chapel Stile to the road end at the head of the valley. It turns around by the peerless **Old Dungeon Ghyll Hotel** (☎015394/37272; ⑨, ⑥ with dinner), the traditional accommodation for anyone visiting Great Langdale – lashings of hot water for tired limbs, a cosy lounge, great three-course dinners (£18) in its restaurant (book in advance), and a stone-flagged hikers' bar with roaring range and

Walks from Great Langdale

Walking in Great Langdale isn't necessarily an expeditionary undertaking, but you do need to be more aware than usual of time, weather conditions and your own ability before setting off on a hike. Once you leave the valley bottom there's nothing much that's simply a stroll – then again, of the classic routes picked out below, all save Jack's Rake are within the average walker's competence.

Pavey Ark

Behind Stickle Tarn stands the fearsome cliff-face of **Pavey Ark** (2297ft), which can actually be climbed relatively easily if you approach it up the grassy path to its rear (north). Gung-ho walkers make the more dramatic climb up **Jack's Rake** trail which ascends the face right to left, and is the hardest commonly used route in the Lake District – in parts it's effectively rock-climbing and requires a head for heights and steady nerves. An alternative climb, up Easy Gully (it isn't), starts from near the base. However you get up, count on it taking an hour from Stickle Tarn.

The Langdale Pikes

From the top of Pavey Ark it's a straightforward walk on to **Harrison Stickle** (2414ft), down to the stream forming the headwaters of Dungeon Ghyll and then slowly up to **Pike of Stickle** (2326ft). To make a long walk of it, aim then for **Stake Pass** to the northwest and return down the old Langdale packhorse route. You could of course walk the Pikes the other way round, finishing with a descent from Stickle Tarn. Either way, the walking is around seven miles and takes about five hours.

Crinkle Crags and Bowfell

The orthodox route up to the distinctive **Crinkle Crags** (2816ft) – the name, as you'll see, is deserved – is from the Old Dungeon Ghyll Hotel via Oxendale, Brown Howe and Red Tarn. From the summit, a ridge walk south along the "crinkles" drops down to Three Tarns (from where there's a possible descent down The Band to Langdale) or you continue north instead up to the conical summit of **Bowfell** (2960ft) – one of Wainwright's favourite half-dozen fells. From Bowfell, descend via Ore Gap to Angle Tarn, and then back to the Old Dungeon Ghyll Hotel down Rossett Gill and Mickleden Beck. A nine-mile (six-to-seven-hour) circuit

See Basics, p.19, for general walking advice in the Lakes; recommended maps are detailed on p.9.

filling food (it's also open summer weekends from 9am for hikers' breakfasts). The only other option at this end of the valley is the National Trust's very popular *Great Langdale* **campsite** (☎015394/37668); under a quarter of a mile south of the hotel, it has a laundry and drying room, a well-stocked shop and offers bike rental.

A mile back down the road at **Stickle Ghyll**, beneath the Langdale Pikes, the *New Dungeon Ghyll Hotel* (☎015394/37213,

Great Langdale

enquiries@dungeon-ghyll.com; ⑤, ⑥ with dinner) has similar levels of comfort to its older namesake, with rooms that feature dramatic fell views. You can eat in the restaurant here, or on the sunny terrace of the adjacent *Sticklebarn Tavern* (☎015394/37356; ①; two-night minimum stay at weekends), which has comfortable **camping-barn** beds available – centrally heated, carpeted, and very popular – and serves big breakfasts every day, and bar meals all year round. Finally, the *Greenhowe Caravan Park* (☎015394/37231; ②; closed Nov–Feb), a couple of hundred yards to the south, has a range of static caravans for rent for groups of two and upwards.

Travel details

From Grasmere

Bus #555/556 (hourly service, every 2hr on Sun) to: Dove Cottage (2min), Rydal (5min), Ambleside (20min), Brockhole (30min), Windermere train station (35min), Kendal (1hr); or to Keswick (20min).

Bus #599 (every 20–30min): to Dove Cottage (2min), Rydal (5min), Ambleside (20min), Brockhole (30min), Windermere train station (35min), Bowness piers (45min). Service operates April–Oct only.

To Langdale

Bus #516 from Ambleside (5–6 daily) to: Skelwith Bridge (10min), Elterwater (17min), Chapel Stile (20min), Old Dungeon Ghyll Hotel (30min). Service operates April–Oct daily; Nov–March Mon–Sat only.

Chapter 3

Coniston Water, Hawkshead and the South

Coniston Water – five miles west of Windermere as the crow flies – is not one of the most immediately imposing of the lakes, yet it's one of the oldest settled parts of lakeland. For as long as there has been human habitation, there has been industry of sorts around Coniston, whether fishing in the lake by the monks of Furness Abbey, copper-mining and slate-quarrying in the north-western valleys and fells, or coppicing and charcoal-making in the forests to the south and east. The lake's understated beauty – and very possibly its association with these traditional lakeland trades – attracted the Victorian art critic, essayist and moralist John Ruskin, who moved here in 1872. Brantwood, his isolated house on the lake's

---

ACCOMMODATION PRICE CODES

Hotel and **B&B** accommodation is priced on a scale of ① to ⑨ (see below), indicating the **average price** you could expect to pay per night for a **double or twin room** in high season. **Youth hostels** are not given a price code since they fall within a fairly narrow price band. For more accommodation details, see Basics, p.12.

① under £40	④ £60–70	⑦ £110–150
② £40–50	⑤ £70–90	⑧ £150–200
③ £50–60	⑥ £90–110	⑨ over £200

CAFÉ AND RESTAURANT PRICE CODES

Cafés and restaurants listed in this guide have been assigned one of four price categories:

Inexpensive under £10
Moderate £10–20
Expensive £20–30
Very expensive over £30

This is the price you can expect to pay per person for a three-course meal or equivalent, excluding drinks and service.

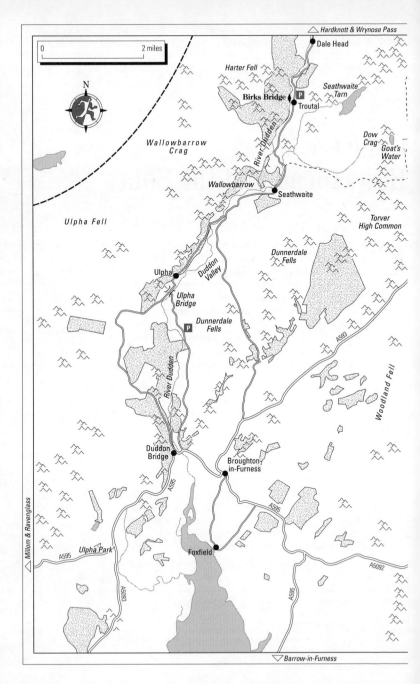

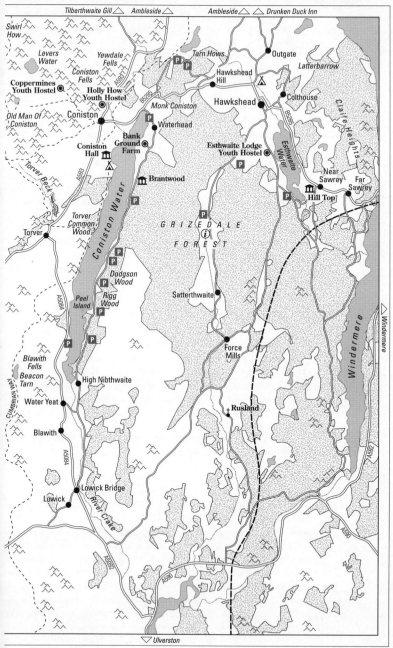

northeastern shore, provides the most obvious target for a trip, though boat rides on the National Trust's elegant steam yacht, *Gondola*, or on the lake's wooden motor-launches, also provide a powerful incentive for a visit.

Those wanting to stay in the area usually look no further than the cute cottages and cobbled streets of **Hawkshead**, three miles east of Coniston Water, with its connections to the big two literary lakeland anchors of William Wordsworth (who went to school here) and Beatrix Potter (whose husband's former office has been turned into an art gallery). Certainly, the former mining village of **Coniston** itself has to work hard to keep visitors in the face of such stiff competition, but it grows on some after a while and is the usual base for an ascent of the **Old Man of Coniston**, the distinctive peak which backs the village. Wherever you stay, there are easy side trips: to the renowned local beauty spot of **Tarn Hows**, the paths and sculptures of **Grizedale Forest**, or Beatrix Potter's former house of **Hill Top** – the latter one of the most visited attractions in the Lake District. Routes south towards the Furness peninsula take you through the pretty **Duddon Valley** – immortalized by Wordsworth in a series of sonnets – and to the quiet market town of **Broughton-in-Furness**, on the southern edge of the National Park.

Coniston

Its dimensions are nothing out of the ordinary – five miles long, half a mile across at its widest point – and its only village is the plainest in the Lakes, but the glassy surface of **Coniston Water** weaves a gentle spell on summer days. Wooded on its eastern shores (and traced by a minor road from the south), with much of the western side accessed only by the Cumbria Way footpath, it's easy to lose the worst of southern lakeland's crowds around the lake. At the end of the nineteenth century, **Arthur Ransome** spent his childhood summer holidays at the still serene southern end, near Nibthwaite, and was always "half-drowned in tears" when it was time to leave. His vivid memories of messing about on the water, camping on the islets, making friends with the local charcoal-burners and playing make-believe in the hills surfaced later in his children's classic, *Swallows and Amazons*, when **Peel Island** became the "Wild Cat Island" of the book. The sheltered waters also attracted speed-adventurers **Sir Malcolm and Donald Campbell**, father and son, who between them set a series of records on Coniston Water, starting with Sir Malcolm's world water-speed record of 141mph in 1939. After raising the record in successive years, Donald reached 260mph here in 1959 (and 276mph in Australia five years later) but on January 4, 1967, having set out once again to better his own mark, his jet-powered *Bluebird* hit a patch of turbulence at an estimated 320mph, which sent the craft into a somersault. Campbell's shoes, helmet, oxygen

For a life of Arthur Ransome, see p.90.

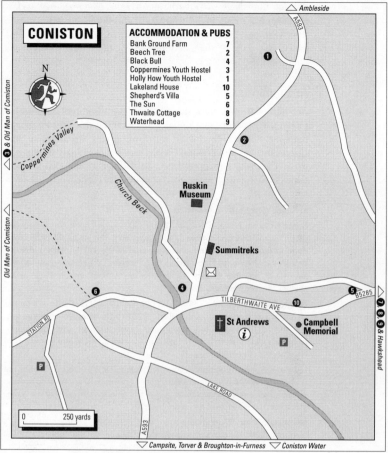

mask and teddy-bear mascot were recovered from the water, but his body and boat were destroyed completely.

Arrival and information

Buses – principally the #505/506 (from Kendal, Windermere, Ambleside or Hawkshead) – stop on the main road (B5285) through the village, though some of the services also run down to the ferry pier at the lake. A Ruskin Explorer ticket (£8) gets you return bus travel on the #505/506 from any point between Bowness and Coniston, plus use of the Consiston Launch and free entrance to Brantwood – buy the ticket on the bus. Drivers either come in on the A593 (Ambleside road) or the B5285 (from Hawkshead), which runs

Coniston services:

bike rental p.20;

post office p.11;

taxis p.7;

water sports p.21.

through the village as Tilberthwaite Avenue. The main **car park** is signposted; it's right in the centre (off Tilberthwaite Avenue), next to the **National Park Information Centre**, on Ruskin Avenue (April–Oct daily 9.30am–5.30pm; Nov–March limited weekend hours; ☎015394/41533).

Accommodation

Accommodation is plentiful and, for the most part, reasonably priced. Holiday **cottages** are fairly thick on the ground, too, though none so intricately linked with the area's heritage as *The Coppermines* (☎015394/41765), a series of converted dwellings in the old saw mill in Coppermines Valley, behind the Coppermines **youth hostel**; note that the road up here is largely unsurfaced.

B&Bs, guest houses and hotels

Bank Ground Farm, Coniston Water, east side, north of Brantwood (☎015394/41264, *bankground@kencomp.net*). The model for Holly Howe Farm in *Swallows and Amazons* (and used in the 1970s' film), sixteenth-century *Bank Ground Farm* has its own shoreline, rooms with lake and Old Man views, and four holiday cottages. Rooms without en-suite facilities are slightly cheaper. Parking. ③.

Beech Tree Guesthouse, Yewdale Rd (☎015394/41717). Coniston's former vicarage, 150 yards north of the village, makes a charming, no-smoking, vegetarian base. Decorated with zest, rooms either share a bright bathroom or have their own shower; there's a garden, with fell views, where you can have tea. Parking. No credit cards. ②.

Lakeland House, Tilberthwaite Ave (☎015394/41303). A slightly shabby but friendly enough place (opposite the Campbell memorial), accustomed to walkers and their ways, with an attached café and laundry service. Half the rooms share bathroom facilities. No credit cards. ②.

Shepherds Villa, Tilberthwaite Ave (☎015394/41337). One of Coniston's most popular B&Bs has a decent sense of space, an approachable owner and comfortable rooms, some of which retain their original fireplaces. Some are also en-suite, but there's a bathroom and shower on every floor. Packed lunches and parking available. No credit cards. ②.

Sun Hotel (☎015394/41248). Coniston's best inn lies 200 yards uphill from the bridge in the centre of the village. This sixteenth-century pub has its guest rooms in an Edwardian country-house-style adjunct – fell views, a cosy lounge, and parking. Two-night minimum stay at weekends. ④.

Thwaite Cottage, Waterhead (☎015394/41367). Half a mile east, set back from the Hawkshead road; there are three well-appointed rooms available in this peacefully located slate-flagged house. Parking. No credit cards. ②.

Waterhead Country Guest House, Waterhead (☎015394/41442). Just 200 yards from the north end of the lake, and with views to the Old Man of Coniston, it's easy to see why this small guest house fills quickly. Rooms aren't huge, but they are decently furnished and there's a garden, bar and parking. No credit cards. ②.

Walks from Coniston

The classic walk from Coniston village is to the top of the Old Man of
Coniston, which is tiring but not overly difficult – Wainwright's flippant
reference to ascending crowds of "courting couples, troops of earnest Boy
Scouts, babies and grandmothers" isn't that far wide of the mark. Other
Coniston walks are similarly accessible to most abilities, ranging from
lakeside strolls to ghyll scrambles.

Old Man of Coniston

Most walkers can reach the summit of the **Old Man of Coniston** (2635ft)
in under two hours from the village, following the signposted path from
Church Beck. It's a steep and twisting route through abandoned quarry
works and their detritus, past Low Water tarn, but the views from the top
are tremendous – to the Cumbrian coast and Morecambe Bay, and across
to Langdale and Windermere.

Old Man circular routes

Hardier hikers combine the Old Man in a ridge-walk loop with **Swirl How**
(2630ft) and **Wetherlam** (2502ft) to the north – a seven- or eight-mile
walk (5–7hr). Wetherlam too is pitted with caves, mines and tunnels,
requiring caution on the various descents to Coppermines. Or instead of
heading north you can loop around to the south, descending via **Goat's
Hause** and Goat's Water tarn, under the fearsome **Dow Crag** (a famed lure
for rock climbers). This eventually deposits you in Torver (see below),
with the full circuit back to Coniston being something like eight miles
(5hr).

Lakeside walks

From Coniston village the Cumbria Way footpath provides access to
Coniston Water's west side. The route runs past sixteenth-century
Coniston Old Hall (note its traditional circular chimneys) and through
Torver Common Wood to **Torver**, where there are a couple of pubs and
the possibility of climbing up Torver Beck to see its waterfalls. There are
also several park-and-walk spots on the lake's **east side** – nearest to the
village is the northern pier of Monk Coniston – with trails and picnic tables
in the National Trust woodland.

Tilberthwaite Gill and Yewdale

North of Coniston the crags, beck and tarn of **Yewdale** offer a multitude
of short walks. **Tilberthwaite Gill** is a quiet, narrow glen set among
dramatic old quarry workings – there's free parking up a signposted
lane off the Ambleside road (one-and-a-half miles from Coniston), or
you can walk here from Coppermines Valley via Hole Rake. **Yew Tree
Tarn**, right on the Ambleside road (two miles from Coniston), is another pretty spot.

*See Basics, p.19, for general walking advice in the Lakes; recom-
mended maps are detailed on p.9.*

Campsite and youth hostels

Coniston Hall Campsite, Haws Bank, off A593 (☎015394/41223). The most convenient campsite for the village is a mile south of town, set in spacious grounds by the lake. Booking is essential; closed Nov–Easter.

YHA Coniston Coppermines, Coppermines Valley (☎015394/41261). The hikers' favourite (perfectly placed for ascents of the Old Man and Wetherlam) is in a dramatic mountain setting a steep mile from the village – follow the "Old Man" signs past the *Sun Hotel* or take the small road between the *Black Bull* and the Co-op; both routes lead to the hostel. It's simpler, and cheaper, than Holly How, with bunks in eight- and ten-bedded rooms.

YHA Coniston Holly How, Far End, A593 (☎015394/41323). Closest hostel to the village, in a slate house (with some four-bedded rooms) set in its own gardens just a few minutes' walk north of Coniston on the Ambleside road.

Coniston village

Copper has been taken from the Coniston fells since the Bronze Age, though the Romans were the first to mine it systematically. The industry again flourished in the seventeenth century, and by the nineteenth century hundreds of workers were employed in the local copper mines – producing ore used for the "copper-bottoming" of the wooden hulls of ships. Together with slate-quarriers – first recorded here in the seventeenth century – Coniston's industrious miners established themselves in the village of **CONISTON** (a derivation of "King's Town"). That it was originally a mining village, pure and simple, is clear from the rather drab, utilitarian, rows of cottages and later Victorian shop-fronts which make up the slate-grey/green settlement. By the late nineteenth century the copper-mining business was in terminal decline and the railway, built in 1859 to remove the mined copper and quarried slate, began to bring the first tourists, who then, as now, nearly all made time to ascend the craggy, mine-riddled bulk of **The Old Man of Coniston**, which looms to the north-west. It may sound an odd name, but "Man" is a common fell term hereabouts, signifying a peak or summit, while "Old" is merely a corruption of the Norse "alt", or high. Even if you're not game for the climb, it's worth the initial stroll from the village up Church Beck and over the old Miner's Bridge – along what's known as **Coppermines Valley** – to get a glimpse of the scars and gouges from the industrial past.

The village is a functional kind of place, with an eye on tourism and plenty of accommodation and cafés. It keeps to itself to such an extent that some first-time visitors are surprised to find it has a lake – the water is hidden out of sight, half a mile southeast of the village. A memorial plaque to Donald Campbell (and his chief mechanic, Leo Villa) dominates the small green in the centre. Having studied this and the **grave of John Ruskin**, which lies in St Andrew's churchyard beneath a beautifully worked Celtic cross, you've exhausted all that Coniston has to offer save the superb museum.

Belle Isle, Windermere

Frosted jetty, Windermere

Bridge House, Ambleside

Dove Cottage, Grasmere

Timber sculpture, Grizedale Forest Park

Autumn in Little Langdale

Climbing Napes Needle, Great Gable   Cumberland wrestling, Langdale

Sheep grazing at Great Rigg, northeast of Grasmere

Castlerigg stone circle, Keswick

Hiking in Borrowdale

The Ruskin Museum

Yewdale Rd, ☎015394/41164. Open Easter to mid-Nov daily 10am–5.30pm. Admission £3. Bus #505/506 stops nearby in the village.

Coniston's **museum** – named after its most famous resident but devoted to all aspects of local life and work – is the most thought-provoking in the Lakes. The village's first museum had its genesis in the memorial exhibition held following John Ruskin's death in 1900. Organized by his long-time secretary and literary assistant W.G. Collingwood, the exhibition appropriated manuscripts and mementoes from Ruskin's house at Brantwood and raised sufficient funds for a permanent museum, largely devoted to Ruskin himself. This was housed in Coniston's Mechanics Institute, a local cultural society supported by Ruskin during his life. The latest building stands at the back of this, and is still first port-of-call for anyone interested in tracing Ruskin's life and work. In relating his ideas and theories to local trades and pastimes the museum also doubles as a highly effective record of Coniston's history through the ages.

For more on W.G. Collingwood, see p.83; and for an account of Ruskin's life and work, see Brantwood, p.83.

The museum begins with a walk-through timeline, placing the village and Ruskin within the wider historical context. Stone and Bronze Age artefacts give way to an exposition of the local geology, essential for an understanding of why Coniston became an important mining and quarrying district. The slate quarried locally has been used for centuries to roof buildings and build bridges and walls – here in the museum, it flags the floors. You'll learn about sheep-farming and about the traditonal trades which Ruskin himself promoted as a means of sustaining local employment, notably wood-carving and the making of Langdale linen and the famous Ruskin lace – examples of these are contained in slide-out panels and drawers. In the museum's separate **Ruskin Gallery** are found

---

Ruskin linen and lace

Encouraged by Ruskin, who had his own theories about the sanctity of traditional labour (see Brantwood, p.83), a local woman, Marion Twelves, revived the trade of flax hand-spinning in Elterwater in 1884. It had almost died out in the Lake District, and the flax itself had to be imported from Ireland. The linen trade flourished, assisted financially by Ruskin's own Guild of St George, though contemporary tastes dictated that the finished article would be more attractive to purchasers if it was embroidered. Ruskin provided a series of designs inspired by those of Renaissance ruffs, and the hand-cut lace was attached to the plain linen to make cushion and sideboard covers and bedspreads. Ruskin's own name was used to promote the work after 1894; and his funeral pall (displayed in the museum) was a particularly fine example. The industry continued until the 1930s, though by then few were relying upon it as a principal means of income.

---

artefacts from the original memorial exhibition (including a pair of his socks and his matriculation certificate from Oxford), alongside a mixed bag of letters, manuscripts, sketchbooks and a series of Ruskin's own watercolours. Most enterprisingly of all, an interactive side-gallery lets you view pages of Ruskin's sketchbooks at the click of a mouse.

Coniston Water

It's a ten-minute walk down Lake Road from the village to **Coniston Water** and its piers. The *Bluebird Café* sells ices and drinks, while the adjacent **boating centre** can provide the wherewithal for fooling around on the water in rowboats, sailing dinghies, canoes, electric launches or motorboats.

For boating details on Coniston Water, see p.21.

Boat speeds are now limited to 10mph, a graceful pace for the sumptuously upholstered and quilted **Steam Yacht Gondola** (Easter–Oct 4–5 departures daily; ☎015394/36003), first launched in 1859 but fully restored by the National Trust. This leaves Coniston Pier for hour-long circuits (£4.75 round trip), calling at Park-a-moor landing stage (£2.80 one-way) – for access to some fine wood and fell walks – then Ruskin's Brantwood (£4 one-way). **Evening cruises** (every Tues, 6pm; £8.50) last an hour and a half and include wine and nibbles; advance reservations recommended.

The other lake service is the **Coniston Launch** (Easter–Oct hourly departures 10.30am–4.30pm; Nov–Easter up to 4 daily depending on demand and weather, call ☎015394/36216 or ☎0797/010 8778), whose two wooden vessels operate on two routes around the lake – north to Monk Coniston, Torver and Brantwood (£3.40 return) or south to Torver, Lake Bank and Brantwood (£5.40 return). You can stop off at any pier on either route. **Special cruises** (Easter–Oct up to 2 weekly; call for details) concentrate on the various sites associated with *Swallows and Amazons* (£7) and the speed-racing Campbells (£5).

Eating and drinking

Eating opportunities outside Coniston's pubs are limited to a few basic cafés, but in any case you shouldn't look much further than the *Sun Hotel*, whose traditional bar (or hotel restaurant) serves pastas, grills and home-made pies. The *Sun* is also the cheeriest place for a drink (an outdoor terrace looks on to the fells), though the *Black Bull* by the bridge in the centre is the oldest in the village and has outdoor tables in the former coachyard. Donald Campbell stayed in both pubs during his attempts on the water-speed record: contemporary photographs and newspaper accounts are on display at the *Sun* while the *Black Bull* brews its own Bluebird beer.

Brantwood

Brantwood

Brantwood, off B5285 ☎015394/41396. Open mid-March to mid-Nov daily 11am–5.30pm; mid-Nov to mid-March Wed–Sun 11am–4.30pm. Admission: house £4 (50p discount for Gondola ticket-holders); gardens £2; combined ticket (available on the Coniston Launch) for house, gardens & launch £7.

Nestling among trees on a hillside above the eastern shore of the lake sits **Brantwood**, the magnificently sited home of John Ruskin (1819–1900). It's only two and a half miles by road from Coniston, though the approach is greatly enhanced if you arrive by either steam yacht or motor launch. Ruskin lived here from 1872 until his death: at first sight he was captivated, though by the stunning mountain and lake views and not by the house itself which he complained was "a mere shed". Indeed, the house today bears little resemblance to the eighteenth-century cottage bought for £1500 in 1871 from Radical engraver William James Linton. Ruskin spent the next twenty years expanding it, adding another twelve rooms and laying out its gardens. Thus adapted, Brantwood – "brant" is a Cumbrian dialect word meaning steep – became Ruskin's lair, where the grand old eminence of Victorian art and letters gardened, wrote, painted and pontificated.

Ruskin was from a wealthy background and could afford to indulge his passion for art from an early age. He made his name as

Ruskin fans may be interested in the Ruskin Passport (£8.50), which covers entry to Brantwood and Coniston's Ruskin Museum, as well as use of the Coniston Launch.

The Collingwoods

Few families have had as sure a feel for the Lake District as the Collingwoods, whose home was at Lanehead at the northern end of Coniston Water. Local scholar, historian and artist William Gershorn (W.G.) Collingwood (1854–1932) was born in Liverpool, but visited the Lake District on holiday as a child and moved here as soon as was practicable. He became an expert on lakeland archeology, the Vikings and early Northumbrian crosses (his *Northumbrian Crosses of the Pre-Norman Age*, published in 1927, is a classic), writing his own guide to *The Lake Counties* (1902) and even a lakeland saga, *Thorstein of the Mere*, largely set around Coniston. While at Oxford University, Collingwood had studied under John Ruskin (who was Professor of Fine Art) and was immediately impressed by his mind and ideas; later, Collingwood became Ruskin's trusted secretary and literary assistant. It was W.G. who designed Ruskin's memorial cross, and established the first Ruskin Museum in Coniston. The family befriended the young Arthur Ransome, who was of a similar age to W.G.'s son Robin Collingwood (1889–1943). Robin was later to become an Oxford professor of philosophy, influential historiographer and an authority on Roman Britain – he excavated the Galava site and fortifications at Waterhead near Ambleside. W.G.'s wife Edith and two daughters, Barbara and Dora, were also highly talented: Edith and Dora as painters, Barbara as a sculptor. Barbara's bust of the elderly Ruskin is on display in Ambleside's The Armitt. The family graves all lie, with Ruskin's, in Coniston's churchyard.

an art critic with the publication of the first part of his precocious *Modern Painters* (1843), conceived as a defence of J.M.W. Turner, whose work he had admired (and collected) since his student days. Later a champion of the Pre-Raphaelites and, after his European travels, a proponent of the supremacy of Gothic architecture, Ruskin came to insist upon the indivisibility of ethics and aesthetics. He was appalled by the conditions in which the captains of industry made their labourers work and live, while expecting him to applaud their patronage of the arts. "There is no wealth but life," he wrote in his study of capitalist economics, *Unto the Last*, elaborating with the observation: "That country is richest which nourishes the greatest number of noble and happy human beings."

Drawing a distinction between mere labour and craftsmanship, he intervened in the lakeland economy by promoting a revival of wood-carving, linen and lace-making, and ventures like this as well as his architectural theories did much to influence such disparate figures as Proust, Tolstoy, Frank Lloyd Wright and Gandhi. Nonetheless, not all Ruskin's projects were a success, partly because of his refusal to compromise his principles. A London teashop, established to provide employment for a former servant, failed since Ruskin refused to advertise; meanwhile, his street-cleaning and road-building schemes, designed to instil into his students (including Arnold Toynbee and Oscar Wilde) a respect for the dignity of manual labour, simply accrued ridicule. Perhaps more relevant today is the very Ruskinian notion of ecological conservation – some see him as the first "green" – espoused in his opposition to the expansion of the railways and the creation of Thirlmere reservoir.

His marriage had ended in 1854 (the divorce a cause-célèbre of the day, sensationally alleging his impotence) and Ruskin was looked after at Brantwood by his married cousin Joan Severn, receiving visits from the Victorian great and good. Here he worked until the 1890s – his last work his autobiography, *Praeterita* – though the last ten years of his life were punctuated by bouts of depressive illness and mental breakdown. Ruskin caught influenza and died on January 20, 1900.

House and gardens

Once you've paid to go in the **house**, you're free to wander around the various rooms. Ruskin's study (hung with handmade paper to his own design) and dining room boast superlative lake views; they are bettered only by those from the Turret Room where Ruskin used to sit in later life in his bathchair – itself on display downstairs, along with a mahogany desk and Blue John wine goblet, amongst other memorabilia. A twenty-minute video expands on the man's philosophy and whets the appetite for rooms full of his watercolours, as well as for the surviving Turners from Ruskin's collection which weren't sold off after his death. Other exhibition rooms and the Coach House

Gallery display Ruskin-related arts and crafts, while the *Jumping Jenny* tearooms – named after Ruskin's boat – have outdoor terrace-seating for meals and drinks. There's also a well-stocked **bookshop** for those who want to bone up on the Pre-Raphaelites or the Arts and Crafts Movement; there's a summer **theatre** season held in the grounds; and various other lectures, recitals and walks scheduled throughout the year – call the house for a brochure.

The 250-acre estate surrounding the house boasts a nature trail, while paths wind through the lakeside meadows and **gardens**, where Ruskin pottered about, attending to his native flowers and fruit and his moorland shrubs and ferns.

Hawkshead

HAWKSHEAD, midway between Coniston and Ambleside, wears its beauty well, its patchwork of whitewashed cottages, cobbles, alleys and archways backed by woods and fells and barely affected by twentieth-century intrusions. This is partly due to the enlightened policy of banning traffic in the centre. Huge car parks at the village edge take the strain and when the crowds of day-trippers leave, Hawkshead regains its natural tranquillity. The village sits at the head of **Esthwaite Water**, a skinny lake less than two miles long which empties into Windermere. This isn't troubled by too many visitors, though it's said to have good trout-fishing and Wordsworth is known to have rambled and splashed around its perimeter as a boy.

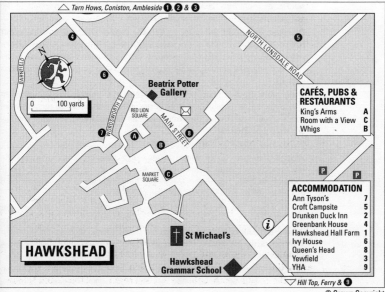

© Crown Copyright

Hawkshead

Best view of the water is from the car-park access point on the far southwestern shore, two miles from Hawkshead.

Arrival and information

Hawkshead services:

bike rental p.20;

pharmacy p.23;

post office p.11.

The main **bus service** to Hawkshead is the #505/506 between Bowness, Ambleside and Coniston. On reaching Hawkshead, three or four services a day loop down to Near Sawrey and back for the Beatrix Potter house at Hill Top. The B5285 between Coniston and Sawrey skirts the eastern side of Hawkshead; no traffic is allowed in the village itself. The **National Park Information Centre** is at the main **car park** off Main Street (Easter–Oct daily 9.30am–6pm; Nov–Easter Sat & Sun only 10am–4pm; ☎015394/36525); everything lies within five minutes' walk of here.

Accommodation

Book a long way ahead if you want to stay in Hawskhead during the peak summer season. The information centre can help if the places we recommend below are full. As well as the local campsites, there's also **camping** in nearby Grizedale Forest, and at Low Wray, either of which are more remote, relaxed options.

B&Bs, guest houses and hotels

Ann Tyson's Cottage, Wordsworth St (☎015394/36405). Wordsworth briefly boarded here, and the street and house have changed little since. Choose between variously sized rooms in the main house (oak beams, low ceilings) – ask for the room with Ruskin's bed in it – the adjacent barn conversion, or the self-catering Top Cottage. No credit cards. ②.

Drunken Duck Inn, Barngates crossroad, 2 miles north of Hawkshead off B5286 (☎015394/36347, *drunkenduckinn@demon.co.uk*). Well-known pub on the brow of a hill with sweeping views – plus a cheery welcome, fine rooms, deservedly popular bar food, own-brewed beer and occasional folk/jazz gigs. ⑤.

Greenbank House, Main St (☎015394/36497). Modernized seventeenth-century house at the northern edge of the village, with views to the fells from some of the small rooms. Only four have en-suite showers, for which you pay slightly more. Parking. ④.

Ivy House, Main St (☎015394/36204, *Ivyhousehotel@btinternet.com*). Elegant Georgian house whose rotunda lights up the country-house-style interior. Six rooms in the main house, five more in the lodge behind (some rooms with bath, not shower). Parking. Rate includes dinner, though B&B available (④) on request. Closed Nov to mid-March. ⑤.

Queen's Head, Main St (☎015394/36271). The pick of the pubs, at least as far as the comfortable rooms go – thoroughly modernized, with good beds and repro antique furnishings. Though not huge, the family rooms can sleep three or four. Downstairs, the sixteenth-century reasserts itself in the oak-and-panel interior. A self-catering cottage (sleeps three), around the back, is available too. ④.

Yewfield, Hawkshead Hill, 2 miles west of Hawkshead off B5285 (☎015394/36765). Vegetarian guest house set amongst organic vegetable gardens, orchards and wild-flower meadows; the old coach house and stables in the grounds are also rented out as self-catering apartments. Closed mid-Dec to Jan. ③.

Campsites and youth hostel

Croft Caravan and Campsite, North Lonsdale Rd, beyond the car parks on the edge of the village (☎015394/36374). Closest campsite to the centre is this busy and expensive spot; bike rental available. Closed Nov to mid-March.

Hawkshead Hall Farm, half a mile north of Hawkshead on the Ambleside road (☎015394/36221). Escape some of the crowds: bus #505/506 passes the farm on the way into Hawkshead. Closed Dec–Feb.

YHA Esthwaite Lodge (☎015394/36293, *hawkshead@yha.org.uk*). The local hostel is a mile to the south down the Newby Bridge road, on Esthwaite Water's west side, housed in a Regency mansion with good-sized family rooms.

The village

The Vikings were the first to settle the land here, Hawkshead probably founded by and named after one Haukr, a Norse warrior. In medieval times it became an important wool market, the trade controlled by the monks of Furness Abbey, whose last remaining manorial building – Hawkshead Courthouse (not open to the public) is sited half a mile north of the village, where the Ambleside and Coniston roads meet.

This early wealth explains the otherwise puzzling presence in such a small community of **Hawkshead Grammar School** (Easter–Sept Mon–Sat 10am–12.30pm & 1.30–5pm, Sun 1–5pm; Oct same days, but closes 4.30pm; £2), whose entrance lies opposite the tourist office. This was founded in 1585 and – even by Wordsworth's day, when the wool trade had much declined – was considered to be among the finest schools in the country. Wordsworth and his brother Richard were sent here following the death of their mother in 1778 to acquire an expensively bought education; "grammar" of course being the Latin grammar, knowledge of which was the mark of every gentleman. In the simple, yet rather forbidding, school room the Wordsworth boys were taught geometry, algebra and the classics at time-worn wooden benches and desks (some date back to the school's foundation); you'll be shown the desk on which the rapscallion William carved his signature – a foolhardy stunt given the anecdote that miscreants were suspended from a pulley in the centre of the room to be birched. He also wrote his first surviving piece of poetry, a paean to the bicentenary of the school's foundation, before leaving in 1787 to go up to Cambridge. The only other things to see are the headmaster's study upstairs, a small exhibition on the history of English grammar schools, and a few quills and nibs. The school closed in 1909.

The poem written by the 15-year-old Wordsworth in honour of his school is on display in Dove Cottage, Grasmere.

During his schooldays Wordsworth attended the fifteenth-century church of **St Michael's** above the school, which harks back to

Hawkshead

Norman and Romanesque designs in its rounded pillars and patterned arches. It's chiefly of interest for the 26 pithy psalms and biblical extracts illuminated with cherubs and flowers, painted on the walls during the seventeenth and eighteenth centuries. Wordsworth's other connection with the village is that during termtimes he lodged with a local woman, **Ann Tyson** – someone he remembered kindly as "my old Dame" in *The Prelude*. Her Hawkshead cottage is now a guest house (see p.86), though the Tyson family, and Wordsworth, actually lived for longer in another (unknown) house after 1783 when they moved half a mile east to Colthouse.

From its knoll the churchyard gives a good view over the village's twin central squares, anchored by a couple of pubs and several cafés. Past the Queen's Head on Main Street, the **Beatrix Potter Gallery** (Easter–Oct Mon–Thurs & Sun 10.30am–4.30pm; £2.90; NT; ☎015394/36355) hoovers up all Hawkshead's remaining visitors; in summer, its popularity is such that timed-entry tickets are issued. The gallery occupies rooms once used by Potter's solicitor husband, William Heelis, whom she met while purchasing land in the Hawkshead area. There had been a Heelis law firm in the village since 1861 and William was a partner in the family firm from 1900 until he died in 1945, when the building passed to the National Trust. If you were ever going to crack the enduring mystery of his wife's popularity you'd think this would be the place, since the upstairs rooms contain an annually changing selection of Potter's sketchbooks, drawings, watercolours, letters and manuscripts – Heelis's prewar office is maintained downstairs. But to a non-believer, the original paintings and drawings are pleasant without ever being more than mere fluff: the less devoted will find displays on her life as a keen naturalist, conservationist and early supporter of the National Trust more diverting. Potter bought eighteen fell farms and large parcels of Lake District land, which she bequeathed to the Trust on her death.

There's still a Heelis law firm in the Lakes, with offices in Ambleside and Penrith.

For more on the Beatrix Potter's life and work, see Hill Top, p.89.

Eating and drinking

Hawkshead's **pubs** provide the main eating options, not bad at either the *Queen's Head* (Main Street) or *King's Arms* (Market Square), both of which have bar meals and outdoor tables, as well as more formal restaurants. Of the **tearooms**, *Whig's* on Market Square (closed Thurs; also Wed in winter & all Jan) serves its eponymous speciality chewy white rolls flavoured with caraway seeds; try them toasted with garlic butter, or as a rarebit with cheese. *Room With a View* (☎015394/36751; closes 9pm & all Mon) overlooks the square – the entrance is around the corner, below the church, by Hawkshead Crafts and Woollens – and serves vegetarian roasts, rice dishes, roulades and tarts for lunch and dinner, accompanied by organic wines and beer.

Tarn Hows

A minor road off the Hawkshead–Coniston road (B5285) winds the couple of miles northwest to **Tarn Hows**, a body of water surrounded by spruce and pine and circled by paths and picnic spots. The land was donated by Beatrix Potter in 1930 – one of several such grants – since when the National Trust has carefully maintained it. It takes an hour to walk around the tarn, during which you can ponder on the fact that this miniature idyll is in fact almost entirely artificial – the original owners enlarged two small tarns to make the one you see today, planted and landscaped the surroundings and dug the footpaths. It's now a Site of Special Scientific Interest – keep an eye out for some of the Lakes' (and England's) few surviving native red squirrels.

This is one of the Lake District's most popular beauty spots and a free National Trust **bus** runs here from Hawkshead and Coniston on Sundays between Easter and the end of October (5 services, roughly 9.30am–5pm). Otherwise, you'll have to pay to use the designated car park, or make the two-mile **walk** on paths and country lanes from either Hawkshead or Coniston.

Hill Top

Hill Top, Near Sawrey ☎015394/36269. Open Easter–Oct Mon–Wed, Sat & Sun 11am–5pm. Admission £4. NT. Bus #505/506 or #525 from Hawkshead.

It's two miles down the eastern side of Esthwaite Water from Hawkshead to the twin hamlets of Near and Far Sawrey, overlooked by the woods and tarns of Claife Heights. Near Sawrey in particular – a cluster of flower-draped whitewashed cottages in a shallow vale – receives an inordinate number of visitors since it's the site of Beatrix Potter's house, **Hill Top**.

This is an almost mandatory stop on many tours of England (London, Stratford, Hill Top) and the house furnishings and contents have been kept as they were during Potter's occupancy – a condition of her will. The small house is always thronged with visitors, so much so that numbers are often limited. In summer, expect to have to wait in line. The carved oak bedstead and sideboards, the small library of bound sets of Gibbons and Shakespeare, and the cottage garden are all typical of well-to-do, if unexceptional, Edwardian taste – though the few mementoes and curios do nothing to throw light on Potter's character. But if you love the books then Hill Top and the Sawrey neighbourhood will be familiar (the *Tower Bank Arms*, next door, for instance, is the inn in *The Tale of Jemima Puddle-Duck*). And where better to buy a Mrs Tiggy-winkle salt-and-pepper shaker or a Peter Rabbit calendar?

A Londoner by birth, **Beatrix Potter** (1866–1943) spent childhood holidays in the Lakes, first at Wray Castle on Windermere and later in houses with grand gardens, at Holehird (Troutbeck) and Lingholm

Arthur Ransome

Arthur Ransome (1884–1967) was born in Leeds and spent early child-hood holidays with his brother and sisters at Nibthwaite by Coniston Water. His boyhood holiday pursuits were all put to use in his books, though it was the friendship he made with the outgoing Collingwood family as a young man of twenty which cemented his love affair with the Lakes – sailing with them on Coniston Water, picnicking on Peel Island, and visiting the local copper mines.

Ransome's first job was with a London publisher, though he was soon published in his own right, producing critical literary studies of Edgar Allan Poe and Oscar Wilde, and an account of London's Bohemia. He met and married Ivy Constance Walker and they had one daughter, Tabitha, in 1910, but the marriage was never happy. In part this prompted a bold solo move to Russia in 1913, after which his marriage was effectively at an end. Ransome was keen to learn the language and had a special interest in Russian folklore – a well-received translation and adaptation of various fairytales (*Old Peter's Russian Tales*) appeared in 1916.

During World War I, ill-health prevented him joining up and he was hired as a war correspondent by the *Daily News*. Consequently, when the Russian Revolution broke out, he was well-placed to report on events. Ransome clearly knew his Russian politics, and was a sympathetic but critical observer of the Bolshevik Revolution, producing two books of on-the-spot reportage. He interviewed Lenin and other leading figures, and was introduced to Trotsky's secretary, Eugenia, who – on the final break-up of his first marriage – became his second wife.

Ransome spent much of the following ten years in Russia and the Baltic states, latterly as special correspondent for the *Manchester Guardian*,

(Derwent Water). Her landscape and animal sketching was encouraged by Canon Rawnsley, a family friend, who inspired her to produce her first book, *The Tale of Peter Rabbit*, published in 1901. With the proceeds, Potter – remembering her happy holidays – bought the lakeland farmhouse at Hill Top in 1905. Half a dozen of her later books are set in and around Hill Top, though she still lived for much of the year in London. Following her marriage to a local solicitor in 1913, Potter retained the house as her study but installed a manager at Hill Top to oversee the farm. Only known locally as Mrs Heelis the farmer (rather than Beatrix Potter the author), she lived down the road in another house, Castle Cottage (not open to the public), but visited Hill Top most days, usually to work on business associated with her increasing portfolio of farms, which took up more and more of her time. She actually wrote very few books after her marriage, preferring to develop her interest in breeding the local Herdwick sheep, for which she won many prizes at local shows. When she died, her ashes were scattered locally by the Hill Top farm manager: the place has never been identified and there's no other memorial to her, save the house.

You can reach Hill Top by bus in summer, though it's also a lovely hour's walk from the Sawrey car-ferry pier on the west side of for whom he travelled widely. In 1925 he bought his first lakeland house at Low Ludderburn, in the Winster Valley and, having eventually abandoned journalism, it was here he wrote *Swallows and Amazons* (published in 1930). This was the first of twelve books he produced in the series (the last in 1947), most, but not all, set in the Lake District – spells in Norfolk and Suffolk provided the background for *We Didn't Mean To Go To Sea* and *Coot Club*.

Ransome was inspired to write for and about the five children of the Altounyan family, whose father, Ernest, brought them to the Lake District on holiday in 1928. Ernest Altounyan, married to Dora Collingwood, a long-time Ransome family friend, bought two boats (one called *Swallow*) and he and Ransome first taught the children to sail. That the Altounyan children were models for the "Swallows" is now accepted – the first edition of the book was dedicated to them – though when the relationship cooled in later years, Ransome denied this and withdrew the dedication. Other friends and local characters appeared in the books, while Coniston locations figured heavily – Peel Island as "Wild Cat Island", the Coniston fells and mines in *Pigeon Post*, and the Old Man of Coniston as "Kanchenjunga". Ransome and Eugenia lived in Coniston itself between 1940 and 1945, but settled in retirement at a house called Hill Top in Haverthwaite. He died on June 3, 1967.

Eugenia donated various effects and mementoes of her husband's to Abbot Hall in Kendal, which maintains an Arthur Ransome exhibition and doubles as the HQ of The Arthur Ransome Society (TARS), whose zealous members keep his flame alive by means of literary events, publications and activities. For more information, contact the museum or visit the expansive Arthur Ransome Web site: *arthur-ransome.org/ar/index.html*

Windermere, on a route which climbs steeply up Claife Heights and passes first through **FAR SAWREY**. It must be the only hike in England signposted in Japanese (the Japanese have a special fondness for Potter). You can revive yourself in Far Sawrey's *Sawrey Hotel*, which has a beer garden, before swinging around to the church and across the hay fields to **NEAR SAWREY**, where the *Tower Bank Arms*, next to Hill Top (☎015394/36334; ③), serves good sandwiches, lakeland game pie and local sausages. You'd be lucky to score a room here in the summer, though there are a couple of other local possibilities: B&B at gorgeous *Buckle Yeat* cottage (☎015394/36446, *info@buckle-yeat.co.uk*; ③) – illustrated in Potter's *The Tale of Tom Kitten* – or Victorian grace and comfort a hundred yards down the road at *Sawrey House Country Hotel* (☎015394/36387, *enquiries@sawrey-house.com*; ⑥, ⑦ with dinner), which looks down over Esthwaite Water.

Grizedale Forest

Historically, much of the land between Coniston and Windermere was thickly forested, as indeed it is today, though by the eighteenth century successive generations of charcoal-making, coppicing and iron-smelting had taken its toll and stripped the fells and dales virtually bare. Twentieth-century regeneration by the Forestry Commission has restored thick oak, spruce, larch and pine woodland to **Grizedale Forest**, whose visitor centre, trails, sculptures and other diversions make a great day out in good weather.

Pick up a map from the forest visitor centre (see below) and you can set out on one of several marked hiking or biking trails, or just follow a nature trail to one of the picnic spots. Red deer are seen here occasionally, and the forest also provides a habitat for badgers and squirrels, grouse, woodcock and woodpeckers. The **Silurian Way** (10 miles; 4–5hr) links the majority of the eighty remarkable stone and wood sculptures scattered amongst the trees. Since 1977 artists have been invited to create a sculptural response to their surroundings using natural materials. Some of the resulting works are startling, as you round a bend to find pinnacles rising from a tarn, sculpted wooden ferns, a hundred-foot-long wave of bent logs or a dry-stone wall slaloming through the conifers.

Access to the forest is easiest from Hawkshead, which is just two-and-a-half miles northeast of the visitor centre. There's an hourly bus service (#525) – on weekends and school holidays between Easter and the end of October – from Hawkshead or the Sawrey ferry pier (for Bowness). The bus stops at the **Grizedale Forest Centre** (Feb–Dec daily 10am–5pm; free; ☎01229/860010), where there's also plenty of parking, a tearoom, art gallery and theatre. **Bikes** are a good way to get around: Grizedale Mountain Bikes at the centre (daily 9am–5pm; call ☎01229/860369 to reserve in advance) provides bikes, maps and gear. If you're planning to use the **campsite** (☎01229/860257; closed Oct–Feb), just past the visitor centre, call ahead as it's very popular.

Two miles south down the road from the visitor centre, the forestry hamlet of **SATTERTHWAITE** has a pub, the *Eagle's Child*, while some clever route-finding in the narrow lanes the same distance beyond brings you to rustic **Rusland** church. Surrounded by undulating grazing land, it's a serene setting for the simple graves of children's writer **Arthur Ransome** and his wife Eugenia.

Broughton-in-Furness

Southwest of Coniston Water, a quiet triangle at the southern edge of the National Park is anchored by the small market town of **BROUGHTON-IN-FURNESS**. It dates back to medieval times, though its aspect is pure Georgian. Tall houses surround an attractive square, complete with spreading chestnut tree, commemorative obelisk, stone fish slabs and stocks. In the eighteenth century the market was a staging post for wool, wood and cattle, shipped out of the area from the nearby Duddon estuary. Follow Church Street to the edge of town and you'll reach the **church** of St Mary Magdalene, originally twelfth-century though now much restored. The town's only literary connection is a slight one: the scapegrace Brontë brother, Branwell, taught here briefly before terminally pickling himself in Haworth.

Just ten miles from Coniston, Broughton makes a handy local walking base. It's also well-sited for touring the **Furness peninsulas**, which lie just south of the National Park: it's only ten miles south to Dalton-in-Furness (burial place of the artist George Romney) and the South Lakes Animal Park, and another four to Furness Abbey, medieval powerhouse of the lakeland economy (the latter covered on p.164). The most direct route here is along the A593 from Coniston, via Torver, through the gentle charms of the **Woodland Valley** – the way the branch railway line (now dismantled) used to run. **Cumbria Way** hikers cut through an even less frequented sector of the park, as their route takes them above the **Crake Valley**, through the bracken and heather of Blawith Fells, past Beacon Tarn. The A5084 parallels the path, sticking closer to the River Crake as it falls away from Coniston Water; turn west at Lowick for the main road to Broughton.

The most frequent **bus services** to Broughton are from the south, from Ulverston, though there's a twice-daily school service (#507) from Coniston via Torver. The **tourist office** is in the old Town Hall on The Square (Easter–Oct Mon–Fri 10am–4pm, Sat 9am–4pm, Sun 9am–1pm; ☎01229/716115). There are several **B&Bs**, including *Garner House* on Church Street (☎01229/716462; no credit cards; ②; closed Nov–Feb); and there's also accommodation available in a couple of the local pubs – for example, the *Manor Arms*, The Square (☎01229/716286; ②), a nice old local with good beer, and breakfast (and drinks) served in your room. The *Square Café* (☎01229/716388; no credit cards) on the square is the nicest **tearoom**; it also has three B&B rooms above (one with en-suite facilities; ①). *Beswick's*, on the corner of Griffin Street (☎01229/716285; eve only in winter), is a **bistro** with good food and a great wine list. For fell views, walk just out of town up the hill (the Millom road) to the *High Cross Inn* for a drink.

The Duddon Valley

A mile west of Broughton, from Duddon Bridge, the minor road up the stunning **Duddon Valley** – marked **Dunnerdale** on some maps – twists and turns its increasingly dramatic way northeast to the foot of the Wrynose and Hardknott passes. Wordsworth wrote a sequence of 34 sonnets about the valley (published as *The River Duddon* in 1820), his conclusion – "Still glides the Stream, and shall for ever glide"– a comment on the ephemeral nature of man. Lofty thoughts indeed as you navigate around the rocky outcrops and through the wandering sheep crowding the road. On warm days cars line the verges at **Ulpha Bridge**, five miles north of Broughton, as picnics are spread on the river banks and kids plummet from the bridge into the water. At **Seathwaite**, another three miles along the road, there's a pub and a church, and a popular short walk to Wallowbarrow Crag, below which the river tumbles through a gorge. Beyond Seathwaite the road is ever more tortuous, though there's parking a couple of miles further north close to **Birks Bridge**, an ancient bridge which spans a twenty-foot-deep chasm. People picnic here, too, or climb through the forestry land to the west to ascend **Harter Fell** (2240ft). Shortly after Birks Bridge the head of the valley widens dramatically at Dale Head, whose "Big Sky" perspective is quite out of keeping with the confined Lakes – more New Zealand than Cumbria. The river is at its widest here, and at the bridge and junction of **Cockley Beck** – where there's a farmhouse tearoom – you can debate the dubious pleasures of attempting your onward route: west over Hardknott Pass into Eskdale or east over Wrynose Pass to Little Langdale; both passes require careful driving or, in the case of out-of-condition cyclists, an oxygen tent.

There's an early-morning **post bus** once a day (not Sun) from Broughton-in-Furness to Cockley Beck, via Ulpha and Seathwaite.

Travel details

From Coniston

Bus #505/506 (Sun only; summer hourly; winter 3 daily) to: to Hawkshead (20min), Ambleside (30–50min), Brockhole (1hr), Bowness (1hr 5min).

Bus #X12 (Mon–Sat 8 daily, Sun 4 daily) to: Torver (7min) and Ulverston (30min).

Chapter 4

Keswick, Derwent Water and the North

K eswick – main town in the lakeland north – has one of the region's most advantageous settings: standing on the northern shores of beautiful **Derwent Water**, backed by the imposing heights of Skiddaw and Blencathra, and lying at the junction of the main north–south (A591) and east–west (A66) routes through the Lake District. Despite its long history as a market and mining town, it's now almost entirely devoted to the tourist trade, though most of Keswick's visitors are the type who like to rock-hop in the dramatic surroundings rather than clamber from tour-bus to gift shop. Consequently, there's slightly less of the themed lakeland packaging which afflicts the southern towns, and rather more of an

---

ACCOMMODATION PRICE CODES

Hotel and **B&B** accommodation is priced on a scale of ① to ⑨ (see below), indicating the **average price** you could expect to pay per night for a **double or twin room** in high season. **Youth hostels** are not given a price code since they fall within a fairly narrow price band. For more accommodation details, see Basics, p.12.

① under £40	④ £60–70	⑦ £110–150
② £40–50	⑤ £70–90	⑧ £150–200
③ £50–60	⑥ £90–110	⑨ over £200

CAFÉ AND RESTAURANT PRICE CODES

Cafés and restaurants listed in this guide have been assigned one of four price categories:

Inexpensive under £10
Moderate £10–20
Expensive £20–30
Very expensive over £30

This is the price you can expect to pay per person for a three-course meal or equivalent, excluding drinks and service.

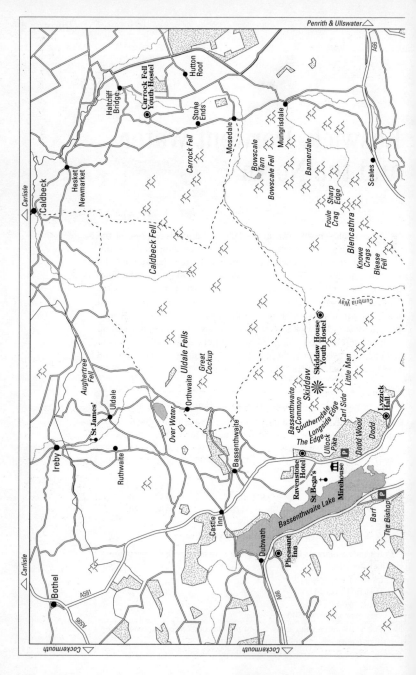

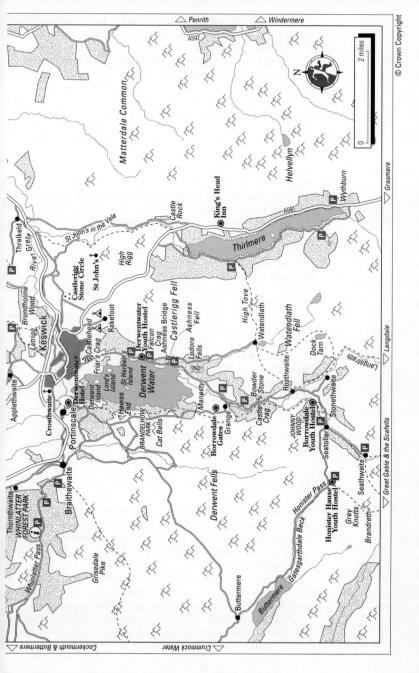

outdoors air, with walkers steadily coming and going from their peregrinations. The town also has solid literary connections – not with Wordsworth for a change, but with the other members of the poetical triumvirate, Samuel Taylor Coleridge and Robert Southey, who both settled in Keswick in the early years of the nineteenth century.

Derwent Water lies just a few minutes' from the town centre, its launch service providing easy access to long-famed beauty spots such as Ashness Bridge, Watendlath and the Lodore Falls. And even with just a day in town you should make the effort to take in the charms of **Borrowdale**, the glorious meandering valley to the south of Derwent Water that's been a source of inspiration to artists and writers over the centuries. There are fellside scrambles, isolated tarns and waterfalls, riverside walks and tranquil farming hamlets, while the lonely settlements of Rosthwaite, Seatoller, Stonethwaite and Seathwaite are the jumping-off points for the many walking routes to the peaks around **Scafell Pike**, the Lake District's (and England's) highest mountain.

Keswick also makes a good base for climbing either of its shadowing northern bulks, **Skiddaw** or **Blencathra** – the first, one of the four Lakes' mountains that clocks in at over the magic 3000-feet mark, but easy to conquer; the second, a couple of hundred feet lower but with several rather more challenging approaches. Also north of town lies **Bassenthwaite Lake**, from where minor roads and footpaths head northeast into the region known locally as **Back o' Skiddaw**, a little-visited neck of the lakes hidden behind Skiddaw itself. This is as off-the-beaten-track as it gets in the National Park, though handsome villages such as **Caldbeck** and the unsung heights of **Carrock Fell** make a trip worthwhile. East of Keswick, the old railway line footpath makes a fine approach to the little village of **Threlkeld**, from where some are drawn south through bucolic **St John's in the Vale** to **Thirlmere**, the Lake District's largest reservoir.

Keswick

The modern centre of **KESWICK**, a town of around 5000 people, sits south and east of the River Greta, though its origins lie around an early medieval church just over the river in Crosthwaite. Scattered farms probably provided its first local industry, if the town's name (*kes*, meaning cheese, and *wic*, meaning dairy farm) – is anything to go by. Granted its market charter by Edward I in 1276 – **market day** is still Saturday – Keswick became an important centre for trading wool and leather until around 1500, when these trades were supplanted by ore-mining and, later, the discovery of local graphite, which formed the mainstay of the local economy until the late eighteenth century. The railway (long defunct) arrived in the 1860s,

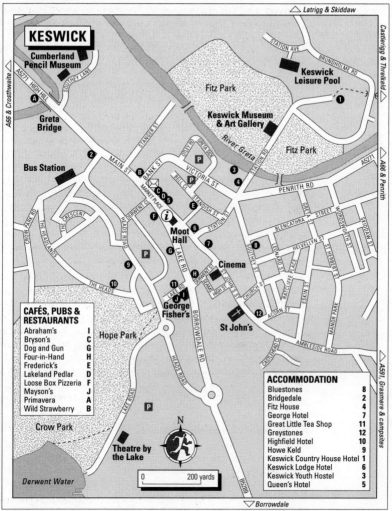

KESWICK

Cumberland Pencil Museum

Greta Bridge

Bus Station

Fitz Park

Keswick Leisure Pool

Keswick Museum & Art Gallery

River Greta

Fitz Park

Moot Hall

Cinema

George Fisher's

St John's

Hope Park

Crow Park

Theatre by the Lake

Derwent Water

CAFÉS, PUBS & RESTAURANTS

Abraham's	I
Bryson's	C
Dog and Gun	G
Four-in-Hand	H
Frederick's	E
Lakeland Pedlar	D
Loose Box Pizzeria	F
Mayson's	J
Primavera	A
Wild Strawberry	B

ACCOMMODATION

Bluestones	8
Bridgedale	2
Fitz House	4
George Hotel	7
Great Little Tea Shop	11
Greystones	12
Highfield Hotel	10
Howe Keld	9
Keswick Country House Hotel	1
Keswick Lodge Hotel	6
Keswick Youth Hostel	3
Queen's Hotel	5

Latrigg & Skiddaw

Castlerigg & Threlkeld

A66 & Crosthwaite

A66 & Penrith

A591, Grasmere & campsites

Borrowdale

0   200 yards

© Crown Copyright

since when Keswick has turned its attention fully to the requirements of tourists. There's plenty of accommodation and some good cafés aimed at walkers, while several bus routes radiate from the town, getting you to the start of even the most challenging hikes. For those not up to a day on the fells, the town remains a popular place throughout the year, with its handsome park, two interesting museums and old pubs – and you're only ever a short stroll away from the shores of Derwent Water.

Arrival and information

*Keswick
services:*
*bike rental
p.20;*
car rental p.7;
hospital p.22;
laundry p.22;
*money
exchange p.11;*
*pharmacies
p.23;*
*post office
p.11;*
*swimming
pool p.23;*
taxis p.7.

Buses (including National Express services) use the terminal at The Headlands, behind the Lakes Foodstore, off Main Street. Parking is easier than in many places: large **car parks** down Lake Road near the lake, and on either side of Market Place, soak up most of the visiting and shopping traffic; while there are no restrictions in the streets off Southey Street (where most of the B&Bs are) or on Brundholme Road behind the park.

The **National Park Tourist Information Centre** is in the Moot Hall on Market Place (daily: July & Aug 9.30am–6pm; April–June, Sept & Oct 9.30am–5.30pm; Nov–March 9.30am–4pm; ☎017687/72645). **Guided walks** – from lakeside rambles to mountain climbs – depart from here (Easter–Oct daily 10.15am; £4; details available from tourist office); just turn up with a packed lunch. George Fisher, at 2 Borrowdale Rd (☎017687/72178), is perhaps the most celebrated **outdoors store** in the Lakes, with a full range of equipment and maps, a daily weather information service and café. But Keswick has a dozen other outdoors stores, most found along the western half of Main Street, between the post office and the bus station.

Accommodation

B&Bs cluster around Southey, Blencathra, Church and Eskin streets, in the grid off the A591 (Penrith road). Smarter places line The Heads, overlooking Hope Park, a couple of minutes' south of the centre on the way to the lake. Nearly all the town pubs offer accommodation too – the best are picked out below – while if you're in the market for a country-house experience, Keswick's environs have plenty of choice.

B&Bs, guest houses and hotels

Bluestones, 7 Southey St (☎017687/74237, *bluestones-keswick@ cwcom.net*). Welcoming guest house, used to families (check out the classic Dinky car collection) and groups of walkers – three of the reasonably spacious rooms have three or four beds; all bar one share a bathroom. And there's fresh fruit and yoghurt at breakfast. No credit cards. ①.

Bridgedale Guesthouse, 101 Main St (☎017687/73914). Keswick's cheapest rooms: the Shirley Bassey-style lamé shower curtain aside, there are no frills (the simplest rooms don't even have a sink or TV), but it's a friendly place to rest your head, get your laundry done (£1) or store your luggage. No credit cards. ①.

Derwentwater Hotel, Portinscale, 2 miles west of town, off the A66 (☎017687/72538, *derwentwater.hotel@dial.pipex.com*). Superior lakeside retreat with comfortable rooms – some de luxe, with CD and video players – lounges and sweeping views, a conservatory and rated restaurant. Two-night D, B&B rates are a good deal. Self-catering apartments available in the grounds. Parking. ⑦–⑧.

Fitz House, 47 Brundholme Terrace, Station Rd (☎017687/74488). B&Bs don't come any more stylish than this beautiful Victorian house overlooking the park, glowing with restored pine, lovely furnishings and artwork. One room has a private terrace, the others have use of a stunning tiled conservatory, while the top twin (②) is roomiest and has a private bath. No credit cards. ①.

The George Hotel, St John St (☎017687/72076). Old coaching inn with bags of character in its public bars, modernized B&B rooms (half with private facilities – ask if you want a bath instead of a shower) and good food (see p.107). Standard rooms are less well-equipped (no TVs). Parking. ②–③.

The Great Little Tea Shop, 26 Lake Rd (☎017687/73545). The rooms could be bigger and a bit smarter – best is the four-poster room with its own private bath – but there's no faulting the relaxed atmosphere, above a no-smoking tearoom-restaurant known for its good cooking. No credit cards. ③.

Greystones, Ambleside Rd (☎017687/73108). Non-smoking terrace house opposite the church. Spick-and-span rooms (one single available) have fell views and there's parking. No credit cards. ③.

Highfield Hotel, The Heads (☎017687/72508). Beautifully restored Victorian stone hotel whose stylish feature rooms include two perky turrets and a converted chapel. Some front rooms have balconies, all have comfortable beds, and there's garden seating, parking, a bar and an inventive restaurant (set dinner £16). ③, ④ for feature rooms.

Howe Keld, 5–7 The Heads (☎017687/72417, *howekeld@globalnet.co.uk*). The Fishers' non-smoking guest house has a reputation for great breakfasts (pancakes and syrup, rissoles and other home-made specialities) inspired by their stint at the vegetarian food chain *Cranks*. Sympathetically styled rooms with fell views and compact shower rooms; and a view-laden lounge with walking books. Parking. ③.

Keswick Country House Hotel, Station Rd (☎017687/72020 or ☎0800/454454). Grand hotel, built for the nineteenth-century railway trade and sitting in landscaped grounds beneath Latrigg Fell. The conservatory is a beauty. Parking. ⑦, includes dinner.

Keswick Lodge Hotel, Main St (☎017687/74584). Old coaching inn with decently priced rooms, and good beer and food downstairs in one of Keswick's better hostelries. Ask about the three-for-two night offers (excludes weekends & Aug). ③.

Lyzzick Hall, Under Skiddaw, A591 (☎017687/72277). A couple of miles northwest of town, this relaxed country-house hotel is a bit heavy on the floral decor but set in its own grounds, with an indoor pool, lounges warmed by log fires and very good restaurant. Parking. ⑤, ⑥ with dinner.

The Queen's Hotel, Main St (☎017687/73333, *TheQueensHotel@ btinternet.com*). The nicest central hotel has a very cosy clubbable bar and a huge variety of rooms, all reasonably sized, many with good views. Some have been upgraded more recently than others, so ask to see first. Parking (fee charged), and free pass to Keswick pool. ⑤.

Ravenstone Hotel, Bassenthwaite, 5 miles northwest of town, A591 (☎017687/76240). A Victorian beauty, with terrific views over Bassenthwaite Lake and enough decorative oak to denude a small forest. Bigger, pricier four-poster rooms available, plus firelit lounge, full-sized snooker table, restaurant and bar. Parking. ⑤, ⑥ with dinner.

Campsites and youth hostels

Castlerigg Farm, Rakefoot Lane, off A591, Castlerigg (☎017687/72479). Mainly for tents (with showers and a small shop), just over a mile southeast of the centre. Closed Nov–Easter.

Castlerigg Hall, Rakefoot Lane, off A591, Castlerigg (☎017687/72437). Large tent-and-caravan site; it's the first one you reach up this road. Closed Nov–Easter.

Derwentwater Camping and Caravan Club Site (☎017687/72392). Less than ten minutes' walk from the centre, down by the lake (which means it's always busy); turn off Main Street, and head past the bus terminal. Closed Dec & Jan.

Derwentwater Youth Hostel, Borrowdale (☎017687/77246, *derwentwater @yha.org.uk*). Based in a two-hundred-year-old mansion with fifteen acres of grounds sloping down to the lake, a couple of miles south of Keswick along the B5289. It's a bit far to walk in and out for the shops and pubs; bus #79 runs past.

Keswick Youth Hostel, Station Rd (☎017687/72484, *keswick@yha. org.uk*). A converted woollen mill by the river, across from the park, which fills quickly in summer. Most rooms have just three or four beds. There's plenty of local hiking and biking info, a lounge with balcony overlooking the river, and free tea and coffee on arrival.

The town

The centre of Keswick fills the space between Main Street and the wide River Greta, which makes a lazy curve through town and park. Most of the main sights – including the Pencil Museum, Crosthwaite church, and Castlerigg stone circle – lie outside this area, but don't abandon the centre without a quick walk around. Many of the buildings are Victorian, including the **Moot Hall** (1813), marooned in the middle of Market Place; formerly the town hall and prison, it now houses the tourist office. Down St John's Street, sandstone **St John's Church** dates from the same year, notable only for its handsome spire (a landmark from all over town) and for the fact that the novelist Sir Hugh Walpole – who set his Herries novels in Borrowdale and the Back o' Skiddaw – is buried in the churchyard: follow the sign to where the "Man of Letters, Lover of Cumberland, Friend of his fellowmen" lies beneath a Celtic cross, looking towards the west side of Derwent Water, where his house still stands.

Keswick Museum and Art Gallery

Station Rd ☎017687/73263. Open Easter–Oct daily 10am–4pm. Admission £1.

Some of Walpole's original manuscripts are on display in Keswick's terrific **Museum and Art Gallery**, on the edge of the riverside **Fitz Park**. Founded in 1780, the museum is a classic of its kind, its elderly glass cases preserving singular archeological, mineral and butterfly collections, as well as stuffed birds, a set of lions' teeth, antique climbing equipment, cock-fighting spurs, packhorse bells and a mas-

Walks from Keswick

Keswick walks fall into two categories: strolls down by the lake or up to scenic viewpoints, and the considerably more energetic peak-bagging of Skiddaw and Blencathra. If you've got time to make only one local hike, there's a case for making it up Cat Bells (see Derwent Water, p.111), which forms the distinctive backdrop to many a Keswick view.

Latrigg

Latrigg (1203ft) gets the vote for a quick climb (45min) to a fine viewpoint – up Bassenthwaite Lake and across Derwent Water to Borrowdale and the high fells. Driving first to the Underscar car park gets you even closer, within twenty minutes of the summit. For a circular walk (4–6 miles; 2–3hr), follow the eastern ridge to Brundholme, returning through Brundholme wood or along the railway line path.

Skiddaw

Easiest of the true mountain walks is the hike up the smooth mound of splintery slate that is **Skiddaw** (3053ft). From the Underscar car park it's a steady (and, it has to be said, boring) walk up a wide eroded track, with a possible diversion up Skiddaw **Little Man** (2837ft), before reaching the High Man summit. Straight up and down is around five miles and takes about five hours, but there's a much better route back, descending to the southwest, along the ridge above Bassenthwaite formed by Longside Edge, **Ullock Pike** (2230ft) and The Edge, before dropping down through Dodd Wood to the A591 (8 miles; 7hr); to avoid walking along the busy road you'll have to catch a bus back to town.

Blencathra

Blencathra (2847ft) – also known as Saddleback – could keep hikers occupied for a fortnight. Wainwright details twelve possible ascents of its summit and though made of the same slate as Skiddaw, it's a far more aggressive proposition. Many use Threlkeld as the starting-point: easiest route is via Blease Fell and Knowe Crags (an ascent that Wainwright pooh-poohs as too dull); the path starts from the car park by the Blencathra Centre. The more adventurous steer a course up any of the narrow ridges, whose names (Sharp Edge, Foule Crag) don't pull any punches – for most of these, the best starting-point is the White Horse pub at Scales, another mile-and-a-half up the A66 (towards Penrith) from Threlkeld.

See Basics, p.19, for general walking advice in the Lakes; recommended maps are detailed on p.9.

sive set of Victorian "musical stones"– cordierite-impregnated slate – which bong in tune when you hit them. Under protective covers in the literary room sit a huge array of letters, manuscripts and poems of Southey, Wordsworth, De Quincey, Hartley Coleridge, Walpole and Ruskin. There's interesting memorabilia too: a cheque for thirty pounds drawn on Ruskin's account, Southey's gloves and leather chair, and a desk filched from Greta Hall (see below).

The Cumberland Pencil Museum

Cumberland Pencil Museum, Southey Works, Greta Bridge ☎017687/73626.
Open daily 9.30am–4pm. Admission £2.50.

For the town's industrial history, you need to pop along to the
Cumberland Pencil Museum, west along Main Street by Greta
Bridge. For centuries Borrowdale shepherds marked their sheep
with a locally occurring substance they knew as wadd and, later, as
plumbago or black-lead. It was, of course, graphite (a pure carbon)
from the Borrowdale fells and after about 1500, when it was discovered that it could also be carved and cut to shape, graphite-
mining became commercially viable. In the early days, graphite
was used in several ways – rubbed on firearms to prevent rusting,
to make cannon-ball moulds and as a medicinal cure for stomach
disorders. With the idea of putting graphite into wooden holders
(prototype pencils were used by Florentine artists), Keswick
became an important pencil-making town – the mines and ship-
ments were so valuable that they were put under armed guard to
thwart smugglers. The town prospered until the late eighteenth
century, when the French discovered how to make pencil graphite
cheaply by binding the common amorphous graphite with clay.
Keswick's monopoly was quickly broken, though its major pencil
mills by the River Greta – first established in 1832 – continued to
thrive. Today, only the factory which owns the museum still survives and even that is under persistent financial pressure. Its future
is far from certain and although pencils are still made here, the
graphite is now imported from the Far East and the wood used is
American cedar. All this, and more than you'll ever need to know
about the pencil-producing business, is explained inside, where a
mock-up of the long-defunct Borrowdale mine heralds multifarious
examples of the finished product, including the world's largest
(six-foot-high) pencil, duly acknowledged as such by the *Guinness
Book of Records*.

Crosthwaite

Over Greta Bridge, it's a fifteen-minute walk down High Hill and
Church Lane to the edge of town and **Crosthwaite Church**, dedicated to St Kentigern (or Mungo), the Celtic missionary who founded
several churches in Cumbria. Evidence suggests that Kentigern
passed through in 553 AD and planted his cross in the clearing
("thwaite") here, though it's unlikely a permanent church was built
on this site until the twelfth century, while the present structure
dates from 1523. The poet **Robert Southey** is buried in the churchyard, alongside his wife and children; his quasi-imperial marble effi-
gy (inscribed by Wordsworth, who attended the funeral) stands
inside the church, as does a plaque honouring Canon Hardwicke
Drummond Rawnsley, one of the co-founders of the National Trust
(see p.110). Both men had strong links with Keswick. Rawnsley was

Coleridge in the Lakes

Samuel Taylor Coleridge (1772–1834) already knew both Robert Southey and William Wordsworth by the time he moved to the Lake District. With Southey, he shared an enthusiasm for the French Revolution and an unfulfilled plan to found a utopian community in America; and in 1795 he'd married Sara Fricker, the sister of Southey's fiancée Edith. Later, while living in Somerset, Coleridge and Wordsworth wrote *Lyrical Ballads* together, which contained Coleridge's *The Rime of the Ancient Mariner*. Coleridge sang Wordsworth's praises at every opportunity; a favour returned by the enamoured Dorothy, who thought Coleridge a "wonderful man . . . [whose] . . . conversation teems with soul, mind and spirit".

Thus, when Wordsworth moved to Grasmere in 1799, Coleridge needed little prompting to follow. Having toured the Lakes, he settled on the newly built Greta Hall in Keswick, leasing it for 25 guineas a year. The Coleridges – Samuel Taylor, his wife Sara, and four-year-old son Hartley – were installed by July 1800; a third son, Derwent, was born in the house that September (the Coleridges' second son, Berkeley, had died in 1798); and daughter Sara followed in 1802.

Coleridge spent much of his first two years at Keswick helping Wordsworth prepare a new edition of the *Lyrical Ballads*, but found plenty of time to explore. His notebooks detail the walks he took, and in the summer of 1802 he embarked on a nine-day walking tour of the Lakes; see Contexts, p.183, for more.

But despite his first flush of excitement at lakeland living, Coleridge wasn't happy. He'd been taking opium for years – if *Kubla Khan* didn't spring from an opium-induced dream no poem ever did – and was in poor health, suffering from rheumatism. What's more, his relationship with his wife was deteriorating – spurred by the fact that Coleridge had fallen hopelessly in love with Wordsworth's sister-in-law, Sara Hutchinson (his "Asra"), by now living at Grasmere. Indeed, his last great poem, *Dejection: an Ode*, was originally sent to Sara as a letter in April 1802.

In September 1803, Southey and his wife arrived to share Greta Hall. As the Southeys had just lost a child Coleridge hoped that the two sisters might comfort each other, but he was also looking for a way to escape so that he might regain his health and inspiration. He left for Malta in June 1804 (where for two years he was secretary to the Governor) and never lived with his family again. Southey assumed full responsibility for Coleridge's wife and children who remained at Greta Hall.

When Coleridge returned to the Lakes it was to live with the Wordsworths at Allan Bank where he produced a short-lived political and literary periodical, *The Friend*, helped by Sara Hutchinson. When she left, and eventually married someone else, a depressed Coleridge – once more dependent on drugs – departed for London. Wordsworth, sick of having him moping around the house, had described Coleridge to someone else as an "absolute nuisance", which Coleridge came to hear about: after this breach in 1810, Coleridge only ever made perfunctory visits to the Lakes, avoiding Wordsworth (though the two were later reconciled). He died in London and is buried in Highgate cemetery.

the vicar at Crosthwaite between 1883 and 1917, while Southey moved into his brother-in-law Samuel Taylor Coleridge's house in the town in 1803 and, after Coleridge moved out, continued to live there for the next forty years. Southey was Poet Laureate from 1813 until his death in 1843 and his house, a Georgian pile known as **Greta Hall**, played its part in the Lakes' literary scene: it had a library stuffed with 14,000 books, which Southey delighted in showing to his visitors – Wordsworth (who tended not to hold with libraries) laments in his memorial inscription, "Loved books, no more shall Southey feed upon your precious lore." Greta Hall is now part of Keswick School (closed to the public) whose playing fields lie across from the church.

Castlerigg Stone Circle

Castlerigg Stone Circle is signposted off both the A66 and A591 on the way into Keswick. The Caldbeck Rambler bus #73/73a runs here twice a day in summer.

Keswick's most mysterious landmark, **Castlerigg Stone Circle**, can be reached by path along the disused railway line to Threlkeld (signposted by the Keswick Country House Hotel, at the end of Station Road) – after half a mile, look for the signposted turning to the right. The site is a mile further on atop a sweeping plateau, dwarfed by the encroaching fells. Thirty-eight hunks of Borrowdale volcanic stone, the largest almost eight feet tall, form a circle a hundred feet in diameter; another ten blocks delineating a rectangular enclosure within. The array probably had an astronomical or timekeeping function when it was erected four or five thousand years ago, but no one really knows. Whatever its origins, it's a magical spot, licked by a summer breeze but particularly stunning in winter when frost and snow blanket the surrounding fells.

Eating, drinking and entertainment

Keswick is a real metropolis compared to anywhere else in the National Park, which means for once that there's no shortage of places to eat and drink. Daytime **cafés** are firmly aimed at the walking and shopping crowd – you won't want for a big bowl of soup or a cream tea – and there are some decent **restaurants** and **pubs** too. If you're planning to be around for any length of time, it's worth a call to see what's on at the local **theatre**, which makes Keswick something of a cultural centre for the Lakes.

Cafés

Abraham's Tea Rooms, in George Fisher's, 2 Borrowdale Rd (☎017687/72178). The top-floor tearoom comes to your aid with warming mugs of *glühwein*, home-made soups, big breakfasts with free-range eggs, and daily specials. Daytime only. No credit cards. Inexpensive.

Brysons, 42 Main St (☎017687/72257). Top-notch bakery and tearooms with breakfasts, traditional main dishes and cream teas. Daytime only. No credit cards. Inexpensive to moderate.

Lakeland Pedlar, Henderson's Yard, Bell Close Car Park (☎017687/74492). Keswick's best caff – a (licensed) wholefoood veggie experience – has fell views from its outdoor tables, great coffee, inspired breakfasts (*burritos*, *huevos rancheros*) and a Mediterranean/Tex-Mex menu featuring *nachos*, pizzas and sandwiches. Daytime only, though open until 8pm in July & Aug; closed Wed. No credit cards. Inexpensive to moderate.

Mayson's, 33 Lake Rd (☎017687/74104). Under the tumbling houseplants is a licensed, self-service café serving bakes, pies and stir-fries (until 8.45pm in summer). No credit cards. Inexpensive.

Theatre by the Lake, Lake Rd (☎017687/74411). Gourmet snacks – rustic breads, smoked salmon, Cumbrian air-dried ham – served between 11am and 5pm in the smart Stalls Bar. No credit cards. Inexpensive.

Wild Strawberry, 54 Main St (☎017687/74399). Known for its teas in their various guises, but also the place for home-made scones, sticky-toffee pudding and meringues. Daytime only; closed Fri afternoon. No credit cards. Inexpensive.

Restaurants

Fredericks, 1 New St (☎017687/75222). The stylish choice for good-value cooking: the three-course *table d'hote* menu changes regularly but uses local ingredients – from black pudding to lamb, and salmon to wild mushrooms – enhanced by Mediterranean flourishes. Booking recommended. Dinner only; closed Tues (& closed Mon too in winter). Moderate.

The George Hotel, St John's St (☎017687/72076). Popular blackboard bistro-style specials in the bar and restaurant, which might be anything from chicken chasseur to mussels with lime and saffron. Plus twenty wines by the glass. Moderate.

Loose Box Pizzeria, King's Arms Courtyard, Main St (☎017687/72083). Popular pizza-and-pasta joint – the house special is *spaghetti rustica* (tomato, garlic, chilli and prawns). Moderate.

La Primavera, Greta Bridge (☎017687/74621). Classic pastas (try the spicy *linguine con peperoncino*), meats and fish in a riverside Italian bistro. Closed Mon. Moderate to expensive.

Pubs, entertainment and festivals

Keswick has lots of **pubs** and weekend nights in summer can be a bit boisterous, to say the least, when Market Place turns into the Wild Wild West. Nicest place for a drink is *The George*, on St John's Street, Keswick's oldest inn which certainly looks the part, its snug bars lined with historic portraits, pictures and curios, and featuring wooden settles in front of the fire. The *Keswick Lodge Hotel*, on Main Street near Market Place, is also good for meals and a beer, and as it's a free house you can escape the grasp of Jennings' brewery for a while. Most of the other pubs pack in the summer crowds for meals, though popular doesn't always mean good: best general choices are the *Dog and Gun*, 2 Lake Rd, which retains its slate floor and oak beams and shows off a series of classic climbing pictures; and the *Four in Hand*, an old coaching inn further down Lake Road, opposite George Fisher's, whose race-horse-owning landlord has festooned the interior with racing pictures. It's always nice to stroll across the fields to Portinscale (20min) for a drink in the conservatory-bar and lakeside gardens of the *Derwentwater Hotel* (see "B&Bs, guest houses and hotels" p.100).

The **Theatre by the Lake** on Lake Road (☎017687/74411) hosts a full programme of drama, concerts, exhibitions, readings and talks. This replaced the Blue Box theatre, a temporary mobile affair which lasted more than twenty years on its lakeside site. The Alhambra **cinema** on St John's Street (often closed Dec–Feb; programme information on ☎017687/72195) shows mainstream releases, but hosts an annual **Film Festival** (February), featuring the best of world cinema.

Otherwise, the biggest events in town are the annual **jazz festival** each May (information on ☎01900/602122), the June **beer festival**, and the traditional **Keswick Agricultural Show** (August bank holiday), which is the place to learn more about sheep-shearing and other rural pursuits.

Derwent Water

Derwent Water may not be that big – three miles long and, at most, a mile wide – but it's among the most attractive of the lakes. What's more, it's only five minutes' walk south of the centre of Keswick, down Lake Road and through the pedestrian underpass. Standing on the northern shore, headed by the grassy banks of **Crow Park** and ringed by glowering crags, you look down the lake to its islets. One of these, **Derwent Island**, was settled by sixteenth-century German miners brought to Keswick to mine its ores. Another, **St Herbert's Island**, in the middle of the lake, is thought to be the site of the seventh-century hermitage's cell of St Herbert, disciple and friend of St Cuthbert of Lindisfarne. Derwent Water is also a relatively shallow lake, eighty feet at its deepest point but averaging more like twenty feet deep; so shallow in fact that roe deer from the surrounding woods sometimes swim across to **Lord's Island**. There's a mysterious floating island, too, which appears only after sustained periods of dry weather.

Derwent Water marks a geological divide, where the slate of Skiddaw gives way to the volcanic rock of Borrowdale, something you'll notice at jutting Falcon Crag, halfway down the east side. Falcons still nest and breed here; indeed, Derwent Water supports several **wildlife** habitats, including those of the sandpiper and yellow wagtail, as well as Britain's rarest fish, the plankton-eating vendace (like the char, an Ice Age survivor). But the otters and wild cats remembered in place names around the lake are long gone.

Human interaction has shaped the lakeside: you can still see the scars from the old mines on the west side, though further damage has been prevented by the intervention of the National Trust, whose first purchased parcel of land in the Lake District was that of **Brandlehow woods** and **park** in 1902. During the eighteenth and early nineteenth centuries, the lake saw regular **regattas**, orchestrated initially by Joseph Pocklington, a wealthy banker, for whom the word eccentric seems woefully inadequate. He built himself a house, church and fortress on Derwent Island (the house is still there, owned and rented out by the National Trust) and appointed himself "Governor and Commander-in-Chief", blasting off brass cannons at the boats. The house that's now Derwentwater Youth Hostel was also his; he had the rocks behind it dynamited to fashion an artificial waterfall.

Cruising and walking around the lake

The **Keswick Launch** (daily: Easter–May & mid-Sept to Oct 10am–6pm; June to mid-Sept 10am–7.30pm; Nov–Easter 2–3 departures only; 75p per stage; £4.95 round-trip; ☎017687/72263) runs right around the lake calling at six points en route. There's also a one-hour **evening cruise** (£5.70) from May Day bank holiday until mid-September; pop down earlier in the day to buy a ticket and ensure a place. You can rent **rowboats** and self-drive motorboats at the piers.

For details of boat rental and water sports on Derwent Water, see p.21.

The hourly departures during the day are frequent enough to combine a cruise with a walk and picnic – the main attractions around the lake are detailed below, in clockwise order (ie, the way the launch goes). You can also make the entire lake loop on foot from Keswick (9–10 miles; 3–4hr); the path around the western side forms part of the Cumbria Way and Allerdale Ramble long-distance routes.

Friar's Crag

The most popular short walk on the lake – no more than ten minutes from the launch piers – is to **Friars' Crag**, a wooded peninsula from where medieval pilgrims left for St Herbert's Island to seek the hermit's blessing. The Friar's Crag land was acquired by the National Trust in 1922, and is held in memory of its founder Canon Rawnsley (see box on p.110), though it's long been a beauty spot. Ruskin's childhood visit to Friars' Crag famously inspired "intense joy, mingled with awe", which is a bit over the top, but the grass banks and little rocky coves nearby are very attractive. For a longer walk, return to Keswick via the **Castlehead** (530ft) viewpoint, from where you can look straight down Derwent Water to Castle Crag, with Scafell Pike rising in the distance. Castlehead is reached from the lake by cutting up to and crossing the B5289 – a round-trip of three miles or one and a half hours from town.

Canon Rawnsley and the National Trust

Hardwicke Drummond Rawnsley (1851–1920) was ordained in 1875, gained his first living in the Lakes (at Wray, near Ambleside) two years later, and was appointed vicar at Crosthwaite, Keswick, in 1883. It was a period of rapid industrial development and the conservation-minded Canon Rawnsley found himself opposing the proposed Braithewaite and Buttermere Railway, fighting footpath disputes and lining up with Ruskin (an old Oxford college friend) against the creation of Thirlmere reservoir – though Rawnsley later accepted the needs of the northern cities for water and even attended Thirlmere's official opening. His time served on the County Council and the newly formed Lake District Defence Society convinced him of the need for a preservation society with money and teeth. In 1893, together with Octavia Hill and Sir Robert Hunter, and the backing of the Duke of Westminster, he established the **National Trust**. This received its first piece of donated land (in Wales) the following year and encouraged subscriptions to buy endangered property elsewhere: between 1902 and 1908 the Trust acquired much of Derwent Water and Borrowdale and is now easily the largest landowner in the Lake District.

Rawnsley remained an active part of the Trust while continuing to preach and write – he produced many collections of lakeland sonnets, poems, histories and guides, including an entertaining book of "reminiscences" of Wordsworth by the local peasantry (none of whom thought the Poet Laureate's poetry was any good). After Rawnsley's wife died in 1916 he retired to Wordsworth's old house at Allan Bank in Grasmere. He married again (1918) but died only two years later on May 28, 1920.

Ashness Bridge to Watendlath

The pier at Ashness Gate provides access to a narrow road branching south off the B5289 which climbs a steep half-mile to the photogenic **Ashness Bridge**, an old dry-stone packhorse bridge providing marvellous Derwent Water views. *Ashness Farm* (☎017687/77361; no credit cards; ②) has a field for **camping**, as well as **B&B**, and there's more rural B&B at nearby *Ashness Cottage* (☎017687/77244; no credit cards; ①).

The road (and a well-used footpath) ends two miles further south at **WATENDLATH**, an isolated farmstead, tearoom and tarn which can be hopelessly overrun at times in summer. In an attempt to combat the ever-increasing road traffic, the National Trust runs a free "Watendlath Wanderer" bus here every couple of hours from Keswick on summer Sundays, via Ashness. Watendlath provided the setting for Hugh Walpole's most famous episode of his Herries Chronicles, *Judith Paris* (1931); you can buy a copy in the tearooms.

From Watendlath tarn, walkers have a few options, all pleasant, all easy: south via smaller Dock Tarn to Stonethwaite in Borrowdale; southwest over the tops to Rosthwaite; or east, up and over High Tove, to the western shore of Thirlmere.

Lodore Falls

At Lodore landing stage there are rowboats for rent. A path at the agreeable *Stakis Lodore Hotel* (☎017687/77285; ⑨, includes dinner) heads to the nearby **Lodore Falls**, though these are only really worth the diversion after sustained wet weather. Then, you'll be able to appreciate Robert Southey's magnificent, alliterative evocation of the falls in *The Cataract of Lodore*: "Collecting, projecting, receding and speeding, and shocking and rocking, and darting and parting", and so on, for line after memorable line. Even in dry weather, there's some lovely woodland clambering to be done around here and with a keen sense of direction (or a map) you'll be able to find the Watendlath path, east of the falls.

Cat Bells

Asked to pick a favourite Lake District walk and climb, many would plump for **Cat Bells** (1481ft), a renowned vantage-point above the lake's western shore. It's not difficult (possible for all the family), the views from the top are stupendous, and it's easy to combine with the launch to or from Keswick. The name derives from the age-old belief that the fell once harboured a wild cat's den (*bield*, the Norse word for den, was later corrupted to "bells"). Most people climb up and down the badly eroded path from Hawes End (launch pier), where there's also a car park, though the longer haul up from Manesty to the south (High Brandlehow launch) has its merits. Return to either launch pier along the lakeside path through Manesty Park and Brandlehow woods and park, allowing, say, two-and-a-half hours for the entire walk. Walpole fans should note that Sir Hugh lived and worked for many years in the lee of Cat Bells, at the house he called **Brackenburn**, by Manesty Park.

Borrowdale

Beautiful **Borrowdale** stretches beyond the foot of Derwent Water, south of Keswick, and it's difficult to overstate the attraction of its river flats, forested crags, oak woods and yew trees. Early visiting writers and poets, including Thomas Gray who marvelled at the prospect in 1769, saw it as an embodiment of their Romantic fancy; Turner and Constable came to paint it; and Wordsworth praised its yews, "those fraternal Four of Borrowdale, joined in one solemn and capacious grove." But the dale's sonorous place names suggest a more prosaic heritage. The numerous "thwaites" were the site of Norse clearings, while by the thirteenth century the monks of Furness Abbey were farming the valley from their "grange" (an outlying farmhouse), grazing sheep and smelting iron-ore along the becks. The valley's higher reaches were later extensively mined and quarried, activities which

Derwent Water

Bus #79 from Keswick runs daily (every 30min–1hr) to Lodore.

impinged upon the indigenous wood cover. Borrowdale's oak woods once, effectively, formed part of a temperate rainforest – the surviving fragments are still known for their mosses, ferns, liverworts and lichens, and provide cover for a wide range of berries and birds, including warblers and flycatchers.

In summer there's a pretty steady stream of traffic taking hikers to the head of the valley, overshadowed by the peaks of Scafell and Scafell Pike (the two highest in the Lakes) and Great Gable, the latter one of the finest-looking mountains in England. Public transport access is by **buses #77a** (along the minor road on the west side of Derwent Water) and **#79** (along the B5289), which both run south to Grange and Seatoller.

Grange and around

The riverside hamlet of **GRANGE-IN-BORROWDALE**, four miles south of Keswick, sits back from an old twin-arched packhorse bridge, under which the River Derwent tumbles from the narrower confines of Borrowdale and runs across the flood plain to the lake. And flood it does on occasion, which is why the raised wooden walkways snake across the flats between here, Lodore and Manesty. *Grange Bridge Cottage* in a great spot, right by the bridge (☎017687/77201; no credit cards; ①), has just one double room available and an attached tea garden. There are a couple of other local B&Bs, as well as the superbly sited *Borrowdale Gates* (☎017687/77204, *hotel@borrowdale-gates.com*; ⑦, ⑧ with dinner; closed Jan), a country-house hotel with a deserved reputation for its food; it's 200 yards up the western shore road, past the church.

South of Grange, the valley narrows at a crag-lined gorge known as the **Jaws of Borrowdale**. Until the eighteenth century, the route beyond was considered wild and uncertain, and there was no permanent road through until the mid-nineteenth century, when travellers other than locals first began to venture into the valley. The views are famed from **Castle Crag** (985ft), one of the western "teeth" of the Jaws, which you can reach on paths from Grange or Rosthwaite. Across the valley from the crag, also around a mile from Grange, stands the 1870-ton **Bowder Stone** (there's a car park on the B5289), a house-sized lump of rock scaled by wooden ladder and worn to a shine on top by thousands of pairs of feet. Controversy surrounds the origin of this rock, pitched precariously on the edge. Some say it came from the fells above, others contend it was brought by glacier movement during the last Ice Age.

Rosthwaite and Stonethwaite

The riverside path and the B5289 lead on to the straggling hamlet of **ROSTHWAITE**, two miles south of Grange. Its whitewashed stone

Skiddaw fells

Launching boats, Portinscale, Derwent Water

St James Church, Uldale

Hawkshead church

Striding Edge, Helvellyn

Burnthwaite, Wastwater

Brougham Castle, near Penrith

Newlands pass, Buttermere

Mosedale Beck, Wasdale Head

GREG EVANS

Furness Abbey, Dalton-in-Furness

JOE CORNISH

Yewbarrow, Great Gable and Ling Mell, view from Wastwater

buildings, backed by the encroaching fells, sustain the most concentrated batch of **accommodation** in the valley. As well as two or three B&Bs – such as *Yew Tree Farm* (☎017687/77675; no credit cards; ②), which also has a tearoom – there are comfortable rooms at the hiker-friendly *Royal Oak Hotel* (☎017687/77214; ⑤, includes dinner), where a hearty lakeland dinner is served promptly at 7pm. Weather conditions are posted daily, packed lunches and filled flasks supplied, but if the rain comes down you may prefer to repair to the firelit sitting room for tea and scones, or to the stone-flagged bar. The neighbouring *Scafell Hotel* (☎017687/77208; ⑤) is a little smarter: its attached *Riverside Inn* – the only local pub – serves popular bar meals (including smoked trout and grilled salmon), while the set dinner (£20) in the hotel restaurant is a good deal. At the Rosthwaite **village shop** – the only one in the valley – you'll be able to put together a basic picnic. A purpose-built **youth hostel**, *Borrowdale Longthwaite* (☎017687/77257, *borrowdale@yha. org.uk*), lies a mile south of Rosthwaite, on the riverside footpath to Seatoller; while across the river, on the eastern side of the B5289, is the *Chapel House Farm* **campsite** (☎017687/77602), a simple site though with showers available.

   STONETHWAITE, a place of some antiquity just to the southeast of Rosthwaite and half a mile up a side road, is the trailhead for those aiming to walk into Langdale via bleak Langstrath and the watershed of Stake Pass. There's more foot-traffic than you might expect, since it's on the route of both the Cumbria Way and the Coast-to-Coast walk. Pretty whitewashed stone cottages huddle around the *Langstrath Inn* (☎017687/77239; no credit cards; ③), a fine place to hole up, with a cosy bar and popular meals. There are basic **camping** facilities (toilets and cold water), too, at *Stonethwaite Farm* (☎017687/77234). The inn features in the Lake District section of Ian McEwan's Booker prize-winning novel *Amsterdam* (1998), which is short enough to read overnight if you've come armed with a copy, before tackling the Langstrath valley – "one long frown set in stone" – as walked by McEwan's character, Clive Linley.

Seatoller and Seathwaite

Another mile or so up the valley from Rosthwaite, and eight miles from Keswick, lies the old farming and quarrying settlement of **SEATOLLER**. Most stop long enough to call in at the **National Park Information Centre** at Seatoller Barn (Easter–Nov daily 10am–5pm; ☎017687/77294) to check the programme of events, craft displays, talks and local walks; there are also drinks and snacks on sale, and a good book, map and guide selection. Outside, you can walk from the car park into **Johnny Wood** to see the moss-covered boulders and lichen-draped trees. Opposite, a few slate-roofed houses cluster around the moderately priced *Yew Tree* **restaurant** (☎017687/

Scafell, Scafell Pike and Great Gable

In good weather, the minor road to Seathwaite is lined with cars by 9am as hikers take to the paths for the rugged climbs up the three major peaks of **Scafell**, **Scafell Pike** and **Great Gable**. Technically, they're not too difficult; as always, though, you should be well-prepared and reasonably fit.

Scafell and Scafell Pike

The summit of **Scafell Pike** (3205ft), the highest point in England, is close to **Scafell** (3163 ft), the second highest point in the Lakes; an eight-mile (six-hour) loop walk taking in both leaves Seathwaite via Stockley Bridge to the south, branching up Styhead Ghyll to **Styhead Tarn**. This is as far as many get, and on those all-too-rare glorious summer days the tarn is a fine place for a picnic.

Great and Green Gable

A direct but very steep approach to **Great Gable** (2949ft) is possible from Styhead Tarn, though most people cut west at Seathwaite campsite up Sourmilk Ghyll and approach via **Green Gable** (2628ft), an eight-mile (six-hour) return walk. However, the easiest Great Gable climb is actually from Honister Pass (see p.115), following a six-mile (four-hour) route past Grey Knotts and Brandreth to Green Gable, before rounding Great Gable and returning along an almost parallel path to the west.

See Basics, p.19, for general walking advice in the Lakes; recommended maps are detailed on p.9.

77634; closed Mon in winter, & all Jan), fashioned from seventeenth-century quarrymen's cottages and serving a menu strong on Cumbrian produce. For **accommodation**, you can't beat *Seatoller House* (☎017687/77218; no credit cards; ③, ⑤ with dinner; closed Dec–Feb) next door, a well-maintained seventeenth-century farm-house with plenty of original panelling, a library, parlour and fire, an honesty bar, and very popular communal meals (not Tues) served in the former kitchen. The house is owned by the family of the historian G.M. Trevelyan, who first visited a century ago as a Cambridge undergraduate and later organized "hare and hound" hunts on the fells above – stalking people rather than animals – which are still held here each year.

A minor road south runs to **SEATHWAITE**, twenty minutes' walk away. This is a popular base for walks up the likes of **Great Gable** and **Scafell Pike** (see box above): *Seathwaite Farm* (☎017687/77394; no credit cards; ②) at the end of the road has **rooms**, a fine **café** (Easter–Sept daily 10am–6.30pm), serving fresh grilled trout, cakes and sandwiches, and a basic **campsite** used extensively by Great Gable climbers. Prospective campers might like to know that Seathwaite has a reputation for being the wettest inhabited place in England, with an average of over 120 inches of rain recorded a year.

Honister Pass

Overlooked by the steep Borrowdale Fells, the B5289 cuts west at Seatoller, up and over the dramatic **Honister Pass**, dominated by the dread thousand-foot heights of Honister Crag. From the top of the pass the road down to Buttermere is an absolute beauty, following tumbling Gatesgarthdale Beck. **Bus #77a** comes this way, making the initial, steep mile-and-a-quarter grind from Seatoller to the car park at the top of Honister Pass; nearby is the supremely isolated *Honister Hause* **youth hostel** (☎017687/77267).

Slate-quarrying on the pass was well-established by the mid-eighteenth century – the local green roofing slate was soon much sought-after – and though full commerical quarrying ceased in 1986 you can't miss the vicious scars of the old workings. Until well into the nineteenth century, the slate was either carried down the severe inclines in baskets on men's backs, or guided on heavy hand-pulled wooden sledges, since pit ponies couldn't get a foothold on the scree. Needless to say, this was ridiculously dangerous work. You can get an idea of what life was like by donning a hard hat and lamp and descending the re-opened **Honister Slate Mine** (tours: March–Oct daily at 10.30am, 12.30pm & 3.30pm; £6; ☎017687/77230) at the top of the pass, by the hostel. The mine also has a **visitor centre** (10.30am–5pm), refreshments and ornamental slate for sale.

Threlkeld to Thirlmere

The A591 between Keswick and Grasmere runs directly past **Thirlmere**, and this is the way the buses go. But if you're in no particular hurry, it's more pleasant to detour east to **Threlkeld** first and then turn south along the minor road through **St John's in the Vale**. You can come this way entirely on foot too – it's an extremely attractive route (7 miles; 4hr) – and pick up the #555/556 **bus** back up the A591 to complete the circuit back to Keswick.

Threlkeld

Keswick's disued railway path (signposted by the Keswick Country House Hotel on Station Road) runs straight to **THRELKELD**, three miles east of Keswick; or it's a quick ride on **bus #X4/X5** or the summer **#73/73a**. The riverside walk's a delight, enhanced by the promise of a drink in one of Threlkeld's old pubs at the end, either the *Horse & Farrier* or the *Salutation*, both of which serve bar meals. Across the A66 (follow the signs) you can delve further into the mechanics of the local mining industry at **Threlkeld Quarry**

On the way to Threlkeld, there's a possible detour to Castlerigg Stone Circle (see p.106).

(March–Oct daily 10am–5pm; Nov–Feb call for times; £2.50;
☎017687/79747), which produced granite for road- and railway-
making until 1982. The entrance price gets you into the museum of
mining artefacts and the locomotive shed and machine shop, while
for another £2.50 you can descend into a recreated mine for a forty-
minute hard-hat-and-torch tour.

St John's in the Vale

A bucolic walk from Threlkeld cuts south from the railway path,
across Threlkeld Bridge, and through the fields into **St John's Vale**;
the B5322 shadows the same route. The old chapel of St John's and
views of the Blencathra ridges behind are the draws, with the south-
ward path hugging the base of **High Rigg** (1163ft) and eventually following the river to *Low Bridge End Farm* (☎017687/79242),
where there's a summer tea garden (serving home-made lemonade)
and camping. From here the A591 is under a mile away – on the way,
keep an eye out for climbers scaling **Castle Rock** across the river,
Walter Scott's model for the fairy castle in his poem *Bridal of
Triermain*.

Thirlmere

Thirlmere, a five-mile-long reservoir at the southern end of St John's
in the Vale, was created from two smaller lakes at the end of the nineteenth century when Manchester's booming population and industry
required water. Over a hundred miles of gravity-drawn tunnels and
pipes still supply the city with water from here. In a campaign that
foreshadowed the founding of the National Trust, the losing fight
against the creation of Thirlmere was led by Ruskin and other proto-
environmentalists, outraged at a high-handed raising of the water
level which drowned the hamlet of Armboth and various small farms.
No one was best pleased either by the subsequent regimental
planting of thousands of conifers around the edge (to help prevent
erosion), which dramatically changed the local landscape. The century since the creation of the reservoir has softened the scene – these
are among the oldest planted trees in the park – and you'd be hard
pushed now to tell that Thirlmere was man-made.

The only side served by public transport (take any bus along the
A591 between Grasmere and Keswick) is the eastern one, from which
some choose to make the climb up Helvellyn and back – in which
case, you'll be pleased at the thought of a pint in the popular *King's
Head* at **THIRLSPOT** (☎017687/72393; ④). But to enjoy the reservoir's waterside paths, forest trails (through planted conifers and
mixed woodland) and viewpoints, you need to be on the minor road
which hugs the western shore. The #555/556 bus can drop you at
Wythburn church, at the foot of the reservoir, handy if you wanted to
walk the six miles up the western side and round to Thirlspot.

Braithewaite, Thornthwaite and Whinlatter Pass

Just under three miles west of Keswick, the cottage gardens of **BRAITHEWAITE** line the banks of Coledale Beck, with **Grisedale Pike** (2593ft) towering above. As an alternative walking base to Keswick, it provides access to the fells between Derwent and Crummock waters, notably on the heavy-going **Coledale Horseshoe** (9–11 miles; 6–8hr), which takes in up to eleven grassy tops in a long day's walking. There's B&B **accommodation** in and around the village but the best lodgings are at the fine *Coledale Inn* (☎017687/78272; ④) on the hillside above Braithewaite. Once a mill, this is now a cosy lakeland inn with fell views, sheltered garden and home-cooked food. They'll make you up a packed lunch for your day's walking.

A mile north up the minor road shadowing the A66, **THORNTH-WAITE** looks across the Derwent basin to the Skiddaw range. The **Thornthwaite Galleries** here (March–Nov Mon & Wed–Sun 10.30am–5pm; free; ☎017687/78248) exhibit a good range of lakeland arts and crafts – from paintings and sculpture to jewellery and fabrics – and some of the artists demonstrate their work during special sessions in the summer. A barn conversion under the gallery, *Gallery Mews* (☎01946/861018), provides three cottages for rent which sleep from two to six people.

The B5292 climbs west past Braithewaite to the **Whinlatter Pass** (1043ft), on the way to Buttermere or Cockermouth. A couple of miles up are the woodland plantations of **Whinlatter Forest Park**, England's only true mountain forest, whose visitor centre (daily: winter 11am–4pm; rest of year 10am–5pm; free; parking fee; ☎017687/78469) can put you on track for a day's exploration. There are walks (up to Spout Force falls, for example) and viewpoints, plus waymarked trails for hikers and cyclists (bike rental available across the main road at Revelin Moss) and a permanent orienteering course. The **café's** worth a stop in any case, with a terrace that looks over the plantations and down the valley.

Bassenthwaite Lake

Pub-quiz bores love **Bassenthwaite Lake** as it's the only lake in the Lake District (all the others are known as waters or meres). It's also the northernmost of the major patches of water, but it doesn't receive much attention otherwise, partly because of the difficulty in actually reaching its shores. Although just three miles from Keswick, and linked by the River Derwent which flows across the broad agricultural plain between the two, most of the shoreline is privately owned. Power boats are banned and there are no-boating zones, restrictions which are intended to preserve the lake's rich variety of plants and animals. The shoreline habitat is the best-preserved example in the National Park, where over seventy species of birds and wildfowl winter and breed, while Bassenthwaite (with Derwent Water) is the only place in Britain where the vendace, a nine-inch fish related to other arctic species, is found.

There's a permitted three-mile path up the **west shore** as far as Dubwath, but as this is paralleled by the busy A66 the noise of traffic is ever present. The best thing to do on this side is to park at the Swan Hotel (two miles up the minor road from Braithewaite) for the climb up (yes, really) **Barf** (1536ft), whose distinctive craggy protuberance – usually painted white – is known as "The Bishop". Back in your car, it's worth knowing about the *Pheasant* (☎017687/76234; ⑥), just before Dubwath, signposted up a left-turn off the A66 – a classic old **coaching inn** with a terrific period bar.

The main interest is really on the **east shore** of the lake, though again access is restricted to certain sections, all clearly marked on maps; bus #X4/X5 runs this way from Keswick. The only place to park is at **Dodd Wood**, heavily planted Forestry Commission land, through which there are four marked trails of varying length. Keep an eye out: roe deer and some of the Lakes' few surviving red squirrels are occasionally seen around here. Some of the crowded pines, planted in the 1920s, are now 120ft high, which makes the climb (3 miles; 3hr return) to the heights of **Dodd** (1612ft) itself a rather disorientating experience.

Parking at the *Old Sawmill Tea Rooms* (mid-March to Oct daily 10am–5pm) – one of the Dodd Wood access points – also provides access to the **Mirehouse** across the road (April–July, Sept & Oct Sun & Wed 2–4.30pm; Aug Wed, Fri & Sun 2–4.30pm; gardens same days 10am–5.30pm; house & gardens £3.75; gardens only £1.50; ☎017687/72287). This lakeland home of the Spedding family has been passed down the generations for three hundred years (Sir James was a friend of Tennyson, who is supposed to have sought inspiration for his *Morte d'Arthur* here) and the current members open up the interior a couple of days a week for a view of the contents and portraits. The gardens and lakeside walk are more worthwhile – there are adventure playgrounds for the kids – while you don't need to pay for the best sight of all, the glorious chapel on the shores of Bassenthwaite. Look for the footpath to the side of the entrance, which runs down through the fields in twenty minutes to the **church of St Bega**, originally Norman, heavily restored and completely serene, protected by the flanks of Skiddaw.

Other than the *Old Sawmill Tea Rooms* and the café at Mirehouse, the only sustenance is in the small village of **BASSEN-THWAITE**, a couple of miles east of the top end of the lake. It's easily missed (coming off the A66, follow the signs for Castle Inn), but if you track it down, you'll find that the *Sun* retains its seventeenth-century air and serves good food, including a mean lasagne.

Back o' Skiddaw

People often complain that the Lake District is too crowded, that tourists (including themselves) have overwhelmed the infrastructure and transformed the villages – none of which, happily, is true of the **Back o' Skiddaw**, the local name for the arc of fells and valleys which stretches around the back of Skiddaw mountain, tucked into the northernmost section of the National Park. For the most part it's countryside that really does deserve the epithet "rolling", with farmland tumbling down from Skiddaw's gentle humps to encircle small hamlets and villages that see little tourist traffic. The only **public transport** is the #73/73a Caldbeck Rambler bus, which runs daily in the school summer holidays, on weekends from June to September and on Saturdays throughout the year.

Uldale and Ireby

From the Castle Inn junction, half a mile from the northern edge of Bassenthwaite Lake, the sweeping road into Uldale ends three miles further on at **ULDALE** village where the cow dung on the road announces its farming credentials. Farming in the Lakes is a precarious business at the best of times: what it must have been like in the past in "wolf's dale" doesn't bear thinking about. Walpole used the quiet village and moorland surroundings as the backdrop in the middle two Herries novels, *Judith Paris* and *The Fortress*, with the fictional Fell House as the Herries family lair. There's a pub – the *Snooty Fox* – and a tearoom in the old Victorian school, now the **Northern Fells Gallery** (March–Oct daily 10.30am–5pm; Nov & Dec Fri–Sun 10.30am–5pm; free), which displays a collection of north Cumbrian work: photography, watercolours, ceramics, stained glass, knitwear and jewellery. A mile and a half south of the village lies tiny **Over Water**, the northernmost splash of water in the Lake District, with the farms of Orthwaite beyond. Only bad things await, surely, on the heights of **Great Cockup** (1720ft), an easy two-mile walk east from Orthwaite.

In the other direction, Uldale's **St James church** lies a full mile from the village on the Ireby road, a pretty building with some interesting old gravestones and uninterrupted fell views. Another mile beyond is sleepy **IREBY**, with its lion's head drinking trough. You can eat well in the venerable beamed-and-nooked *Sun*, whose small beer garden is a restful spot on a sunny day.

Caldbeck and Hesket Newmarket

Prosperity came easily to **CALDBECK**, six miles east of Ireby and just twelve from Carlisle, and it remains one of lakeland's most appealing villages. The fast-flowing "cold stream" from which it takes its name provided the power for the rapid expansion in the number of mills here in the seventeenth and eighteenth centuries. Corn, wool and wooden bobbins flowed out, lead and copper from the fells was carted in; and the many surviving contemporary buildings (look for the dates carved on the lintels above the doors) attest to its wealth. A signposted quarter-mile walk from the car park up to the limestone gorge known as **The Howk** shows you the river in all its rushing glory, as well as the restored ruins of one of the old bobbin mills.

The village is anchored by its **church of St Kentigern**, dedicated to the sixth-century saint better known as Mungo, who journeyed from Scotland through Cumberland to Wales to preach the gospel to the heathen Saxons and Celts. The well he is supposed to have used for baptism lies by the packhorse bridge, next to the churchyard.

Caldbeck's most famous resident these days is mountaineer and writer Chris Bonington.

The first stone church here was built in the twelfth century but though a medieval tombstone survives in the chancel today's church bears the brunt of heavy nineteenth-century restoration. No matter, since all the interest is outside in the churchyard, where you'll easily find the ornate tombstone of **John Peel** of Ruthwaite (died 1854), emblazoned with reliefs of hunting horns and his faithful hound. Peel's is a name synonymous with fox-hunting, yet he was just one of several hardened and hard-drinking nineteenth-century hunting men of local repute; his fame today derives squarely from the song ("D'ye ken John Peel…") written about him by one of his friends. Eighteen paces from his grave, walking away from the church, is the tombstone of the Harrisons of Todcrofts: Richard was a simple farmer; it's his wife Mary (died 1837) who is better known – as Mary, the Maid of Buttermere, the most celebrated beauty of her day (see p.139).

Caldbeck makes a peaceful night's stop and there's plenty of local **accommodation** to choose from. B&B at *Todcrofts Farm* (☎016974/78485; no credit cards; ②), on the Uldale road, 250 yards from the village, lets you sleep in Mary of Buttermere's old house; while *Parkend* (☎016974/78494; ③), another mile beyond, is a well thought of farmhouse-hotel which serves dinner. The village **pub**, the *Oddfellows Arms* (☎016974/78227; ②), has rooms in a converted mill at the back and many of Caldbeck's other old mills and buildings are also in use. **Priest's Mill**, near the church, has been turned into a little arts centre (mid-March to Oct Tues–Sun 11am–5pm), with a jeweller and a secondhand bookshop among the outlets; the riverside *Watermill* **restaurant** here (☎016974/78267; closed Jan to mid-Feb) specializes in vegetarian cuisine, open throughout the day for snacks, organic hot chocolate and herbal teas, and serving dinner by arrangement.

There's a path from Caldbeck a mile-and-a-half southeast through the fields to the small eighteenth-century village of **HESKET NEW-MARKET**, which straddles a long village green overlooked by the *Old Crown* pub. The beer in here is great, a variety of ales brewed by the local Hesket Newmarket Brewery.

Carrock Fell, Mosedale and around

The road south from Caldbeck and Hesket Newmarket winds the eight miles back to the A66, effectively down the eastern boundary of the Lake District. Away to the east lie fields not fells, and beyond is the Eden Valley and Yorkshire. The bulk looming to the west, behind Blencathra and Bannerdale, is **Carrock Fell** (2174ft), best climbed from Stone Ends Farm – you can park by the road – three miles from Hesket Newmarket. The fell is riddled with abandoned mines (keep back – exploration is dangerous), while a huge tangle of fallen rocks litters the hillside: Charles Dickens and Wilkie Collins had a particularly disastrous time climbing Carrock Fell, described in *The Lazy Tours of Two Idle Apprentices* (1857).

Two **youth hostels** provide good bases for any lengthy walking tours of the area. *Carrock Fell* (☎016974/78325), at High Row, Haltcfliff, provides simple farmhouse accommodation just a mile north of Stone Ends. This is isolated enough, but eight miles to the southwest – and only reachable on foot, up **Mosedale** – is *Skiddaw House* (postal bookings only, or phone *Carrock Fell*), a former shooting lodge and one of the most remote buildings in England. It's on the Cumbria Way (six miles from Keswick by path) so it sees a fair amount of traffic, but be warned that the bedrooms are unheated (though there's a log fire in the lounge) and there are limited food supplies; bring your own (and a torch).

Day-walkers in Mosedale will probably go no further than **Bowscale Tarn**, scooped dramatically out of Bowscale Fell and ringed by crags. It's 1600ft up, and the summit of **Bowscale Fell** is another 700ft on top of that, a hefty five-mile (four-hour) return climb from the road, after which you'll be ready for a drink in the *Mill Inn* at **MUNGRISDALE**, just a mile down the road from the foot of Mosedale.

Travel details

From Keswick

Bus #73/73a (2–3 daily) circular route to: Castlerigg Stone Circle (7min), Threlkeld (15min), Mungrisdale (25min), Mosedale (30min), Hesket Newmarket (45min), Caldbeck (50min), and on to Mirehouse (1hr 20min); or to Mirehouse (10min), Uldale (25min), Ireby (35min), Caldbeck (40min), and on to Mungrisdale (1hr 10min). Service operates mid-July to Aug daily; June & Sept Sat & Sun; rest of year Sat only.

Bus #77/7a (2 daily) circular route to: Grange (20min), Seatoller (30min), Honister Pass (40min), Buttermere (50min), Whinlatter Pass (1hr 20min); or to Whinlatter Pass (15min), Buttermere (45min), Honister Pass (1hr), Seatoller (1hr 5min), Grange (1hr 15min). Service operates May–Oct only.

Bus #79 (every 30min–1hr) to: Lodore (15min), Grange (20min), Rosthwaite (25min), Seatoller (30min).

Bus #555/556 (hourly service) to: Thirlspot (10min), Grasmere (25min), Ambleside (45min), Windermere (1hr), Kendal (1hr 30min); and also (3 daily) to Carlisle (1hr 10min).

Bus #X4/X5 (Mon–Sat hourly; Sun 3–4 daily) to: Threlkeld (15min) and Penrith (35min); and also to Bassenthwaite (15min) and Cockermouth (30min).

Chapter 5

The western fells and valleys

G reat Gable and the Scafells stand as a formidable last-gasp boundary between the mountains of the central lakes and the mostly gentler land to the west, which smooths out its wrinkles as its descends to the Cumbrian coast. Here, in the **western fells and valleys**, lies some of the National Park's most diverse scenery – the stunning lakeland vistas you'd expect around Wast Water and Buttermere, tempered by the forested swathes of Ennerdale, the deeply rural hamlets of Wasdale and Eskdale, and a little-known coastline. Indeed, it's the west Cumbrian **coast** that impinges most upon this part of the region. The old industrial ports of Whitehaven, Workington and Maryport all lie outside the National Park but their

---

ACCOMMODATION PRICE CODES

Hotel and **B&B** accommodation is priced on a scale of ① to ⑨ (see below), indicating the **average price** you could expect to pay per night for a **double or twin room** in high season. **Youth hostels** are not given a price code since they fall within a fairly narrow price band. For more accommodation details, see Basics, p.12.

① under £40	④ £60–70	⑦ £110–150
② £40–50	⑤ £70–90	⑧ £150–200
③ £50–60	⑥ £90–110	⑨ over £200

CAFÉ AND RESTAURANT PRICE CODES

Cafés and restaurants listed in this guide have been assigned one of four price categories:

Inexpensive under £10
Moderate £10–20
Expensive £20–30
Very expensive over £30

This is the price you can expect to pay per person for a three-course meal or equivalent, excluding drinks and service.

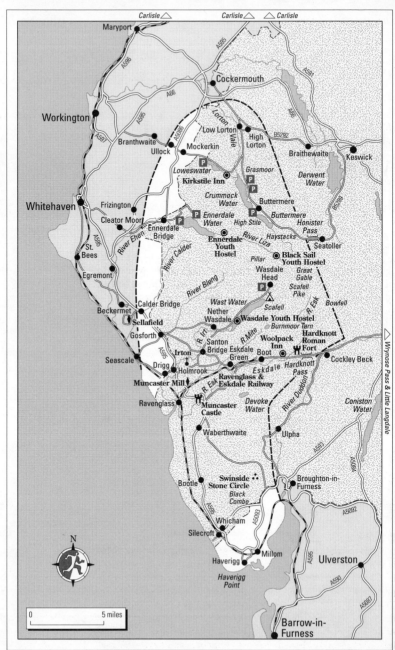

© Crown copyright

influence is felt in subtle ways: for one hundred and fifty years water has been drained from Ennerdale to supply the towns and only a spirited defence in the late 1970s by environmental protesters prevented a scheme to build a higher weir at Ennerdale Water and raise the water level. The driving force behind the proposed increase in water extraction was the other engine of change in the region, the Sellafield nuclear reprocessing plant, a major local employer which lurks on the coast just north of Ravenglass. It's changed its name twice, from Calder Hall to Windscale and then to Sellafield, in what might seem, to a cynic, an attempt to hide its manifest dangers.

The main road, the **A595** between Broughton-in-Furness and Workington, is the principal means of approach for the western fells and valleys. It runs along the coastal plain, with minor roads striking off north and east into the valleys, and it's this limited access which preserves the region's relative isolation – only Eskdale and Buttermere can be reached by road from the central fells. **Eskdale**, for that reason, is among the most popular targets, though the narrow-gauge **Ravenglass & Eskdale Railway** has as much to do with it. **Wast Water**, which points its slender finger towards Great Gable, remains one of the most isolated of the lakes and a night at the inn (or campsite) at **Wasdale Head** is unlikely to be forgotten. It's a toss-up whether Wast Water or **Ennerdale Water** is the better-looking lake, though Ennerdale is, if anything, even more remote. En route north to Cockermouth, a few interested visitors are drawn to tiny **Loweswater**, though the biggest attractions are the twin lakes of **Crummock Water** and **Buttermere**. These are situated on a well-defined circuit from Keswick but there's enough grandeur in their surrounding fells to make the summer crowds bearable.

Public transport is limited. You can reach Wast Water, Ennerdale Water and Loweswater by bus but only on summer weekends and public holidays, and the daily Buttermere service from Keswick is summer-season only too. At all other times, you're going to find yourself walking between the lakes and villages, over mountain passes and across fells whose names (Pillar, Great Gable, the Scafells) are among the most resonant in the region.

The coast and Black Combe

The short section of the **west Cumbrian coast** that falls within the National Park – the twenty miles between Silecroft and Ravenglass – is neither particularly dramatic nor appealing. Its one unique feature is the bulky **Black Combe** (1857ft) which dominates the southern part of the coast, the only Lake District fell to fall straight to the sea. This gives climbing it a certain appeal, since the views are tremendous and, unusually for the Lakes, only run out with the horizon. The A595 makes a V-shape around the massif, with the angle at the hamlet of **WHICHAM**, where there's a pub (on the main road) and a path up to the summit which starts from the minor Kirkbank road, behind the church. The fell's northeastern side shelters the **Swinside stone circle**, though this is best reached from back up the A595 towards Broughton-in-Furness: look for the minor Broadgate turn-off, park by the farm buildings and walk the mile up the rough fell track to the ancient standing stones.

Road and rail shadow the coast from **MILLOM** (just outside the National Park), a former iron-ore mining town at the mouth of the River Duddon whose claim to fame is that the poet Norman Nicholson spent his life here. The local beach at **HAVERIGG**, a mile to the south, is typical of what's to come – a lengthy, duned stretch that leads a quiet existence, even in summer.

Next decent sweep of beach is at **SILECROFT**, four miles northwest of Millom. The coastal scrub here is a habitat for the natterjack toad; and, as elsewhere along the Cumbrian coast, terns, oyster-catchers and ringed plovers nest and breed, scraping the shingle over their camouflaged eggs. At **BOOTLE**, five miles further on, the sandstone-faced church is split from its cemetery by the road; the *King's Head* is a venerable eighteenth-century local. Bootle's nearest beach is three miles to the northwest, at **ESKMEALS**, which has a stony foreshore, though when the tide is out a large expanse of sand is exposed, from which you can admire the views as far north as St Bees Head. North of here, as far as Ravenglass, the coastline itself is off-limits – red flags fly over an experimental firing range – while beyond lie the hard-to-miss towers and buildings of Sellafield. Whether you'd choose to swim anywhere in the vicinity of a nuclear-reprocessing plant is, of course, entirely a matter for you.

Ravenglass and around

The principal coastal stop before the headland of St Bees is **RAVEN-GLASS**, a sleepy village at the estuary of three syllabically challenged rivers, the Esk, Mite and Irt. The village is the starting point for the narrow-gauge Ravenglass & Eskdale Railway (see below), which is why most people pass through, but it merits a closer look before you take the train. Its single main street preserves a row of plain nineteenth-century cottages. These back on to estuarine mud flats and dunes, which are accessible when the tide's out – the northern section, across the Esk, is a nature reserve where black-headed gulls and terns are often seen. The Romans, who used the estuary as a harbour, established a supply post at Ravenglass in the first century AD for the northern legions manning Hadrian's Wall. Nothing remains of what the Romans knew as Glannaventa save the remarkably complete buildings of their **bathhouse**, part of a fort which survived in Ravenglass until the fourth century. It's on the road out of the village, just past the station, 500 yards up a (signposted) single-track lane.

The Ravenglass & Eskdale Railway

Ravenglass & Eskdale station, adjacent to the Furness coastal line station. Information on ☎01229/717171, *www.ravenglass-railway.co.uk*. Departures: June–Sept daily 9am–5pm, every 30min–1hr; April, May & Oct 10.30am–4.30pm, hourly; Nov–March 1–2 daily. Fares: one-way £3.70, return £6.50.

The **Ravenglass & Eskdale Railway** (known affectionately as La'al Ratty) opened in 1875 to carry iron-ore from the Eskdale mines to the coastal railway. Long converted to tourist use and running on a 15-inch gauge track, the tiny train takes forty minutes to wind its way through seven miles of forests and fields, first along Miterdale under Muncaster Fell and then into the valley of the River Esk, where it terminates at Dalegarth station, near Boot. You can break your journey with a return ticket, allowing you to get off and walk from one of the five stations en route; the full return journey, without a break, takes an hour and forty minutes. There's parking at Ravenglass station, a small **railway museum** (same days and times as rail service; 50p), a short video showing you the route, a café on the platform and a shop, where budding engine drivers can buy an all-important driver's cap. Over by the main station, the *Ratty Arms* has good beer and sandwiches.

Muncaster Mill and Castle

Muncaster Mill (Easter–Oct daily 10am–5pm; Nov–March Sat & Sun 11am–4pm; £1.60; ☎01229/717232) stands where the A595 crosses the railway line, a mile from Ravenglass; it's first stop on the Ravenglass & Eskdale Railway. The machinery in this restored eighteenth-century water-mill turns every day, milling organic flour which then ends up in bread, scones and cakes in the teashop or for takeaway sales. Special weekend breaks at the mill provide tuition for wannabe Windy Millers, who get to take home their own milled flour.

From the mill there's a path south through the pine woods (where you might see red squirrels) which meets the A595 a mile east of Ravenglass, just before the entrance to **Muncaster Castle** (Easter–Oct Mon–Fri & Sun 12.30–4pm; gardens & owl centre year round daily 11am–6pm. Castle, gardens & owl centre £5.50; gardens & owl centre £3.80; ☎01229/717614). Built around a medieval pele tower, the castle has been home to the Pennington family since the thirteenth century and very agreeable it is too, worth the entry fee if you make a day of it. An audio-tour points out the family treasures (a Gainsborough here, a Reynolds there) and the oft-renovated interior, though it's the terrific gardens that win plaudits (best in spring and autumn), boasting a stupendous view from the terrace. The owl centre, meanwhile, hosts a daily lecture and display, showing off some of the two hundred birds from fifty different species in the collection. A two-mile **circular walk** links the castle with the Roman bathhouse at Ravenglass, either returning through the fields to the main road near the castle, or extending the walk to include the mill.

Eskdale

Eskdale, accessed most easily from the Cumbrian coast, is just twelve miles long from start to finish, but what a finish it provides – in the dramatic high-fell surroundings of Hardknott Pass. It's a fairly gentle valley in its early stages, with various approach roads (from Ulpha in the Duddon Valley, from Wasdale or along the River Esk itself) meeting at the elongated hamlet of **Eskdale Green** (a stop on

---

Walks from Eskdale

Eskdale is a great choice for a walk at any time of year: you'll rarely come across many other people on the walks outlined below, even on the shorter strolls. There's parking at Dalegarth station and in Boot, and as the train runs year-round the valley makes a fine off-season day out.

Dalegarth Force and the River Esk

Footpaths along both sides of the **River Esk** between Eskdale's St Catherine's church and Doctor Bridge (near the Woolpack Inn) allow an easy two-mile (1hr) riverside walk – in low water you can cross the river below the church by stepping stones, or there's a bridge further up. You can combine this with the steep climb up the wooded ravine which holds the impressive sixty-foot falls of **Dalegarth Force** (also known as Stanley Ghyll Force), in full spate for much of the year.

Hardknott and the Esk Falls

It's harder going east of Doctor Bridge, where a path to the foot of the **Hardknott Pass** keeps to the south side of the River Esk beneath Birker Fell, before cutting up, via the farm at Brotherikeld, to the Roman fort. Keeping to the Esk, you can hike on up the narrow valley between overhanging crags to **Lingcove Bridge**, beyond which tumble the **Esk Falls** – an eight-mile (5hr) round-trip that requires fine weather and good visibility, otherwise you risk getting bogged down and lost.

The Woolpack Round

The most strenuous hike from Eskdale is the sixteen-mile (8–10hr) **Woolpack Round**, a tough circuit topping the two highest mountains in England (the Scafells) and several others which aren't much lower. It is not easy going and a certain amount of scrambling is required, but the views and the varied terrain make this one of the finest lakeland walks. Traditional start- and finishing-point is the Woolpack Inn.

See Basics, p.19, for general walking advice in the Lakes; recommended maps are detailed on p.9.

---

the Ravenglass & Eskdale Railway), on a rise above the valley. From Eskdale Green, the valley road continues east, passing **Dalegarth station** (terminus of the Ravenglass & Eskdale Railway), which lies just a short walk from the valley's isolated church and from Eskdale's other hamlet, **Boot**. Here there's an old mill to explore, an excellent inn and several more local hikes, not to mention the drive up and out of the valley to the superbly sited **Hardknott Roman Fort**.

Eskdale Green

First village stop on the Ravenglass & Eskdale Railway is **ESKDALE GREEN**, where you can access short walks into nearby Miterdale Forest or even plan on hiking back along the spine of Muncaster Fell to Ravenglass. This is around four miles and shouldn't take more than a couple of hours. For drinks before you go, the *Bower House Inn*, at the western end of the hamlet by the Santon Bridge turn-off (☎019467/23308, *info@bowerhouseinn.freeserve.co.uk*; ⑤), is a cut above the usual rural inn. Heading the other way, the *King George IV*, at the eastern end, by the turn-off to Boot (☎019467/23262; ②), is more of a traditional pub. In between the two is *Forest How Guest House* (☎019467/23201; ②), with a couple of en-suite rooms, and a small post office-general store.

Dalegarth station and Boot

By the time the valley road and train line reach **Dalegarth station**, two miles east of Eskdale Green, the fells beyond can be seen more clearly and eyes are drawn ever upwards to the singular skyline. Passengers pile off the train for the walk to Dalegarth Force (see box on p.128), heading down a track opposite the station which leads in a couple of hundred yards to Eskdale's **St Catherine's church**. Its riverside location is handsome in the extreme and in the small cemetery you can't miss the distinctive gravestone of Thomas Dobson (died 1910), former hunt Master of the Eskdale and Ennerdale Hounds whose likeness grins from the top of the stone, above a carved fox and hound. Dobson actually died in the *Three Shires Inn* in Little Langdale, which involved his coffin being carted to Eskdale over the gruelling Wrynose and Hardknott passes. If he hadn't already been dead the bearers would probably have killed him for his thoughtlessness.

It's another 350 yards up the valley road from Dalegarth station to the turning for the dead-end hamlet of **BOOT**. The few stone cottages here, cowering beneath the fells, mark the last remnant of civilization before the road turns serious. The mines near Boot that supplied ore for the railway to Ravenglass never really paid their way, and closed in 1913. But there's been industry of sorts here for centuries, since the Furness Abbey monks first introduced a corn mill into Eskdale. Over the packhorse bridge at the back of the ham-

Dry-stone walls

"A dry-stone wall
Is a wall and a wall,
Leaning together
(Cumberland and Westmorland
champion wrestlers),
Greening and weathering,
Flank by flank,
With filling of rubble
Between the two ..."

from *Wall*, by Norman Nicholson

The hundreds of miles of **dry-stone walls** which criss-cross the Lake District are one of the region's most characteristic sights. Although the earliest farmers had identified boundaries and enclosed fields, these tasks assumed greater significance with the medieval expansion of sheep farming. As early as the thirteenth century the monks of Furness Abbey were enclosing extensive tracts of moorland within stone-built walls, traces of which can still be seen in upper Eskdale. Walls provided the means of converting unproductive high land into enclosed sheep farms: separating grazing areas, providing flocks with shelter (and preventing them straying), and facilitating sheep-driving and collection (by means of stone-built "pounds"). At first built on an ad hoc basis, walls tended to follow irregular patterns to suit local needs – often they were no more than dumping grounds for stones cleared from new pastures.

Irregularly walled enclosures gave way to systematic patterns during the eighteenth and nineteenth centuries as the Enclosure Acts (1801) prevailed – basically, statutes sanctioning the grabbing of once common or wild land by the bigger, richer landowners. Not only was common land seized, but small farmers were deprived of traditional grazing, cropping and wood-gathering rights, forcing them either to become tenants or to move. Behind this larceny was a rapidly increasing demand for food and wool, driven by the mushrooming population of the newly industrialized cities and the effect of the blockades during the Napoleonic War which kept food prices high. For many, the resulting walls – now an integral part

let, the sixteenth-century **Eskdale Mill** (April–Sept Tues–Sun 11am–5pm; £1.25; ☎019467/23335) preserves its wooden machinery and you can picnic near the waterfalls which power the wheels.

Boot has a fair smattering of **accommodation** and services, which makes it the obvious base for extended walks in the valley. By the junction with the valley road, *Brook House Inn* (☎019467/23288, *brookinn@aol.com*; ④) serves meals in its *Poachers Bar* and also has a separate, moderately priced restaurant. A couple of hundred yards away, in Boot itself, the *Burnmoor Inn* (☎019467/23224, *enquiries@burnmoor.co.uk*; ③) is the traditional hikers' choice, a very comfortable place whose rooms (half with baths, not showers) have lashings of hot water. The food's great and not particularly of the landscape, but then a novelty – symbolized the growing hardship of the small farmer. Nineteenth-century English "peasant poet" John Clare wrote bitterly that: "Enclosure came, and trampled on the grave of labour's rights, and left the poor a slave."

The increased demand for walls outstripped the capabilities of most farmers and inspired a new trade, undertaken by bands of itinerant craftsmen (not strictly masons, but skilled nonetheless). Sleeping on the fells and using the stone they found *in situ* – which explains the homogeneous, almost organic quality of lakeland walls – these "wallers" would set about erecting what are known locally as "dykes". A good waller could build seven yards of wall a day, though often less as many walls in the Lakes are unnecessarily thick – surplus stone had to be used up to maximize the grazing land. Tools and methods varied: shovel or spade, pick and stone hammer were common utensils; many wallers preferred to rely on sight rather than use builder's "lines"; others used a "walling frame" (two boards fastened with cross-pieces) to establish the height of the wall and the slope of its sides.

As its name makes clear, a dry-stone wall has no mortar to hold it together. Instead, it's built on the cavity-wall principle, ie, as a double wall with the space between packed with small stones (guts). Ideally a two-person job (someone working alone has to keep changing sides), the wall starts off at anything up to 3ft wide, narrowing to around a foot wide at the top. Long stones (throughs) are placed at intervals through the width for stability; while the walls are topped by slanted stones (cams) so that the rain drains off. To allow sheep access from one pasture to another, a space (hogg hole) might be left in the base of a wall. A waller requires a good eye, both for the line of the wall and the selection of stones, which must either have a smooth side or be suitable for corners. The finished product is remarkably hardy: dry-stone walls might last fifty or one hundred years without shifting or collapsing, often longer.

While not exactly a growth industry these days, new dry-stone walls are still needed on modern sheep farms, and existing walls require maintenance. The old skills have been kept alive by a dedicated band of wallers: you'll see them in action at annual agricultural shows (see p.16), while there are also dry-stone wall-building demonstrations every summer, co-ordinated by the National Park Centre at Brockhole.

expensive, there's a peaceful beer garden, and a holiday cottage for rent over the road which sleeps four. A small general store in Boot sells lakeland ice cream.

Further up the valley road, past the Boot turn-off, it's 200 yards to *Hollins Farm* **campsite** (☎019467/23253) and then another three-quarters of a mile to the popular *Woolpack Inn* (☎019467/23230, *woolpack@eskdale.dial.lakesnet.co.uk*; ③), with a well-kept selection of real ales, a garden and mountainous portions of inexpensive home-cooked food. Aside from the rooms (a category cheaper without en-suite facilities), there's also a purpose-built, centrally heated **bunkhouse** (bring your own sleeping bag) where the price includes breakfast. Finally, another 400 yards beyond the pub you'll find

Eskdale youth hostel (☎019467/23219), in a comfortable detached house nestling under Eskdale Fell.

Hardknott Fort and Pass

The Lake District's other major Roman fort – nothing like as dramatic as Hardknott – is at Ambleside, see p.48.

Three miles beyond Boot, and 800ft up the twisting road, the remains of **Hardknott Roman Fort** (free access) – known as Mediobocdum to the Romans – command a strategic and panoramic position just below Hardknott Pass. If ever proof were needed of how serious the Romans were about keeping what they had conquered, then Hardknott proves the point. This full-scale fortification was built during the reign of Hadrian by a cohort of Dalmatian (Croatian) troops, who gave it walls twelve feet thick and a double-towered gateway, and endowed it with granaries, bathhouses and a plush, stone-built *praetorium* or commandant's quarters. The troops had to endure the discomforts of timber barracks, though since the *praetorium* was built along Roman lines – rooms ranged around an open courtyard – the commandant probably cursed his luck at his assignment every time the wind blew (about every ten seconds up here). Much of the lower part of the defensive wall is original Roman work; elsewhere, the foundations of the granaries and various other buildings have been re-erected to indicate their scale. Needless to say, the views back down into Eskdale and up to the Scafells are stunning.

Past the fort, after negotiating the appalling, narrow switchbacks of **Hardknott Pass**, the road drops to Cockley Beck (for the Duddon Valley; see p.93), before making the equally alarming ascent of Wrynose Pass, gateway to Little Langdale (p.69).

Wast Water and around

Nothing prepares you for the first sight of **Wast Water**, England's deepest lake, and certainly not the gentle approach from the south-west through the forestry plantations and farmland between the Wasdale hamlets of **Santon Bridge** and **Nether Wasdale**. Bracken-covered walls hide the fields from view, while the roads cross little stone bridges and pass farm shops selling jars of bramble jelly or bags of new potatoes. A mile and a half east of Nether Wasdale the lake comes into view, and the initial glimpse of the water brings gasps – not for the lake itself (just three miles long and less than three hundred feet deep) but for the crowding fells which surround it and the awesome **screes** which plunge to its eastern shore. These tumble 1700ft from Ulgill Head, separating Wast Water from Eskdale to the south, while the highest peaks in England – Great Gable and the Scafells – frame **Wasdale Head**, the tiny settlement at the head of the lake. You'll have seen the view up the lake to Great Gable, unwittingly, countless times already since the National Park Authority uses the outline as its logo on every publication, signpost and notice board. For a true measure of your own insignificance, take a walk along the eastern lakeshore path, beneath the impassable, implacable screes, and look up. Thomas Wilkinson, an over-awed eighteenth-century Quaker, fancied that he was gazing upon "the Pyramids of the world, built by the Architect of the Universe".

Wast Water and around

Isolated Wasdale Head and its famous *Wasdale Head Inn* are very much the main events in Wasdale, though you should also make time to see the ancient cross in **Gosforth**, a village just off the **A595** – west of the lake – which provides an alternative approach to Wast Water. Whichever way you approach, the road beyond Nether Wasdale is single-track for the most part and hugs Wast Water's western shore, with occasional parking spots by bosky groves, stony coves and little promontories. There's no **public transport** to Wasdale Head, though a summer-only bus (#13) runs on Saturdays from Seatoller in Borrowdale, via Keswick, as far as Wasdale Hall youth hostel (see Nether Wasdale below), at the foot of the lake.

Wasdale Head

The road ends a mile beyond the lake at **WASDALE HEAD**, a Shangri-La-like clearing between the mountain ranges, where you'll find the **Wasdale Head Inn** (☎019467/26229, *wasdaleheadinn@ msn.com*; ⑤), one of the most celebrated of all lakeland inns. British mountain-climbing was born here in the days when the inn's landlord – and champion liar (see below) – was the famous Will Ritson (1808–1890): black-and-white photographs pinned to the panelled rooms inside show Victorian gents in hobnailed boots and flat caps scaling dreadful precipices with nonchalant ease. The inn's gone a bit upmarket since those days, but still attracts a genuine walking crowd: the compact rooms (no TV reception) all have supremely comfortable beds, the breakfasts are legendary, and though there are reasonable meals in *Ritson's Bar*, the imaginative four-course dinner in the restaurant (£18) is one of the Lake District's best buys. For more space, ask for one of the "superior rooms" in the adjacent cottage conversion, which have a kitchenette and full baths; there are also six self-catering apartments in a converted barn (sleeps two to four). The Barn Door Shop (☎019467/26384) next to the inn has basic foodstuffs, Kendal mint cake, and outdoor clothes and equipment; check in here before pitching a tent at the adjacent field **campsite** (no reservations; open all year). The only other local accommodation is at the **National Trust campsite** (☎019467/ 26220), a mile to the south at the head of the lake, which provides tent space, showers and a laundry room beneath the trees.

For more on the birthplace of British mountain-climbing, see p.183.

What's reputed to be England's smallest church, **St Olaf's**, lies a couple of hundred yards from the inn, encircled by evergreens and dwarfed by the surrounding fells. The small cemetery contains graves and memorials to several of those killed while climbing them. There's been a church at Wasdale since medieval times and though no one knows quite how old this plain chapel is, its current appearance – moss-grown slate roof and all – dates from a complete overhaul in 1892.

The Scafells and Great Gable are popular **hiking** targets from Wasdale Head, as are the routes over the various passes, into Borrowdale, Ennerdale or Eskdale. That over Eskdale Moor, via **Burnmoor Tarn**, was the former "corpse road" along which the dead were carried for burying in Eskdale church, since St Olaf's had no consecrated churchyard until 1901.

Nether Wasdale and Santon Bridge

There's a decent hotel in **NETHER WASDALE**, a mile and a half from the lake: *Low Wood Hall* (☎019467/26100, *lowwoodhallhotel@ btinternet.com*; ⑥), a restored Victorian country house whose gardens look toward the fells; weekend "walkers' specials", when available, provide a room in the associated lodge, plus dinner, for the same price. Meanwhile, Wast Water's **youth hostel**, *Wasdale Hall* (☎019467/26222), a country house in a wooded hollow, set in its own lakeside grounds, lies a mile and a half east of Nether Wasdale. From here, it's just under three miles to the head of the lake.

SANTON BRIDGE, two miles to the southwest of Nether Wasdale, has *The Bridge Inn* (☎019467/26221; ③), a more modest country pub by the River Irt, with Italian bistro meals and weekend walkers' breakfasts. It also hosts the annual "Biggest Liar in the World" competition every November, a tradition started by Will Ritson of Wasdale Head who told famously tall tales of country life to his guests and neighbours.

Gosforth and around

At the Wasdale turn-off from the A595, **GOSFORTH** – a large if unremarkable village, with a couple of pubs, a bank and petrol station – has one extraordinary attraction: the tall, carved **stone cross** in the churchyard of **St Mary's** on the eastern edge of town. Signposted as the "Viking" cross, it's a rare example in Cumbria of the clash between pagan and Christian cultures, with the four faces of the slender shaft carved with Norse figures from the Sagas, which are surmounted by a Christian cross. A scale model inside the church picks out the detail more clearly. There's been a church on this site since at least the tenth century, though it's been rebuilt many times since: nineteenth-century restoration revealed the church's other treasures, the two Viking "hogback" **tombstones**, found buried in the foundations. If your imagination is captured by the Gosforth cross, you should really drive the three miles south back down the A595, through Holmrook, and take the left turn signposted to Santon Bridge. A mile up the ruler-straight road, a signposted track – accessible with care for cars – leads to isolated **St**

Paul's, Irton, which has a worn tenth-century stone cross in its churchyard.

More on the crosses and tombs can be found if you delve through the secondhand and antiquarian books in Archie Miles's **bookshop**, on Gosforth's main street on the way to the church; it's also good for first editions and rare copies of old lakeland guides. For somewhere **to stay** *Gosforth Hall* (☎019467/25322; ⑤), behind the church, has a well-preserved Jacobean mansion at its core; its moderately priced restaurant is a popular night out, with a menu that tours the world. The two old **pubs** in the centre, *Ye Olde Lion & Lamb* and the *Wheatsheaf*, can also provide a bite to eat, as can the *Lakeland Habit Café*, above the village shop.

Ennerdale

Ennerdale, the next major valley north of Wasdale, is about as far off the beaten track as you can get in the western fells and valleys. There's only one very small village, limited public transport and no road at all around nearby **Ennerdale Water**, which makes it one of the most inaccessible of the lakes – or one of the best for walkers, depending on how you look at it. Having made the effort, you'll find Ennerdale Water is among the most alluring of the lakes, its quiet two-and-a-half mile length (fiddle-shaped according to Coleridge) ringed by crags and dominated at the head by the dramatic heights of **Pillar** (2927ft). If you haven't seen this peak before, you'll not recognize it from the name alone – the bulky fell takes its name instead from one of its northern crags, the devilish Pillar Rock, the proving-ground of British mountaineers for over a century.

The village, **ENNERDALE BRIDGE**, straddles the River Ehen, a mile or so west of the lake, encircled by a bowl of rounded fells and tucked just inside the National Park boundary. It's only ten miles from Cockermouth – from where there is a regular **bus** service (every 2hr, not Sun) – and seven from the coast, but seems much further from anywhere, especially in the peaceful shaded churchyard; still "girt round with a bare ring of mossy wall", as Wordsworth described it at the beginning of *The Brothers*. Two **pubs** do the honours: the *Fox & Hounds* and the *Shepherd's Arms*, the latter a popular overnight stop on the Coast-to-Coast walk (☎01946/861249; ③).

Up at the western end of the lake two car parks provide access for day-walkers. The eight-mile (4hr) **circuit of the lake** is an enjoyable low-level walk, with the option of a scramble up **Angler's Crag** on the southwestern promontory. Traffic is allowed as far up the lake as a third car park at **Bowness Knott**, midway along the northern shore, terminus of the summer-only "Ennerdale Rambler" bus #263 from Buttermere and Loweswater.

Afforestation

There's nothing new about conifer plantations in the Lake District. Wordsworth was already complaining about the spread of larch and fir plantations in his *Guide to the Lakes*; a "vegetable manufactory" he called it, which thrust every other tree out of the way. In the early days afforestation was carried out as much for aesthetic reasons as for profit, though once the battle for Thirlmere was lost another was joined as the water authorities planted the shores of the new reservoir with regimented conifers to prevent erosion. With the formation of the Forestry Commission in 1919, the planting of soft woods for profit picked up pace, with Ennerdale, Bassenthwaite and the Duddon Valley heavily forested by the 1930s. Only local resistance prevented Eskdale, Wast Water and Buttermere going the same way.

The problem is the very nature of the forests. In England's mild climate larch, spruce and pine plantations grow quickly, blocking out the light and carpeting the valley floors with slow-decomposing acidic needles. As a consequence, wild plants (and therefore animals) are forced out of their natural habitat. However, almost a century of commercial planting has taught the Forestry Commission several lessons and their planting policy has changed accordingly over the years. Their information centres are keen to explain matters, and to point out that plantations imposed upon previously bare fellsides help soil conservation and encourage animal and bird shelter. Managed forests, moreover, help preserve the surviving indigenous broadleaved woods, which were increasingly threatened by the local practice of wintering sheep among the trees (which then ate the seedlings). Behind the mission to explain is the undeniable economic sense of afforestation: Britain currently imports eight percent of the timber it uses and in a bid to even out the figures, over £1 billion has been invested in timber-processing since 1990.

A series of forest trails at Bowness Knott announces the start of Ennerdale's thick blanket of **Forestry Commission** land. It may now be an accepted part of the landscape but before 1930 the upper part of Ennerdale was a desolate, rocky wilderness, devoid of trees. The mass imposition of uniform conifer plantations irrevocably changed the landscape, and though time and more enlightened planting policies (mixing in broad-leaved trees and following the contours instead of straight lines) have softened the scenery, many still wish Ennerdale had been left untouched. You can decide for yourself as you make your way up the forest track, following the River Liza beyond the head of the lake, to the first of two **youth hostels**. Gas-lit *Ennerdale Gillerthwaite* (☎01946/861237), two-and-a-half miles from Bowness Knott, has been converted from two old forestry cottages. A long four miles on through the plantations, *Black Sail Hut* (☎0411/108450) is even more isolated and basic, a former shepherd's bothy with no electricity and no heating in the bedrooms. But from either hostel the walking is marvellous: classic routes can be followed up Pillar and Great Gable, or over Scarth Gap to Buttermere or Honister Pass to Borrowdale.

Lorton Vale and Loweswater

Southeast of Cockermouth the B5292 rolls into the pastoral **Lorton Vale**, turning east to tackle the Whinlatter Pass on the way to Keswick. Keeping south on the B5289, the fells – and Buttermere – are beckoning but a diversion to **Loweswater**, six miles from Cockermouth, provides an opportunity to see one of the region's smallest, shallowest and least-known lakes. You'll never be bothered by crowds here. There's no village to speak of, rather a collection of houses and a telephone box, with a couple of signs pointing you towards the *Kirkstile Inn* (☎01900/85219; no credit cards; ③), a welcoming sixteenth-century riverside inn with decent bar meals and rooms that, while cosy enough, have seen better days. Loweswater itself is a mile beyond and really the only thing to do is to walk around it, a gentle low-level route (4 miles; 1hr 30min) which stays under a woodland canopy for much of the duration. A detour in Holme Wood up to **Holme Force** adds a bit of interest after sustained rain; while the best views of the water are from Waterend, at the northern end of the lake. The distinctive volcano-shaped peak which towers above the southern end of Loweswater is **Mellbreak** (1676ft), fairly easily climbed from the Kirkstile Inn in around an hour or so.

There are a couple of small parking places at Waterend, and a National Trust car park (unmarked on most maps) near Watergate Farm at the southern end. The Ennerdale Rambler **bus** from Buttermere also passes Loweswater, running along the northern shore road past Waterend.

Crummock Water and Buttermere

A glance at the map shows that **Crummock Water** and **Buttermere** – separated by only a half-mile of slightly elevated flood-prone land – were once joined as one lake. In the main, they're visited as one, with nearly all the day-traffic concentrated in and around **Buttermere village**, a small settlement in the middle of the two lakes with an outlying church, two inns and the rest of the local facilities.

The two lakes, however, have entirely different aspects: small Buttermere ("Boethar's lake") is ringed by crags and peaks, culminating in the desolate heights of Gatesgarthdale; more expansive Crummock Water ("crooked lake") is almost twice as long (at two and a half miles) and half as deep again, yet peters out in the gentle flat lands of Lorton Vale. It's a contrasting beauty that brought back that most obsessive of fell walkers, Alfred Wainwright, again and again. A plaque in the small parish **church of St James**, on a hillock above Buttermere village, asks you to pause and remember him and

There's more on the life of Alfred Wainwright on p.158.

then lift your eyes to Haystacks, his favourite peak (see box below), where his ashes are scattered. In *Fellwanderer*, his account of the writing of his famous *Pictorial Guides*, he's typically and playfully brusque: "If, dear reader, you should get a bit of grit in your boot as you are crossing Haystacks in the years to come, please treat it with respect. It might be me."

The grandeur of the locality was well-known even before Wainwright gave it his seal of approval. With the Lakes in vogue amongst travelling men in the late-eighteenth century, many made their way over the passes to what was then a remote hamlet with a reputation for good fishing in the twin lakes. A certain Captain

Walks from Crummock Water and Buttermere

Many hikers have their fondest memories of the fells around Buttermere and Crummock Water, and one – Haystacks – is the final resting place of the greatest walker of them all, Alfred Wainwright. It's easy to gain height quickly around here for some terrific views, though the low-level circuits of the two lakes are also very rewarding.

Crummock Water and Scale Force

Any circuit of **Crummock Water** should include the diversion to the 170ft drop of **Scale Force**, among the most spectacular of Lake District waterfalls. You can then either regain the western shore and stick close to the lake for the rest of the circuit (8 miles; 4hr), or climb past the falls and follow the Mosedale valley path to Loweswater (where there's a pub, the Kirkstile Inn) before completing the circuit (10 miles; 5–6hr).

Around Buttermere

The four-mile stroll circling **Buttermere** shouldn't take more than a couple of hours – in wet weather, the waters tumbling a thousand feet down Sour Milk Ghyll are amazing. And you can always detour up **Scarth Gap** to **Haystacks** (see below) if you want more of a climb and some views. It's worth knowing that, in summer, there's usually an ice-cream van parked by Gatesgarth Farm at the southern end of the lake.

Red Pike to Haystacks

The classic Buttermere circuit (8 miles; 6hr 30min) climbs from the village up **Red Pike** (2479ft) and then runs along the ridge, via **High Stile** (2644ft), **High Crag** (2443ft) and **Haystacks** (1900ft), before descending to the lake – either by back-tracking and heading down Scarth Gap or by picking your way down off Haystacks, rounding Inominate Tarn and decending via **Warnscale Bottom**. For a fuller experience, add another hour to the beginning of the hike by first climbing up Scale Force from Buttermere (see above) and working your way across to Red Pike from there.

See Basics, p.19, for general walking advice in the Lakes; recommended maps are detailed on p.9.

Budworth – resident at the *Fish Inn*, the only inn in those days – waxed lyrically about the beauty of the landlord's daughter in his bestseller, *A Fortnight's Ramble in the Lakes*. Within a couple of years, curious sightseers – Wordsworth and Coleridge included – were turning up to view **Mary Robinson, the Maid of Buttermere**. One such visitor was Alexander Augustus Colonel Hope, Member of Parliament and brother to an earl. Flush with money and manners, he wooed and married Mary – only to be revealed as the bigamous impostor, John Hatfield, whose whole life had been one of deception and fraud. Arrested and tried for forgery (franking letters as an MP without authority was a capital offence), Hatfield was hanged at Carlisle in 1802 – the entire scandal recorded for the *Morning Post* by Coleridge in investigative journalist mode. Mary became a cause célèbre, the subject of ballads, books and plays, before retiring from the public gaze at the *Fish* to become wife to a Caldbeck farmer. She died there, as Mary Harrison, in 1837.

Buttermere village

Provided you get there early enough in summer, **BUTTERMERE** village is the best base for walks. There's a **car park** behind the Fish Hotel and another is 300 yards up the road to Crummock Water; other parking places are signposted on the Crummock Water lakeshore road. The main **bus** service is the #77/77a, which runs between May and October (4 daily) on a circular route from Keswick via Borrowdale, Honister Pass and Whinlatter Pass (two in each direction).

The village has two **hotels** (and no TV reception in either). The *Bridge Hotel* (☎017687/70252; ⑥, ⑦ with dinner) has a selection of cheerfully decorated superior rooms (⑦) with large bathrooms, some with balconies; and there are south-facing, self-catering apartments across the beck. The smaller *Fish Hotel* (☎017687/70253; two night minimum stay; ④) has history, romance and price on its side. There's simple **camping** at *Syke Farm* (☎017687/70222) right by the lake; the farm also offers B&B (①) during the summer. The local **youth hostel** (☎017687/70245) overlooks the lake, a quarter-mile south of the village on the road to Honister Pass; there's more **camping and B&B** a mile further on at *Dalegarth* (☎017687/70233; no credit cards; ②; closed Nov–March) and, a mile beyond that, at *Gatesgarth Farm* (☎017687/70256; no credit cards; ②).

The popular **bar and beer garden** at the *Bridge* is the best place to eat, though there's a wide restaurant menu too; alternatively you could sit on the benches outside the *Croft House Café* and munch on filled rolls. *Dalegarth* also has **rowboats** for rental, and there are more available on Crummock Water, where the day rate includes a fishing permit.

Travel details

For Ravenglass & Eskdale Railway, see p.127.

From Seatoller, Borrowdale

Bus #13 (1 daily) to: Wasdale YHA (1hr 50min). Service operates July & Aug Sat only.

From Keswick

Bus #77/7a (2 daily) circular route to: Honister Pass (40min), Buttermere (50min), Whinlatter Pass (1hr 20min); or to Whinlatter Pass (15min), Buttermere (45min), Honister Pass (1hr). Service operates May–Oct only.

From Buttermere

Bus #263/Ennerdale Rambler: (3–4 daily) to: Loweswater Waterend, Ennerdale Bowness Knott (45min). Service July & Aug Sat, Sun & bank hol Mon only.

From Barrow-in-Furness

Furness coastal rail line (7 daily) to: Millom (25min), Silecroft (30min), Bootle (37min), Ravenglass (45min); and then via St Bees, Whitehaven and Workington to Carlisle. Service operates Mon–Sat only.

Chapter 6

Ullswater

Wordsworth declared **Ullswater** "the happiest combination of beauty and grandeur, which any of the Lakes affords", a judgment that still holds good. At almost eight miles long, Ullswater is the second longest lake in Cumbria and much of its appeal derives from its serpentine shape, a result of the complex geology of this area. The glacier that formed the two-hundred-foot deep trench in which the lake now lies had to cut across a couple of geological boundaries, from granite in the south, through a band of Skiddaw slate, to softer sandstone and limestone in the north. The resulting fells are a dramatic sight, while the shores are stippled with woods of native oak, birch and hazel – one of the best surviving examples of pre-plantation lakeland scenery. The surrounding grandeur is matched by the means of transport on the lake: lake

There are boat rental and water sports facilities at Glenridding and Water-millock; see p.21, for full details.

ACCOMMODATION PRICE CODES

Hotel and B&B accommodation is priced on a scale of ① to ⑨ (see below), indicating the **average price** you could expect to pay per night for a **double or twin room** in high season. **Youth hostels** are not given a price code since they fall within a fairly narrow price band. For more accommodation details, see Basics, p.12.

① under £40	④ £60–70	⑦ £110–150
② £40–50	⑤ £70–90	⑧ £150–200
③ £50–60	⑥ £90–110	⑨ over £200

CAFÉ AND RESTAURANT PRICE CODES

Cafés and restaurants listed in this guide have been assigned one of four price categories:

Inexpensive under £10
Moderate £10–20
Expensive £20–30
Very expensive over £30

This is the price you can expect to pay per person for a three-course meal or equivalent, excluding drinks and service.

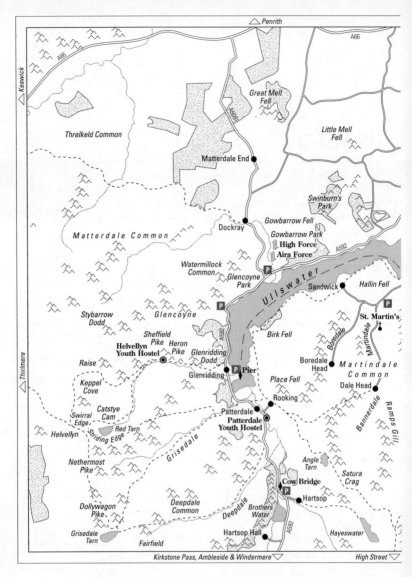

steamer services on Ullswater started in 1859 and the same two vessels, *Lady of the Lake* (1877) and *Raven* (1889), have been in operation for almost as long – though both were converted to diesel in the 1930s.

On spring and summer days the A592 up the western side of the lake is packed with traffic, everyone looking for space in one of the

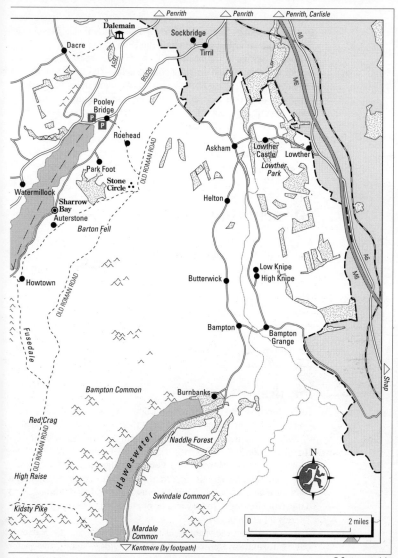

© Crown copyright

few designated car parks. Twin lakeside settlements, **Patterdale** and **Glenridding**, less than a mile apart at the southern tip of Ullswater, soak up most of the visitors intent upon the local attractions: namely **cruises** from Glenridding, the falls of **Aira Force**, the Wordsworthian daffodils of **Gowbarrow Park** and the considerable heights of **Helvellyn**, the most popular of the four tallest mountains in Cumbria. From **Howtown** on the lake's eastern side, much less-tramped walking routes run up glorious hidden valleys such as Fusedale and Martindale and along the High Street range.

Pooley Bridge at the head of Ullswater is the last lakeshore stop before Penrith, though outlying sights such as the historic house at Dalemain or the rolling Lowther parklands might delay you further. However, only real lake aficionados or keen walkers are likely to make the effort to reach **Haweswater**, easternmost and very possibly the least-visited of all the lakes.

Aside from the lake services, **public transport** to Ullswater is limited to the summer-only (May–Oct) buses linking Penrith with Pooley Bridge, Gowbarrow, Glenridding and Patterdale; and Bowness and Windermere with Patterdale and Glenridding, via the Kirkstone Pass.

Glenridding

A fast-flowing beck, flanked by stone buildings and cottages, tumbles through the centre of **GLENRIDDING**, the biggest and busiest of Ullswater's lakeside settlements. Set back from the lake is a huge car park, a couple of tearooms, large general store, post office, outdoors store and a fair amount of accommodation. There are rowboats to rent, and plenty of places to sit on the grass banks or wade into the water from the stony shore. If it sounds too popular for comfort it isn't particularly, since many visitors just park up for a day's walking, and by early evening the placid lakeshore regains much of its peace and quiet.

Practicalities

Lake services are all with the Ullswater Navigation & Transit Company (Glenridding ☎017684/82229; main office ☎01539/721626), which has steamers operating from Glenridding **to Howtown** (June–Sept up to 9 daily; £2.85 one-way, £3.70 return; 35min); and from Howtown **to Pooley Bridge** (June–Sept 3 daily; £2.05 one-way, £3.70 return; 20min). Combining them adds up to a round-the-lake cruise (£5.80). Services are reduced, though still daily, from mid-April to May and throughout October on all services. There's a bar on board.

Buses stop on the main road through the village. The **National Park Information Centre** (Easter–Oct daily 9am–6pm; Nov–Easter Fri–Sun 10am–4pm; ☎017684/82414) is sited on the edge of the car park, and posts a daily weather report for walkers. Two big traditional slate **hotels** dominate the lakeside: the old-fashioned, faintly neglected *Ullswater Hotel* (☎017684/82444; ⑤) – backdrop of most of the unsavoury goings-on in Jimmy McGovern's TV serial, *The Lakes* – and the classier *Glenridding Hotel* (☎017684/82228; ⑥). The *Hikers' Bar* in the *Ullswater* is the place for a beer, a read of the map and a game of pool; the *Glenridding*, though, has the pick of the facilities, with an indoor pool and sauna, a coffee shop with Internet access, good if pricey restaurant and so-so tavern, *Ratcher's*, serving moderately priced pizza, pasta and grills.

There are several cheaper **B&Bs**, the two most central being the *Fairlight Guest House* (☎017684/82397; ①), by the car park; and *Moss Crag* (☎017684/82500; ②; closed Dec), across the beck near the shops. Both have a couple of en-suite rooms available and attached tearooms. **Gillside Caravan & Camping** (☎017684/ 82346; closed Nov–Feb) lies a quarter-mile up the valley behind the tourist office.

Walkers wanting an early start on Helvellyn stay at the dramatically sited Helvellyn **youth hostel** (☎017684/82269), a mile-and-a-

---

Helvellyn walks

The climb to the summit of **Helvellyn** (3114ft) is among the region's most challenging. You are unlikely to be alone on the yard-wide approaches – on summer weekends and bank holidays the car parks below and paths above are full by 9am – but the variety of routes up and down at least offers a chance of escaping the crowds.

Striding Edge

The most frequently chosen, and most direct, route to the summit is via the infamous **Striding Edge**. Purists negotiate the undulating ridge top of Striding Edge; slightly safer, but no less precipitous tracks follow the line of the ridge, just off the crest. However you get across (and some refuse to go any further when push comes to shove) there's a final, sheer, hands-and-feet scramble to the flat **summit** (2hr 30min from Glenridding). People do get into trouble on Striding Edge: if you're at all nervous of heights you'll find it a challenge to say the least.

Swirral Edge, Red Tarn and Catstye Cam

The classic return from the summit is via the less demanding **Swirral Edge**, where a route leads down to **Red Tarn** – the highest Lake District tarn – then follows the beck down to Glenridding past the disused slate quarry workings and the **Helvellyn youth hostel**. Another route climbs back up to **Catstye Cam** and drops down the northern ridge path into Keppel Cove, where you cross the dam and continue to the hostel. Either of these approaches and descents makes a seven-mile or five- to six-hour walk.

Grisedale

South from the Helvellyn summit, you can follow the flat ridge past **Nethermost Pike** and Dollywagon Pike, after which there's a long scree scramble down to **Grisedale Tarn** and then the gentlest of descents down **Grisedale** valley, alongside the beck, emerging on the Patterdale–Glenridding road – a good six hours all told for the entire circuit.

See Basics, p.19, for general walking advice in the Lakes; recommended maps are detailed on p.9.

---

half up the valley track from Glenridding (the last half unmetalled, but suitable for vehicles if taken with care). A hundred yards beyond there's also **bunk-barn** space in the *Striding Edge Hostel & Swirral Barn* (information on: ☎017687/72645), converted from former quarry buildings.

Patterdale

PATTERDALE, less than a mile south of Glenridding down the A592 – a path avoids the road for much of the way – lies at the foot of **Grisedale**, which provides access to a stunning valley hike up to Grisedale Tarn. You're off the lake in Patterdale, but there's some nice **accommodation** strung along the road, not least the popular ski-lodge-style **youth hostel** (☎017684/82394, *patterdale@yha.org.uk*), on the banks of Goldrill Beck, a couple of hundred yards south of the hamlet – very comfortable beds, spacious public areas with open fire, Internet access and good food. It must be the only hostel in England with its own trailing vine. Just before the hostel, on the bend in the road, *Ullswater View* (☎017684/82175, *ext@btinternet.com*; closed mid-Nov to Dec; ②) is an attractive **guest house** with private gardens and parking. Patterdale's only pub, the *White Lion* (☎017684/82214; ③), also has a few rooms available; there's also a public bar at the large *Patterdale Hotel* up the road (☎017684/82231; ④; closed mid-Dec to March) – its little front garden fills up quickly on a summer's day. There's year-round **camping** at *Side Farm* (☎017684/82337), across from the church, and the only other service is a small **post office/village shop** opposite the pub.

Aira Force and Gowbarrow

To avoid the crowds trailing up the needle-carpeted woodland paths to **Aira Force**, three miles north of Glenridding (where the A5091 meets the A592), get there first thing in the morning or last thing in the evening. This is one of the prettiest, most romantic, of lakeland forces – a seventy-foot waterfall that's spectacular in spate and can be viewed from stone bridges spanning the top and bottom of the drop. It's only a thirty- to forty-minute round-trip from the car park, though you'll soon leave most of the visitors behind if you extend your walk further up the valley to High Force and on to **DOCKRAY** (where there's a pub, the *Royal*) and back – a three-mile, two-hour, circuit. Back at the Aira Force car park there's a **tearoom** (open daily Easter–Oct).

The falls flank the western side of **Gowbarrow Park**, whose hillside still blazes green and gold in spring, as it was doing when the Wordsworths visited in April 1802. Dorothy's sprightly recollections of the visit in her journal inspired William to write his "Daffodils" poem, though it was not until two years later that he first composed the famous lines (borrowing many of Dorothy's exact phrases). Despite its fame now, nothing much was thought of the poem at the time; it didn't even have a title on first publication in 1807 (in *Poems in Two Volumes*). The walking is tougher going on adjacent **Gowbarrow Fell** itself, but there's another good circuit signposted from the car park. The National Park Authority is trying to cut the number of sheep grazing the fell in an attempt to lure back some of the wildlife, while every spring there's a battle of wits with visitors intent on picking the famous daffs.

Aira Force and Gowbarrow

For more on William and Dorothy Wordsworth, see p.187.

Pooley Bridge and around

POOLEY BRIDGE, at the head of the lake, has a boulder-speckled shore with wonderful views south. It's a cute retreat, rendered less so once the car parks on either side of the bridge are full, but it's not a bad lunch or overnight stop, with a couple of tearooms and three pubs. A **post-bus** comes this way three times a day from Penrith (not Sun), with six services then making the twenty-minute onward ride to Martindale (see p.149).

Practicalities

A few local B&Bs advertise vacancies, or ask for help at the **tourist office** in The Square (Easter–Oct daily 10am–5pm; ☎017684/86530). Best of the **pubs** is the eighteenth-century *Sun Inn* (☎017684/86205; ③), whose beer garden indeed catches the sun. The alpine *Pooley Bridge Inn* over the way (☎017684/86215; two-night minimum stay on summer weekends; ④, ⑤ with balcony) seems to have been plucked out of a Heidi story, but breakfast in the wicker chairs on your own balcony is tempting.

Plenty of local **campsites** make the Pooley Bridge area popular with families. *Hill Croft* (☎017684/86363; closed mid-Nov to Feb) is the nearest, just 100 yards from the Howtown crossroads, though *Park Foot* (☎017684/86309; closed Nov–Feb), has its own lakeside access and club-house facilities (including bar). *Waterside Farm* (☎017684/86332; closed Nov–Feb), a few hundred yards further down the road is right on the water: it's a tent-only site, and has canoes and rowboats for rent.

One of England's finest country-house hotels, in business since 1948, is the **Sharrow Bay** (☎017684/86301, *enquiries@sharrow-bay.com*; ⑨, includes dinner), on the lakeshore two miles down the Howtown road from Pooley Bridge. It's impossible to fault the service or the food (the dining room is open to non-residents) and there are lovely rooms in the main Victorian house, the Edwardian gatehouse and in a converted Elizabethan farmhouse a mile away.

Dalemain

Dalemain ☎017684/86450. Open Easter–Sept Mon–Thurs & Sun 11am–4pm;
gardens & tearoom same days 10.30am–5pm. Admission: house & gardens £5;
gardens only £3.

Two miles north of Pooley Bridge, up the A592, **Dalemain** – home to
the same family since 1679 – started life in the twelfth century as a
fortified tower, but has subsequently been added to by every genera-
tion, culminating with a Georgian facade grafted on to a largely
Elizabethan house. It's set in ample grounds – terraces, roses and
Tudor gardens provide the main interest – while the estate stretches
west to encompass the fourteenth-century keep of Dacre Castle,
which you can reach on a footpath from the house. Inside Dalemain
itself there's the usual run of imposing public rooms, heavy with oak
though lightened by unusual touches such as the eighteenth-century
handpainted wallpaper in the Chinese Room. Outside, the medieval
courtyard and Elizabethan great barn doubled as the grim school-
room and dormitory of Lowood School in a TV adaptation of
Charlotte Brontë's *Jane Eyre*.

Askham and Lowther Park

Three miles east of Pooley Bridge the little village of **ASKHAM** has
two good pubs, the *Queen's Head* and the *Punch Bowl*, at either end
of a sloping village green. The village lies across the River Lowther
from the rolling lands of **Lowther Park**, seat of the eighteenth-
century coal-mining and shipping magnates, the Lowthers, creators
of the Georgian port of Whitehaven. The most notorious family member, Sir James, employed Wordsworth's father as his agent but, when
John Wordsworth died, refused to pay his back-salary to the
Wordsworth children. The Lowther castle is now partly in ruins, but
the grounds sport the **Lakeland Bird of Prey Centre** (March–Oct
daily 10.30am–5.15pm, last display at 4pm; £5; ☎01931/712746),
whose eagles, hawks, falcons and owls are put through their paces
three times a day.

Howtown and Martindale

HOWTOWN – best reached by regular steamer services in summer from Glenridding – is tucked behind a little indented harbour,
four miles south of Pooley Bridge. There are only a few houses and
the *Howtown Hotel* – a good target for lunch – but it's a popular
spot which lies at the start of several fine walks. Many people
cross to Howtown by boat and then walk back (5 miles; 3hr), following the shore of Ullswater around Hallin Fell to Sandwick and
then through the woods and on around the bottom of the lake to
Patterdale.

Walks from Howtown

For some of the nicest but least-vaunted walking in the Lake District, cross Ullswater on the steamer from Glenridding. Various routes radiate from Howtown, including the two described below.

Fusedale

A strenuous route (8 miles; 4–5hr) cuts past the Howtown Hotel and heads up lovely **Fusedale**, at the head of which there's an unrelenting climb up to the **High Street**, a broad-backed ridge that was once a Roman road. The path is clearly visible for miles, and following the ridge south you meet the highest point, **High Raise** (2632ft) – two hours from Howtown – where there's a cairn and glorious views. The route then runs south and west, via the stone outcrops of **Satura Crag**, past **Angle Tarn** and finally down to the A592, just shy of Patterdale's pub and post office.

To Pooley Bridge

Time the steamer services from Glenridding right and you can cross to Howtown, walk **to Pooley Bridge** and catch the boat back. The most direct route (5 miles; 3hr) leaves Howtown pier and runs northeast under Auterstone Crag before cutting up to the **Stone Circle** on the Roman road, south of Roehead, a couple of miles from Pooley Bridge. But for the best views and most exhilarating walk climb up to High Street from Fusedale (see above) and then charge straight along the ridge to the Stone Circle (7 miles; 3–4hr).

See Basics, p.19, for general walking advice in the Lakes; recommended maps are detailed on p.9.

The minor road from Pooley Bridge runs through Howtown and climbs up in switchbacks to a car park at the foot of **Martindale**. The road, in fact, continues another couple of miles up to Dale Head, but it's best to abandon the car and walk the ten minutes along to **St Martin's**, the most beautifully sited of all the Lake District's isolated churches. An Elizabethan stone chapel of great simplicity, all there is inside is a stone-flagged floor, a seventeenth-century altar table and lectern and rows of plain wooden benches. It's barely changed in centuries and, outside, the feeling of time immemorial is emphasized by the vast spreading yew tree, thought to be a thousand years old, whose gnarled branches shroud the tomb of Martindale's nineteenth-century curate George Woodley.

Brothers Water to Haweswater

The northeastern lakes finish with a flourish in the crinkled valleys between the southern foot of Ullswater and the desolate Shap Fells at the eastern edge of the National Park. The A592, heading for the

Brothers Water to Haweswater

Kirkstone Pass and Ambleside, passes **Brothers Water**; otherwise the only roads are the minor lanes south from Askham and west of Shap which meet at **Haweswater**, the Lake District's other main reservoir.

Brothers Water and Hayeswater

The car park at Cow Bridge, two miles south of Patterdale, is the jumping-off point for the short stroll along a quiet stretch of Goldrill Beck to **Brothers Water**. The Water itself (possibly taking its name from a corruption of the Norse name Brothir) is a mere liquid scoop, but the path along the western shore takes you under the canopy of some of the Lakes' oldest oak woodlands. This was the way Dorothy Wordsworth came on Good Friday in April 1802, after her daffodil-spotting excursion of the previous day, and it's easy to trace her exact route from her journal: "I left William sitting on the bridge, and went along the path on the right side of the lake through the wood. I was delighted with what I saw. The water under the boughs of the bare old trees, the simplicity of the mountains, and the exquisite beauty of the path." When she got back to Cow Bridge, William was busy writing a poem, which he later entitled (mistakenly) "Written in March".

The path alongside Brothers Water runs a mile or so up to the 500-year-old Hartsop Hall Farm – standing on land which experts reckon has been farmed since the Bronze Age. You can press further on if you're in the mood for a hike, or return to the car park and cross the main road for the tiny hamlet of Hartsop itself, from where it's a mile-and-a-bit walk east up the valley to **Hayeswater**, a limpid little lake sitting under the High Street range.

Haweswater

With the example of Thirlmere already set, there was less opposition when **Haweswater** was dammed in the 1940s to provide more water for the industrial northwest. The Lake District's easternmost lake became almost twice as long as a result (now four miles in length), while the village of Mardale was completely drowned. Such brutal dealings seem a long way off nowadays: the water company manages the valley and lake as a nature reserve, where woodpeckers and sparrowhawks inhabit Naddle Forest and golden eagles, buzzards and peregrine falcons swoop to the fells. There's a car park at the foot of the lake, where the road ends: from here, walkers climb south over the Nan Bield Pass to Kentmere or west from the pass to High Street for Troutbeck, Patterdale or Howtown. There are no other facilities, save a pub in the small village of **BAMPTON**, which is a couple of miles beyond the head of the lake (and four miles south of Askham). Between May and September, a weekend (and public holiday) **bus service** runs from Penrith to Askham and Bampton and on to the foot-of-the-lake car park.

Travel details

From Penrith

Bus #108 (Mon–Sat up to 2 hourly, Sun 3 daily) to: Pooley Bridge (23min), Gowbarrow Park (35min), Glenridding (45min), Patterdale (50min). Service operates May–Oct only.

From Bowness

Bus #517 (3 daily) to: Windermere (20min), Kirkstone Pass (30min), Brothers Water (45min), Patterdale (50min), Glenridding (55min). Service operates May to mid-July Sat & Sun; mid-July to Aug daily.

Chapter 7

Out of the National Park

When the Lake District National Park boundary was drawn around the lakes and fells, it excluded several peripheral Cumbrian towns, nearly all of the west Cumbrian coast and the southern Furness peninsulas. Most visitors to the Lakes will pass through at least one of these areas – indeed, the usual approaches to the Lake District make it hard to avoid Kendal or Penrith. And there's a case for aiming to see several other destinations not strictly within the National Park on any trip to the region. The distances help: it's not much more than thirty miles between Penrith and Cockermouth, and about the same around the west coast, making it easy to nip from lakeland valley to outlying town if needs must. This chapter highlights half a dozen of the most interesting destinations on the fringes of the National Park, all close enough to be considered part of the Lake

---

ACCOMMODATION PRICE CODES

Hotel and B&B accommodation is priced on a scale of ① to ⑨ (see below), indicating the **average price** you could expect to pay per night for a **double or twin room** in high season. **Youth hostels** are not given a price code since they fall within a fairly narrow price band. For more accommodation details, see Basics, p.12.

① under £40	④ £60–70	⑦ £110–150
② £40–50	⑤ £70–90	⑧ £150–200
③ £50–60	⑥ £90–110	⑨ over £200

CAFÉ AND RESTAURANT PRICE CODES

Cafés and restaurants listed in this guide have been assigned one of four price categories:

Inexpensive under £10
Moderate £10–20
Expensive £20–30
Very expensive over £30

This is the price you can expect to pay per person for a three-course meal or equivalent, excluding drinks and service.

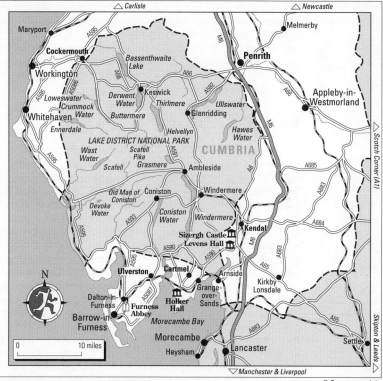

© Crown copyright

District. You may well also pass through the largely industrial towns of the west coast – between Barrow-in-Furness and Maryport – and visit the county capital of Carlisle or the Morecambe Bay resort of Grange-over-Sands; but you won't find those places covered in this guide. For these, you'll need to get hold of a copy of the *Rough Guide to England*.

The towns outside the National Park are all larger than those within, not least **Kendal**, in the southeast, once the county town of Westmorland and still an enjoyable market town with a pair of fine museums. **Penrith**, to the north, is also an ancient commercial centre and, like Kendal, retains the ruins of the castle which defended it during the turbulent medieval border-wars. Religious foundations established in the south at **Cartmel** and **Furness Abbey** had a lasting regional significance; the enterprising Furness monks could be said to have made early Cumbria an economic powerhouse well before the Industrial Revolution. Of the Cumbrian ports and towns which boomed in the eighteenth and nineteenth centuries, only **Ulverston** could really be called attractive (and if the traditional market and old streets weren't enough, Ulverston claims comedian Stan Laurel as its own). Here, and at **Cockermouth** in the northwest – yet another handsome market town – the Georgian well-to-do (including the young Wordsworth family) lived out their comfortable lives.

All the places covered in this chapter are accessible by **public transport** and details are given where necessary. Cumbria County Council's Journey Planner (☎01228/606 000) can provide specific routes and timetables.

Kendal

The self-billed "Gateway to the Lakes" (though nearly ten miles from Windermere), limestone-grey **KENDAL** is the largest of the southern Cumbrian towns with a population of 25,000. Upwardly mobile Norman barons created a medieval market town on the banks of the fast-flowing River Kent and built the first castle here, whose skeletal remains still stand. They also bequeathed to the town its most characteristic feature by establishing uniform building plots along a single main street in an attempt to increase their rents. This resulted in the layout visible today on both sides of Highgate and Stricklandgate: houses and shops to the fore, stables and workshops to the rear in the numerous "yards" and "ginnels". The town became known for its archers – who fought at Crécy and Poitiers in the Hundred Years' War with France – and for its cloth, particularly the "Kendal green" (plant-dyed wool) which earned the town a mention in Shakespeare's *Henry IV*. No wonder that the town motto became the no-nonsense "Cloth is my bread". By the eighteenth century Kendal was a major European cloth distribution centre, while its tanneries (which grievously polluted the River Kent) laid the foundation for today's most important industry, shoe-making. However, you could be forgiven for thinking that **Kendal Mintcake** is what keeps the contemporary coffers filled. This solid, energy-giving block of sugar and peppermint oil, invented by accident in the mid-nineteenth century, has been hoisted to the top of the world's highest mountains and is on sale throughout the Lakes.

Kendal services:
car rental p.7;
hospital p.22;
pharmacies p.23;
police p.23;
post office p.11;
swimming pool p.23;
taxis p.7.

Arrival and information

Kendal's **train station** is the first stop on the Windermere branch line, just three minutes from the Oxenholme main line station. By catching bus #41 or #41a (to the Town Hall) from Oxenholme (Mon–Sat, every 20min) you can avoid the wait for the connecting train. From Kendal station, head across the river and up Stramongate and Finkle Street to reach Highgate, a ten-minute walk. National Express buses stop opposite the **bus station** on Blackhall Road (off Stramongate) on their way south, but opposite the post office on Stricklandgate going north. Locally, the #599 (to Windermere, Bowness, Ambleside and Grasmere) and #555/556 (to Windermere, Ambleside, Grasmere and Keswick, or to Lancaster or Carlisle) are

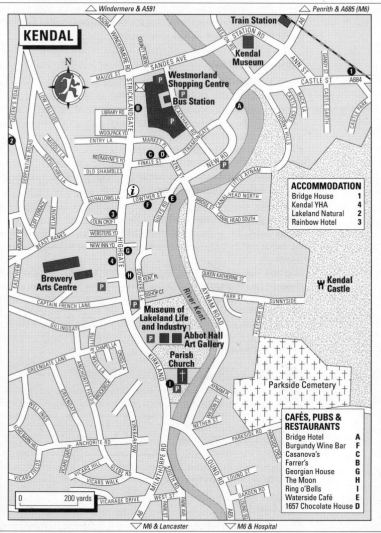

the main services. Driving in from the M6, take junction 38 (north) or 36 (south). There are signposted **car parks** all over town, including one at the Westmorland Shopping Centre (Blackhall Road) and a couple off Highgate, plus free unlimited parking on New Road by the river.

The **tourist office** (Easter–Oct Mon–Sat 9am–5pm, Sun 10am–5pm; Nov–Easter Mon–Sat 9am–5pm; ☎01539/725758) is in the

Town Hall on Highgate (at the junction with Lowther Street). You can book space here on the weekly summer **guided walks** (£2), currently on Wednesdays in July and August.

Accommodation

While Kendal makes a reasonable overnight stop on the way to or from the Lakes, there's no great advantage in basing yourself here, certainly not if you're planning to hike the central fells and valleys (which are all a good drive or bus ride away). In any case, there's not a massive amount of centrally located accommodation, save for the youth hostel and a handful of pubs offering rooms. Most of the local **B&Bs** lie along Windermere Road, north of the centre, and on Milnthorpe Road, to the south, while the most convenient **campsite** lies four miles northwest of town.

B&Bs, guest houses and hotels

Bridge House, 65 Castle St (☎01539/722041). Georgian house, not far from the station, with just a couple of rooms (one with en-suite facilities). No credit cards. ②.

Lakeland Natural, Low Slack, Queen's Rd (☎01539/733011). Best B&B choice by far, this impressive, detached vegetarian guest house stands on high ground above the town, five minutes' walk west of the centre. Expansive views from the lounge, and good breakfasts. Parking. ③.

Rainbow Hotel, 32 Highgate (☎01539/728271). One of a handful of old inns in the centre offering standard B&B rooms; breakfast is served in the oak-beamed dining room. ②.

Campsite and youth hostel

Ashes Lane, Staveley, 4 miles northwest of town (☎01539/821119). The campsite is half-a-mile up Ashes Lane, a left-turn off the A591 (Windermere road), a mile or so before Staveley village; take bus #555 from Kendal bus station. Closed mid-Jan to mid-March.

Kendal YHA, 118 Highgate (☎01539/724066). Straightforward hostel accommodation in a former Georgian town house, attached to The Brewery arts centre. The multi-bunked rooms are a bit barrack-like and the hostel's tight on space, but the location's great (and there's a lively arts centre bar next door).

The town

The old **Market Place** has long since succumbed to development, with the market hall now converted to the Westmorland Shopping Centre (off Stricklandgate), but traditional stalls still do business outside every Wednesday and Saturday. The long main street – Stricklandgate and then Highgate – is backed by the historic yards (many now containing shops and businesses), and strolling along here will eventually take you down to the riverside, past restored almshouses, mullioned shop fronts and old trade-signs like the pipe-smoking Turk outside the snuff factory on Lowther Street.

At Kirkland, by the river at the bottom of Highgate, the wide aisles of the Early English **Parish Church** house a number of family chapels, including that of the Parr family, who once owned the ruined **Kendal Castle** (free access), on a hillock to the east across the river. First erected in the early thirteenth century, it's claimed as the birthplace of Catherine Parr, Henry VIII's sixth wife, but the story is apocryphal – she was born in 1512, at which time the building was in an advanced state of decay. To reach the castle, follow the footpath from the end of Parr Street, across the footbridge just north of the church.

The town museums and art gallery

Kendal museums and art gallery. Information on ☎01539/722464. Open daily: April–Oct 10.30am–5pm; Nov–March 10.30am–4pm. Admission £2.80 per exhibition, or £1 with a ticket from one of the town's other museums.

The **Kendal Museum** on Station Road near the train station is the repository of the district's natural history and archeological finds. It's far from dull, since as well as the usual flints and stuffed birds there are plenty of well-presented displays relating to the town's history and various pieces of ephemera – from a penny-farthing bicycle to a stuffed grizzly bear, shot by the Earl of Lonsdale. Kendal's former borough treasurer, Alfred Wainwright (see box on p.158) was honorary clerk at the museum between 1945 and 1974: his office and a few of his personal effects are preserved, as well as many of the museum artefact labels written in his distinctive hand.

The town's other two museums are in the Georgian **Abbot Hall**, by the river to the south. The main hall, painstakingly restored to its 1760s' town-house origins, houses the **Art Gallery**, whose upper-floor rooms host temporary exhibitions of modern art. The lower-floor galleries are more locally focused, concentrating on the works of the eighteenth-century "Kendal school" of portrait painters, notably Daniel Gardner and, most famously, George Romney. Born in Dalton-in-Furness (and buried there), Romney set himself up as a portrait painter in Kendal in 1757, where he stayed for five years before moving to London to further his career. His society portraits are the pick of the gallery's collection, though you'll also find changing displays of works by those who came to the Lakes to paint, such as Constable, Ruskin, Turner and Edward Lear. Two large paintings of Windermere by Phillip James de Loutherbourg depict Belle Isle and its round house respectively beset by storms and becalmed. In addition, eighteenth-century chairs, writing desks and games tables designed and built by famed furniture-makers Gillows of Lancaster have all survived in Abbot Hall in excellent condition, and there's also a good **café** below the gallery.

Kendal

Alfred Wainwright

If ever a person has changed the way others look at the Lake District hills it's **Alfred Wainwright** (1907–91), whose handwritten walking guides – studied with the intensity normally reserved for religious texts – are among the most common sights on the fells. Wainwright was born in Blackburn in Lancashire, left school at 13 and worked his way up through the Borough Treasurer's office, qualifying as an accountant in 1933. After a first visit to the Lake District in 1930 he became a keen walker, and returned to the Lakes at every possible opportunity. So taken was he with the fells that he engineered a move to Kendal in 1941; he was Borough Treasurer from 1948 until his retirement in 1967.

His love of walking was taken to obsessional lengths, setting off alone at the crack of dawn every weekend to tackle distant fells, peaks and valleys. In 1952, dissatisfied with the accuracy of existing maps of the paths and ancient tracks across the fells, he embarked on a series of seven walking guides, each painstakingly handwritten with mapped routes and delicately drawn views. These *Pictorial Guides* to the Lake District were a remarkable undertaking, especially since the original idea was only for his own amusement. The first book, *The Eastern Fells*, was published in 1955 and was an unexpected success; six others followed by 1966, thus completing the task he had set himself of recording in detail 214 separate lakeland fells. Many other titles followed: a *Pennine Way Companion* (1968), the *Coast-to-Coast* route he devised from St Bees to Robin Hood's Bay (1973), endless sketchbooks and guides to the Lake District, Scotland, Wales, the Yorkshire Dales and the Lancashire hills; fifty-odd books in all. His first wife, Ruth, left him in 1966 and in 1970 Wainwright married Betty McNally, with whom he'd corresponded (and secretly met on his walking trips) for years. He died in 1991, having given away most of his considerable earnings to animal rescue charities, and his ashes were scattered on Haystacks in Buttermere.

The effect his books have had is plain to see. People who don't normally consider themselves walkers are happy to follow his guidance through the Lake District – easy to do since little has changed up on the fells themselves in the forty-odd years since the *Pictorial Guides* were first written. But some decry their popularity, which has led to the ravaging of the land he so adored, especially on his most trekked route, the Coast-to-Coast – much of Wainwright's original route (subsequently amended) was not on designated rights of way and often crossed sensitive wildlife areas and archeological sites. It's also wrong to treat Wainwright as gospel, as many do in their attempts to "bag" the 214 fells he recorded. The number was an entirely arbitrary figure – most of the Wainwright fells are over 1400ft high, but there are plenty of other crags and fells lower than that but just as spectacular, not to mention the lakes, tarns and valleys which he covered only in passing.

A Barbara Hepworth sculpture, *Oval Form*, graces the grass between the hall and its former stables, which now house the **Museum of Lakeland Life and Industry**. Here, reconstructed house interiors from the seventeenth, eighteenth and nineteenth centuries stand alongside workshops which make a fairly vivid presentation of rural trades and crafts, from mining, spinning and weaving to shoe-making and tanning. The museum also contains a room devoted to the life and work of the children's writer Arthur Ransome, whose widow donated his pipes, typewriter and other memorabilia to the collection after his death. John Cunliffe, creator of *Postman Pat*, whose adventures are set just north of Kendal, gets similar treatment in an adjacent room, with a welter of original drawings, a few toys and the author's desk and typewriter on show.

Kendal

For more on Arthur Ransome, see p.90; and for the scenery which inspired the Postman Pat stories, see p.52.

Sizergh Castle and Levens Hall

Three miles south of Kendal stands **Sizergh Castle**, tucked away off the A591 (April–Oct Mon–Thurs & Sun 1.30–5.30pm; gardens same days from 12.30pm; castle & gardens £4.50; gardens only £2.20; EH; ☎015395/60070); take bus #555. Home of the Strickland family for eight centuries, the castle owes its epithet to the fourteenth-century pele tower at its core – one of the best examples of these towers, which were built as safe havens during the region's protracted medieval border raids. The Great Hall underwent significant changes in Elizabethan times, when most of its rooms were panelled in oak with their ceilings layered in elaborate plasterwork. Two miles south of Sizergh, **Levens Hall** (April to mid-Oct Mon–Thurs & Sun noon–5pm; gardens same days from 10am; hall & gardens £5.80; gardens only £3.90; ☎015395/60321), also built around a pele tower, is more uniform in style than Sizergh, since the bulk of it was built or refurbished in classic Elizabethan style between 1570 and 1640. The dining room here is panelled not with oak but with goat's leather, printed with a deep green floral design. Upstairs, the bedrooms offer glimpses of the beautifully trimmed topiary gardens, where yews in the shape of pyramids, peacocks and top hats stand between blooming bedding plants. The #555 bus drops you in the village of Levens, a mile away, across the A590.

Eating, drinking and entertainment

There's no shortage of **cafés and restaurants** in town (see list below), while for evening entertainment the **Brewery Arts Centre**, 118 Highgate (☎01539/725 133), with its restaurant, bar, cinema, theatre, galleries and concert hall, is a good bet. There's live music throughout the year and a renowned annual **jazz and blues festival** every November. Several **pubs and bars** stand out: the *Ring o' Bells* on Kirkland, which, uniquely, stands on consecrated ground by the parish church; the *Bridge Hotel*, a classic old local with small riverside beer garden at the bottom of Stramongate; the *Burgundy Wine Bar*, halfway down Finkle Street, which has a huge list of beers and wines; and the excellent *Vats Bar*, inside the arts centre, more a pub than a bar with good beer on tap.

1657 Chocolate House, Branthwaite Brow, Finkle St (☎01539/740702). Olde-worlde spot which sells little other than hot chocolate (in dozens of guises) and cakes. Daytime only. Inexpensive.

Casanova's, 24a Finkle St (☎01539/720547). Kendal's best Italian restaurant is tucked into an old building up a yard off Finkle Street: *al dente* pasta, authentic pizza and nice staff. Moderate.

Farrers Tea & Coffee Merchants, 13 Stricklandgate (☎01539/731707). Historic merchant's quarters on the main street, with tea and coffee sold by the weight in the shop and by the cup and cafetiere in the café at the back. Daytime only; closed Sun. Inexpensive.

The Georgian House, 99 Highgate (☎01539/722123). The stylish, modernist interior houses a cool bar on the ground floor (serving lunch specials), an art gallery upstairs and a top-floor Modern-British restaurant – reservations recommended at weekends. Restaurant, dinner only. Moderate.

The Moon, 129 Highgate (☎01539/729254). An easy-going bistro with Asian and Mediterranean twists in its inventive, locally sourced, menu – always plenty of vegetarian choice. Closed Mon in winter. Moderate to expensive.

Waterside Café, Gulfs Rd, bottom of Lowther St (☎01539/729743). Veggie wholefood snacks and meals, good coffee and riverside seating. Daytime only. Inexpensive.

Cartmel

CARTMEL grew up around its twelfth-century Augustinian priory and is still dominated by the proud **Church of St Mary and St Michael** (daily: summer 9am–5.30pm; winter 9am–3.30pm; tours Easter–Oct Wed 11am & 2pm; free), the only substantial remnant of the priory to survive the Dissolution. A diagonally crowned tower is the most distinctive feature outside, while the light and spacious Norman-transitional interior climaxes at a splendid chancel, illuminated by the 45-foot-high East Window. The misericords are immaculate, carved with entwined branches, bunches of grapes, tools, leaves and crosses, while chief of the numerous sculpted tombs is the Harrington Tomb – the weathered figure is that of John Harrington, a fourteenth-century benefactor. Another patron of the church was one Rowland Briggs who paid for a shelf on a pier near the north door and for a supply of bread to be distributed from it every Sunday in perpetuity "to the most indigent housekeepers of this Parish". Before you leave, peruse the gravestones on the church floor, reminders of men and women swept away by the tide while crossing the sands – a short cut into the region from Grange-Over-Sands to the south.

The priory was fortified in the fourteenth century to protect it against marauding Scottish raiders; the gatehouse now doubles as a local **Heritage Centre** (Tues–Thurs, Sat & Sun 11am–5pm; free). Everything else in the village is modest in scale, centred on the attractive **market square**, with its Elizabethan cobbles, water pump and fish slabs. Refreshment is at hand at any of the village's four pubs, all on, or close to, the square, and you can then walk down to the **racecourse** whose delightful setting by the River Eea deserves a look even if the races (held on the last weekend in May and August) aren't in action. Given Cartmel's rather twee attraction, you'll not be surprised to find several **antique and craft shops**, as well as weekly antiques fairs (April–Oct) held in the village hall. On the square, Peter Bain Smith's **bookshop** has a huge selection of local books and guides, while the Cartmel Village Shop is known to aficionados for the quality of its sticky toffee pudding.

A couple of miles west of the village, on the B5278, one of Cumbria's most interesting and well-presented country estates, **Holker Hall** (Easter–Oct Mon–Fri & Sun 10am–6pm; last admission 4.30pm; various combination tickets available; hall, gardens, grounds & motor museum £7.25; ☎015395/58328), is still in use by the Cavendish family who've owned it since the late seventeenth century. Only the New Wing is open to the public, and the real showpieces are the cantilevered staircase and the library, which is stocked with more than three thousand leather-bound books, some of whose spines are fakes, constructed to hide electric light switches added later. The 25-acre gardens incorporate a variety of water features, while next to the house the **Lakeland Motor Museum** (Easter–Oct Mon–Fri & Sun 10am–4.45pm; last admission 4.15am) displays more than a hundred vehicles, from 1880s tricycles and wartime ambulances to funky 1920s bubble cars and 1980s MGs. A special exhibition concentrates on the speed-freak Campbells – Sir Malcolm and son Donald. A summer **bus** service, the #534, from Grange-over-Sands to Newby Bridge and Lakeside, runs past the hall.

Practicalities

Cartmel lies a few miles inland of Morecambe Bay, and just five miles south of Lakeside, the southern tip of Windermere. **Trains** stop at Cark-in-Cartmel, two miles southwest of the village; the #530/531 **bus** (originating in Kendal or Windermere) from Cark or from Grange-over-Sands train station runs to the village. The turn-off from the M6 is junction 36; the **car park** is by the racecourse.

Central **B&Bs** include seventeenth-century *Market Cross Cottage* on Market Square (☎015395/36143; no credit cards; ③), which has its own oak-beamed tearooms (closed Mon), and *Bank Court Cottage*, through the arch in Market Square by the bookshop (☎015395/36593; no credit cards; ①). Rooms in both have sinks, though some in cosy *Market Cross Cottage* are en-suite. The celebrated *Cavendish*, through the gatehouse on Cavendish Street (☎015395/36240, *enquiries@thecavendish.co.uk*; ⑤), is an atmospheric inn which retains many of its original sixteenth-century features. For a stay in one of its delightful estate **cottages**, contact *Longlands at Cartmel*, a mile north of the village (☎015395/ 36475, *longlands@cartmel.com*). Guests get free use of a nearby pool, spa and sauna, while well-regarded evening meals are available in the restaurant in the main house on Saturday nights (May–Oct only); at other times (all year), meals prepared in the kitchens are served in the cottages.

The village **pubs**, on and around the square, form the basis of the evening's entertainment. The *King's Arms* has outdoor tables and reasonably priced bar meals, and the *Royal Oak* has a riverside garden. The *Cavendish*, though, is the real winner, the oldest and most characterful of the pubs, sitting on the site of a monastic guest house and offering good (if pricey) food.

Ulverston

The railway line winds westwards from Cartmel to **ULVERSTON** – eleven miles by road – a close-knit market town on the Furness peninsula, which formerly prospered on the cotton, tanning and iron-ore industries. The cutting of Britain's shortest, widest and deepest canal in 1796 allowed direct shipping access into town and boosted trade with the Americas and West Indies, while exports from the heart of the Lake District (from wooden bobbins and linen to copper and slate) passed out through Ulverston and made it wealthy. It's still an attractive place, enhanced by its dappled grey limestone cottages and a jumble of cobbled alleys and traditional shops zigzagging off the central **Market Place**. Stalls set up here and in the surrounding streets every Thursday and Saturday (8am–4pm); on other days the **Market Hall** on New Market Street (9am–5pm, not Wed or Sun) is the centre of commercial life.

What looks like a lighthouse high on a hill to the north of town is the **Hoad Monument**, built in 1850 to honour locally born Sir John Barrow, a former Secretary of the Admiralty. It's open on summer Sundays and public holidays (if the flag's flying) and the walk to the top grants fine views of Morecambe Bay, the town and – to the north – the lakeland fells. To get there, follow Church Walk from the end of King Street, past the parish church.

Ulverston's most famous son is Stan Laurel (born Arthur Stanley Jefferson), the whimpering, head-scratching half of Laurel and Hardy who are celebrated in a mind-boggling collection of memorabilia at the **Laurel and Hardy Museum** up an alley at 4c Upper Brook St (daily 10am–4.30pm; £2; closed Jan; ☎01229/582292), thirty yards off Market Place down King Street. The copy of Stan's birth certificate (June 16, 1890, in Foundry Cottages, Ulverston) lists his father's occupation as "comedian" – young Arthur Stanley could hardly have become anything else. The eccentric showcase of hats, beer bottles, photos, models, puppets, press cuttings and props is complemented by a 1920s-style cinema, with almost constant screenings of the duo's films.

Across King Street, in Lower Brook Street, Ulverston's **Heritage Centre** (Mon, Tues & Thurs–Sat 9.30am–4.30pm; £2; ☎01229/ 580280) is housed in a former eighteenth-century spice warehouse. The other town attraction is the **Lakes Glass Centre** (Mon–Fri 10am–4pm, Sat & Sun 10am–5pm; £2; ☎01229/581385), at Oubas Hill on the A590 as you come into town, by Booths supermarket. Here, you can watch the crystal-glass making process from blowing to painstaking carving; there's also a factory shop on site.

Practicalities

Ulverston **train station**, serving the Furness and Cumbrian coast railway, is only a few minutes' walk from the town centre – walk up Princess Street and turn right at the main road for County Square. **Buses** arrive on nearby Victoria Road from Cartmel, Grange-over-Sands, Barrow, Bowness, Windermere and Kendal. The **Cumbria Way**, the long-distance footpath from Ulverston to Carlisle, starts from The Gill, at the top of Upper Brook Street. The turn-off from the M6 for Ulverston is junction 36; there are **car parks** off Market Street and at The Gill. The **tourist office** is in Coronation Hall on County Square (Mon–Sat 9am–5pm; ☎01229/587120).

Pick of the **B&Bs** are the *White House*, a three-hundred-year-old cottage at the bottom of Market Street (☎01229/583340; no credit cards; ①; closed Nov–March), and *Dyker Bank*, 2 Springfield Rd (☎01229/582423; no credit cards; ②), a Georgian house near the station. There's also a great *Walker's Hostel* on Oubas Hill (☎01229/585588; no credit cards; ①) near the canal basin, on the A590 as you come into town: thirty beds in small shared rooms, with vegetarian breakfasts and evening meals available.

Cafés include the *Hot Mango Café*, 27 King St, a funky joint serving cappuccinos, breakfasts and hot baguette sandwiches, and the more traditional *Ship's Wheel Café*, 11 King St. *Amigo's*, 30 Cavendish St (closed Mon & Tues lunch, plus all Wed & Sun; ☎01229/587616), across from the tourist office, is a moderately priced Mexican restaurant and steak house. Most of the **pubs** serve bar meals – the best located is the *Farmers Arms* in Market Place which has outdoor tables and views down Market Street.

Out of town, follow the A590 briefly and then turn off at the signpost for Canal Foot, running through an industrial estate to reach the beautifully sited *Bay Horse Inn* (☎01229/583972, *reservations@ bayhorse.furness.co.uk*; ⑦, ⑧ with dinner), by the last lock on the Ulverston canal. The cooking here is celebrated far and wide and even if you can't run to lunch or dinner in the waterside conservatory, you can order a coffee, soup or sandwich at one of the outdoor tables.

Furness Abbey

Furness Abbey ☎01229/823420. Open April–Sept daily 10am–6pm; Oct daily 10am–4pm; Nov–March Wed–Sun 10am–4pm. Admission £2.50; EH.

Cumbria's wealth used to be concentrated at **Furness Abbey**, which at the peak of its influence possessed much of southern Cumbria as well as land in Ireland and the Isle of Man. Founded in 1124, the Cistercian abbey had a remarkably diverse industry – it ran sheep farms on the fells, controlled fishing rights, produced grain and leather, smelted iron, dug peat for fuel and manufactured salt. By the fourteenth century it had become such a prize that the Scots raided it twice, though it survived until April 1536, when Henry VIII chose it to be the first of the large abbeys to be dissolved. The Abbot and 29 of his monks, who had hitherto resisted (and indeed, had encouraged the locals to resist Dissolution – a treasonable offence), were pensioned off for the sum of two pounds each.

Now one of Cumbria's finest ruins, the abbey's roofless red sandstone arcades and pillars lie hidden in a wooded vale north of Barrow-in-Furness. It's been a popular tourist diversion since the early nineteenth century, when a train station was built to bring in visitors, among them Wordsworth who was very taken with the "mouldering pile". Borrow an audio-guide from the reception desk to get the best out of the site, since there are no maps or explanatory signs. The transepts stand virtually at their original height, while the massive slabs of stone-ribbed vaulting, richly embellished arcades and intricately carved *sedilia* in the presbytery are the equal of any in England. A small museum houses some of the best carvings, including rare examples of effigies of armed knights with closed helmets and – as medieval custom dictated – crossed legs. Only seven others have ever been found intact. The *Abbey Tavern* at the entrance serves drinks at tables scattered about some of the ruined outbuildings.

The abbey lies a mile-and-a-half out of the industrial town of Barrow-in-Furness, on the Ulverston road (and about six miles from Ulverston). Local **buses** (including the #X35, not Sun) between Ulverston, Dalton-in-Furness and Barrow pass by; details from Ulverston tourist office.

Cockermouth

COCKERMOUTH, midway between the industrial coast and Keswick at the confluence of the Cocker and Derwent rivers, dominates the flat vales which leach out of the northwestern fells, an obvious strategic stronghold. Its Norman castle was at the heart of the medieval border skirmishes, but the town later thrived as a market centre – market day is Monday. Cockermouth tries hard to please, with its impressive Georgian facades, tree-lined streets and riverside setting, but after the dramatic fellside approaches from the south and east it can fall a little flat. However, there's no shortage of local attractions, not least the logical first stop on the Wordsworth trail – the house where the future poet was born.

The town

The single, long, Main Street crosses the River Cocker and runs parallel to the Derwent through the town. At the western end is the **Wordsworth House** (Easter–June, Sept & Oct Mon–Fri 11am–5pm; July & Aug Mon–Sat 11am–5pm; £2.80; NT; ☎01900/824805), a handsome, terracotta-hued Georgian building that was the birthplace of all five Wordsworth children, including William (1770) and Dorothy (1771). It's a house suitable for the professional man that Wordsworth's father was, though he only rented it from his employer, Sir James Lowther, for whom he spent much of his time away on business. The children too, though happy in the house, were often sent to their grandparents in Penrith and when Wordsworth's father died in 1783 – with the children already either away at school or living with relations – the family link with Cockermouth was broken. The building was nearly replaced by a bus station in the 1930s, but was saved and given to the National Trust who have furnished it with imports from their vaults. Some of the original features remain and there are occasional Wordsworthian relics – a chest of drawers here, a pair of candlesticks there – but despite the best endeavours of the enthusiastic staff it's disappointingly lifeless. The kitchen has been put to good use as a café, and on a warm day the walled garden beside the river is a pleasure.

For the story of the rest of William's life, see p.187.

Various rainy-day attractions occupy the historic buildings and yards ranged along the Main Street – including small museums of printing, toys and models, and motoring – while if you follow your nose you're likely to stumble upon **Jennings Brewery** on Brewery Lane by the river confluence. Jennings have been brewers in the town since 1874 and you don't have to step far to sample their product, available in any local pub. For those sufficiently interested in the brewing process to take the ninety-minute-long **brewery tour** (mid-Feb to March & Oct Mon–Fri 11am & 2pm; April–Sept Mon–Sat 11am & 2pm; £3; ☎01900/823214, booking advisable) there's a free tasting at the end.

For more on Cumbrian beer, see p.15.

Also, it's always worth checking to see what's on inside **Castlegate House** (March–Dec Mon, Tues & Fri–Sat 10.30am–5pm, Wed 10.30–7pm; free; ☎01900/822149), a Georgian mansion on Castlegate, opposite the entrance to Cockermouth Castle – itself a private residence and closed to the public. The house supports a changing programme of contemporary art displays, specializing in the work of accomplished local artists. Less rarefied lakeland affairs are dealt with in the out-of-town **Lakeland Sheep and Wool Centre**

Cockermouth

(mid-Feb to mid-Nov daily 10am–5pm; free; ☎01900/822673), a mile south of town on the Egremont road (A66/A5086 roundabout), where various exhibits introduce visitors to the complexities of coun-try life. Most come for the entertaining indoor sheepdog trials and sheep-shearing displays (up to 4 shows daily; £3), during which you'll learn how to be able to spot a Herdwick sheep, the most char-acteristic lakeland breed.

Practicalities

All **buses**, including National Express services, stop on Main Street from where you follow the signs east to the **tourist office** in the Town Hall, off Market Place (April–June & Oct Mon–Sat 9.30am–4.30pm July–Sept Mon–Sat 9.30am–5pm, Sun 2–5pm; Nov–March Mon–Sat 9.30am–4pm; ☎01900/822634). Driving in, the A66 (from Keswick or Workington) bypasses the town to the south; turn in on either the B5292 (Whinlatter Pass road) or A5086 (from Loweswater and Ennerdale). The **car park** in front of the tourist office is the best place to park, since parking on Main Street is limited to an hour (and you need to display a disc in your car, available from local shops).

Central **B&Bs** include *Castlegate Guest House*, 6 Castlegate (☎01900/826749; no credit cards; ②), and *Manor House*, 23 St Helen's St (☎01900/822416; no credit cards; ①), beyond the end of Market Place; you'll share a bathroom at the *Manor House*. Of the traditional **hotels** in town, the *Globe Hotel* on Main Street (☎01900/822126; ③) is the most appealing mid-range spot, but the *Trout Hotel* on Crown Street (☎01900/823591; ⑤), on the banks of the Derwent (the pricier rooms have river views), is the top choice. There are also modern motel-style rooms available in the *Shepherd's Hotel*, out at the Lakeland Sheep and Wool Centre (☎01900/822673; ②). Cockermouth's *Double Mills* **youth hostel** (☎01900/822561) is housed in a seventeenth-century watermill down a track by a bend in the River Cocker: the double wheels (that lend it its name) and grindstones are still *in situ* and though the hostel needs modernizing, it's in a very peaceful spot – fifteen minutes' walk south from Main Street, along Station Road and then Fern Bank.

Of the **cafés**, *Norham Coffee House*, 73 Main St (closed Sun), trades on its history – it was formerly the home of John Christian, grandfather of Mutiny on the *Bounty*'s Fletcher Christian – and its courtyard seating. *Beatfords* (closed Sun), further along Main St in the Lowther Went Shopping Centre, is a bit on the chintzy side but usually has an interesting list of daily specials. Two good moderately priced **restaurants** are the *Quince & Medlar*, 13 Castlegate (☎01900/823579; dinner only; closed Sun & Mon), serving gourmet vegetarian dishes in a wood-panelled Georgian house, and the *Cockatoo*, 16 Market Place (☎01900/826205; dinner only; closed Sun & Mon), whose menu touches base in a dozen countries, serving everything from local lamb to Thai chicken, and poached swordfish to Chinese vegetable stir-fries.

Cockermouth provides the hostelries for one of the more bizarre pub-crawls-of-the-rich-and-famous. Soccer manager Sir Matt Busby, cricketer Ian Botham and (strange but true) crooner and fisherman Bing Crosby have all had a drink in the bar of the *Trout*; while Robert Louis Stevenson plus local lad (and father of atomic theory) John Dalton frequented the *Globe*. Best place for a pint of the local Jennings beer is the *Bush*, halfway along Main Street, though the finest **pub** by far is *The Bitter End* on Kirkgate (off Market Place), housing Cumbria's smallest brewery – try the Cockersnoot or Cuddy Lugs ales. The bar food is popular and there's also a long list of imported bottled beers.

Cockermouth services:

hospital p.22;

pharmacies p.23;

police p.23;

post office p.11;

swimming pool p.23;

taxis p.7.

Penrith

PENRITH – four miles from Ullswater and sixteen east of Keswick – has a long pedigree and an historic significance greater than anywhere else in the Lakes. Probably Celtic in origin, it was capital of the independent kingdom of Cumbria until 1070, a thriving market town on the main north–south trading route from the thirteenth century onwards, and harried by the Scots until the sixteenth century. Its castle, built as a bastion against raids from the north, was one of the northern headquarters of Richard III. It still prospers today as an important local market centre and has positioned itself as one of the main gateways to the Lake District; reasonable enough given that it's a stop on the London–Scotland train route and lies off the M6 motorway and A66 to Keswick. It does, however, suffer from undue comparisons with the improbably pretty settlements of the nearby Lakes and certainly its brisk streets, filled with no-nonsense shops and shoppers, have more in common with the towns of the North Pennines than the stone villages of south Cumbria.

The town

Come on market day, Tuesday, if you want to get to grips with the local economy. The narrow streets, arcades and alleys off **Market Square**, the old **Corn Market** and the open space of **Great Dockray** provide traditional shopping for stalwart Cumbrian families, in the butchers' shops, fishmongers, outfitters, tobacconists and agricultural feed merchants. **St Andrew's Church** (possibly designed by Nicholas Hawkmoor) sits back from the square in a spacious churchyard surrounded by Georgian houses. The so-called "Giant's Grave" is actually a collection of pre-Norman crosses and "hogsback" tombstones. If you walk back round to the square and up Devonshire Street to the **George Hotel** – where Bonnie Prince Charlie spent the night in 1745 – you'll pass Arnison's, the drapers and milliners. The shop stands on the site of the town's old Moot Hall, owned in the eighteenth century by Wordsworth's grandparents. The young William and Dorothy often stayed here and their mother died in the house in 1778 (she's buried in St Andrew's churchyard, though the grave isn't marked).

Beyond the *George*, at the end of Middlegate, the tourist office shares its seventeenth-century school-house premises with a small local **museum** (April–Sept Mon–Sat 10am–6pm, Sun 1–6pm; Oct–March Mon–Sat 10am–5pm; free; ☎01768/867466). After a quick review of the town's history, the only other thing to do is to climb up Castlegate from Corn Market to the immaculately kept sandstone ruin of **Penrith Castle** (Easter–Sept daily 7.30am–9pm; Oct–Easter daily 7.30am–4.30pm; free), opposite the train station. The more impressive local fortification is actually that of **Brougham Castle** (April–Sept daily 10am–6pm; Oct daily 10am–dusk; £1.90; EH), a mile and a half south of Penrith by the River Eamont, and built on the site of an earlier Roman fort. There's a nice walk here – follow the north bank of the river from Eamont Bridge, which lies half a mile from town, just south of the A6/A66 roundabout.

Penrith's latest attraction also harks back to it earliest days. **Rheged** (daily 10am–6pm; information on ☎01768/868000; free parking), at Redhills on the A66, a couple of minutes' drive from the M6 (junction 40), is billed as Britain's largest earth-covered building and is designed to blend in with the surrounding fells. It takes its name from the ancient kingdom of Cumbria, which once stretched from Strathclyde in Scotland as far south as Cheshire, and features an atrium-lit underground visitor centre which fills you in on the region's history by way of a giant-format cinema screen showing a specially commissioned film, *The Lost Kingdom*, documenting "a journey back in time". Allow a couple of hours for a visit: there are also special exhibitions and a useful information centre – plus, of course, restaurant, café, and craft and gift shops to entice you off the road in the first place.

Practicalities

Trains from Manchester, London, Glasgow and Edinburgh pull into Penrith station, five minutes' walk south of Market Square and Middlegate. The **bus station** is on Albert Street, behind Middlegate, and has regular services to Patterdale, Keswick, Cockermouth and Carlisle. Coming in off the M6, take junction 40; there's a **car park** off Brunswick Street and others signposted around town, though spaces are hard to come by on Tuesdays (market day). The **tourist office** is on Middlegate (Mon–Sat 9.30am–5pm, Sun 1–4.45pm; ☎01768/867466).

The bulk of the **B&Bs** line Victoria Road, the continuation of King Street, two minutes' walk south of Market Square. *Victoria Guest House*, at no. 3 (☎01768/863823; no credit cards; ①), and *Blue Swallow*, at no. 11 (☎01768/866335; no credit cards; ②), are the two most convenient choices. The *George Hotel*, on Devonshire Street by Market Square (☎01768/862696; ④), is an old coaching inn with attractive prices, cosy wood-panelled lounges and a decent bar and restaurant – the sort of place where Cumbrian ladies-who-lunch come to take tea and sip sherry. More down-to-earth is the *Agricultural Hotel*, at the top of Castlegate (☎01768/862622; ②), opposite the castle, which serves popular bar meals.

For picnic **food**, the fantastically stocked J. & J. Graham's deli-grocery in Market Square (closed Sun) can't be beaten, while *Chataways Bistro* (closed Mon, plus Sun eve; ☎01768/890233) – serving coffee and cake, an all-day menu of cannelloni, smoked-trout salad and lamb cutlets and the like, plus moderately priced *table d'hôte* dinners – is enhanced by its setting on the edge of pretty St Andrew's churchyard. *Passepartout*, 51 Castlegate (☎01768/865852; dinner only; closed Mon), is the expensive choice, its traditional menu given a modern twist. Or there are inexpensive tapas at *Costa's*, 9 Queen St (☎01768/895550; closed Mon).

Penrith services:

car rental p.7;

hospital p.22;

pharmacies p.23;

police p.23;

post office p.11;

swimming pool p.23;

taxis p.7.

The Contexts

History

The Lake District remained a land apart for centuries, its features – rugged and isolated – mirrored in the characteristics of its inhabitants. Daniel Defoe thought it "eminent only for being the wildest, most barren and frightful of any that I have passed over" – and, as he went on to point out, he'd been to Wales so he knew what he was talking about. Two factors spurred the first waves of tourism: the reappraisal of landscape brought about by such painters as Constable and the writings of Wordsworth and his contemporaries, and the outbreak of the French Revolution and its subsequent turmoil, which put paid to the idea of the continental Grand Tour. Later, as tourism to the Lakes was cemented by the arrival of the railway, Wordsworth – while bemoaning mass travel – wrote in his *Guide to the Lakes* that he desired "a sort of national property, in which every man has a right and interest who has an eye to perceive and a heart to enjoy." His wish finally came to fruition in 1951 when the government established the Lake District as England's largest national park. It's subsequently become one of the most visited parts of England.

Early times

Although human habitation is relatively recent, geologically speaking the Lake District is extremely old. The rocks which make up the Skiddaw and Blencathra massif consist of 500-million-year-old slate, while 100 million years later occurred the immense volcanic activity which shaped the high central mountains. The granite outcrops visible at Ennerdale and Eskdale were formed 350 million years ago. Later still, a tropical sea covered the region (320 million years ago) whose shell remains formed the ubiquitous limestone and sandstone.

At the heart of the region is Scafell, the remnant of a volcanic dome that had already been weathered into its present craggy shape before the last **Ice Age**, when glaciers flowed off its flanks to gouge their characteristic U-shaped valleys. As the ice withdrew, moraines of sediment dammed the meltwater, creating the main lakes, all of which radiate from Scafell's hub – Wordsworth, in a famous image, described them as immense spokes. The gentler terrain to the south was formed after this main burst of activity, with subsequent mini-ice ages (the last around 12,000 years ago) gouging out smaller tarns, flattening the valley bottoms, and modifying the shape and scale of the mountains. Consequently, the Lake District as it appears today comprises a huge variety of terrains and geological material within a compact region.

The first humans

Human interaction has also played a significant part in the shaping of the Lake District. Before **Neolithic peoples** began to colonize the region around 5000 years ago, most of the now bare uplands were forested with pine and birch, while the valleys were blanketed with thickets of oak, alder, ash and elm. As these first settlers learned to shape flints into axes, they began to clear the upland forests for farmland – remnants of shaped stone axes have been found in so-called "factory" sites on Pike of Stickle (in Langdale) and on the slopes of Scafell. During the later **Stone and Bronze ages**, the subsistence existence of Lake District settlers is unlikely to have changed much. Their hunter-gathering lifestyle was augmented by early stock-rearing and planting, though evidence of their lives is sketchy. Bronze tools and weapons have been found (around Ambleside, Keswick and St John's in the Vale), though few burial or settlement sites have been pinpointed. The **stone circles** at Castlerigg (near Keswick), Melmerby (near Penrith) and at Swinside (near Duddon Bridge) are the region's most important sites and even the purpose of these is unclear. Some have suggested they had a time-keeping function or were used for religious purposes; others that the circles were a commercial focus or meeting-place. What's clear is the high degree of co-operation between people required to erect the stones in the first place.

By the third century BC, **Celtic peoples** from the south and east were pushing into the region. From their hill-fort settlements (like that on Carrock Fell) they exploited the local metal deposits and employed advanced farming techniques. Sophisticated religious practices (including burial) and basic systems of law and communal defence (against raiders from the north) were established features of their lives by the time of the Roman invasion of Britain in 55 BC.

The Romans and Celts

The **arrival of the Romans** in the north of England after 69 AD led to the first large-scale alteration of the region's landscape. **Hadrian's Wall**, from the Tyne to the Solway Firth – marking the northern limit of the Roman Empire – was completed by 130 AD. Associated with the wall were roads, forts and supply routes which cut through the heart of the Lakes. There are the remains of fortresses still to be seen at Hardknott Pass and at Waterhead, near Ambleside, while Roman roads can be traced between Kendal and Ravenglass and, most obviously, from Troutbeck to Brougham (near Penrith) along the ridge known as High Street.

The roads and forts were principally a means of subduing the local population. Throughout the Roman period the Lake District was essentially a **military zone**, policed by auxiliaries (recruited from all parts of the Roman Empire) rather than true legionnaires. However, around the bases grew **civilian settlements** as at Ambleside – which formed the basis of later towns and villages. Lead-mining was first practised during Roman times, while upland forests continued to be replaced by agricultural land as cereal crops were planted to supply the various permanent settlements. At Ravenglass, on the Cumbrian coast, are the extant remains of a bathhouse, part of a fort which survived in Ravenglass until the fourth century.

In the face of constant raids and harassment, England had become irrevocably detached from what remained of the Roman Empire by the start of the fifth century AD. The original **Celtic inhabitants** of the northwest had never fully abandoned their traditions and practices in the face of Roman might, and surviving Celtic place-names (Derwent, Blencathra) indicate strong local ties. Indeed, from the Celts comes the word they used to describe themselves – *Cymry* – from which derives the modern place-name Cumbria. **Christianity** secured an enduring toehold in the region too. St Kentigern (or Mungo), the Celtic missionary, founded several churches in the region, passing through Crosthwaite in Keswick in 553 AD.

The Saxon and Norse invasions

The **Saxon invasion** of England's south and east during the sixth century initially had little impact on the Lake District, which slowly fell under the control of the newly established **kingdom of Northumbria**. However, place-name evidence does suggest that Saxon farmers later settled on the lakeland fringes – names ending in "ham" and "ton" betray a Saxon influence, as does the suffix "-mere" attached to a lake.

A greater impact was made by **Norse (ie, Norwegian) Vikings** during the ninth and tenth centuries. Although they eventually supplanted much of the native lakeland population, it would be wrong to see the Norse arrival as a violent invasion. Unlike the Danes, who had sacked Lindisfarne on the east coast in 793, the Norse invasion was less brutal, with Viking settlers (rather than warriors) gradually filtering into the Lake District from their established bases in Scotland, Ireland and the Isle of Man. They farmed the land extensively and left their indelible mark on the northern dialect – dale, fell, force, beck, tarn and the suffix "-thwaite" (a clearing) all have Norse origins. Physical remains are scarce, the finest example being the splendid Norse cross in the churchyard at Gosforth, which combines Pagan and Christian elements in a style reminiscent of similar crosses in Ireland and the Isle of Man. By the end of the eleventh century, wherever they originated, lakelanders were living in small farming communities in recognized shires, or administrative districts, whose names survived for the next nine hundred years: Cumberland and Westmorland.

However, the region began to be disputed in a burgeoning number of turf wars between rival kingdoms. **Dunmail**, a Cumbrian warlord, was defeated in battle in 945 by the Saxon **King Edmund**, who granted control of the region to the kings of Scotland. This heralded six hundred years of political manoeuvring, between Scottish kings keen to push the border south and, after the Conquest, Norman rulers intent upon holding the line at Carlisle. The Lakes themselves, and their farming communities, were largely left alone as the opposing armies marched north and south, but the northern and western lowlands became a cross-border battleground. Castles at Cockermouth, Penrith and Kendal attest to the constant political threat, while raiding "**reivers**" or local clans made the borderlands ungovernable.

Medieval and Elizabethan times

By medieval times, most of the Lake District's traditional industries had been firmly established. The native breed of sheep, the Herdwick (black, with white faces), had proved itself a hardy species since at least Roman times, surviving harsh winters on the fells, while in summer cropping the hills of their wild flowers and preventing the regeneration of the woodland. **Religious houses** bordering the Lake District, such as Furness Abbey in the south, Carlisle in the north and St Bees in the west, came to hold large rural areas, establishing outlying farms – or "granges" – which further exploited the land. The wool produced found its way into markets throughout Europe and beyond, with **packhorse routes** meandering across the region to and from market towns such as Kendal, Keswick, Penrith and Cockermouth. The monks also maintained woods, or **coppices**, whose timber they used to produce charcoal (for iron-smelting) and bark used in tanneries. The **dissolution of the monasteries** in 1536 had little effect on these industries. The new crown tenants and the emerging "**statesman**" **farmers**, who bought their own smallholdings, merely continued the age-old practices, denuding the uplands further with every passing year.

Mining was also altering the contours of the land. Plumbago, or graphite, had been discovered in Borrowdale and in 1564 Elizabeth I gave royal assent to an Anglo-German venture to exploit the ore – invaluable for pencil-making, glazing, black-leading iron weapons (to stop them rusting) and making casting moulds for cannon bore and shot. German miners settled in Keswick, while locals found employment in providing lodging, transport and charcoal. Later, copper-mining took hold in the Keswick and Coniston areas, while slate-quarrying in Borrowdale had always taken place on a local basis and was to boom in later centuries. For most people, though, **domestic life** probably altered very little for three hundred years – clothes were still produced locally, while primitive agricultural methods and poor land kept yields relatively low. The general diet was largely unchanged since Viking times, based around oatmeal cakes or porridge, bread and cheese – potatoes weren't widely cultivated until the eighteenth century. Increasingly, however, houses were being built of durable stone (rather than turf and timber) and many of the Lake District's farms and cottages – including notable examples such as Townend at Troutbeck – can trace their origins back as far as the seventeenth century.

The Picturesque and the Romantic

Until the eighteenth century, it was difficult to persuade the wider world – or at least fashionable England – that the Lake District had anything to offer. Indeed, the old county of Cumberland (containing the northern part of the Lake District) was viewed as a dangerous, unstable corner of the kingdom, too close to lawless Scotland for comfort. William, Duke of Cumberland, the "butcher" son of George II, put down the Jacobite rebellion of 1745, and the fortified towers and castles on the lakeland periphery tell their own story of border raids and skirmishes.

A sea change occurred with the advent of the so-called **Picturesque Movement** in the late eighteenth century, when received notions of beauty shifted from the classical to the natural. Vivid, irregular landscapes were the fashion amongst writers and artists, and it was with a palpable sense of excitement that the era's style arbiters discovered such landscapes on their doorstep. The poet **Thomas Gray** made the first of two visits in 1767 and recorded his favourable impressions in his journal (published in 1775), while in 1778 **Thomas West** produced the first guidebook dedicated solely to the region, waxing lyrical about the "Alpine views and pastoral scenes in a sublime style". These, and a dozen other books or treatises touching on the Lake

District published during the 1770s, merely reinforced the contemporary Romantic view that contact with nature promoted artistic endeavour and human development. **Gainsborough**, **J.M.W. Turner** and, later, **Constable** were all eager visitors to the Lakes, and all drew inspiration from what they saw. The first visitors were encouraged to view the mountains and lakes in a methodical manner – from particular "stations" (ie, viewpoints) and through a "claude-glass" (or convex mirror) to frame the views.

The pre-eminent Romantic, **William Wordsworth**, was born in Cockermouth in 1770, moving to Dove Cottage outside Grasmere in 1799 and, in 1813, to nearby Rydal Mount. He became the centre of a famous, if fluctuating, literary circle – not only one of the so-called **Lake Poets** with **Samuel Taylor Coleridge** and **Robert Southey**, but also friend of the critic, essayist and Opium-Eater **Thomas De Quincey** and of the writer **John Wilson** ("Christopher North" of *Blackwood's Magazine*), and inspiration of future lakeland arrivals such as the Victorian social philosopher and critic **John Ruskin**. Wordsworth's own *Guide to the Lakes* – a mature distillation of all his thoughts on nature and beauty – was first published in 1810 and had gone through four further editions by 1835.

The eighteenth and nineteenth centuries

The **Industrial Revolution** didn't so much pass the Lake District by as touch its periphery. Carlisle was a cotton manufacturing town of some repute, while the coastal ports became important shipping centres and depots for nearby coal and iron industries. Georgian Whitehaven was Britain's third busiest port for a time in the late eighteenth century; Barrow-in-Furness is still an important shipbuilding town.

Within the Lakes themselves, sheep-farming remained the mainstay of the economy. Textile production still tended to take the form of homespun wool, as it had for centuries. However, the manufacture of wooden **bobbins** for the northwest's cotton mills later became an important local industry. There were also improvements in farming as turnips were introduced widely as a crop, which meant that cattle and sheep could be kept alive throughout the winter. Meanwhile, the French Revolution and the ensuing **Napoleonic wars** (1803–1815) not only preclud-

ed European travel (in part explaining the growing popularity of the Lakes with the English gentry) but also pushed food prices higher. As a consequence, farmers began to reclaim the once-common land of the hillsides, a tendency sanctioned by the General Enclosure Act of 1801. Most of the region's characteristic dry-stone walls were built at this time.

Copper-mining at Coniston became increasingly important, as did **slate-quarrying** at Honister Pass and around Elterwater. The still-visible scars, shafts and debris on the Old Man of Coniston and at Honister Pass are evidence of these booming trades.

Transport and communications improved slowly. Roads and packhorse routes that had been barely altered since Roman times saw improvement following the passing of the Turnpike Acts in the 1750s. High passes opened up to the passage of stagecoaches; while England's burgeoning canal system reached Kendal in 1819. The **railway age** arrived late, with early railway lines associated with the mining and quarrying industries. The first passenger line, in 1847, connected Kendal with Windermere – and prompted a furious battle with the elderly Wordsworth who, having spent years inviting appreciation of the Lake District by outsiders, now raged against the folly of making the region easier to visit. Not only was it easier to visit, but after 1869 the Lake District even had its very own indigenous candy to sweeten the tooth of visitors – **Kendal Mintcake**, a peppermint candy that's been the mainstay of climbing expeditions ever since. It's still made in Kendal today.

With the passing of Southey (1843) and Wordsworth (1850), the mantle of local literary endeavour passed to writer **Harriet Martineau** who lived at Ambleside between 1845 and 1876, and **Ruskin**, who settled at Brantwood near Coniston in 1872. Meanwhile, a seemingly endless succession of men and women of letters continued to visit or take a house, pronounce upon and then write about the region – **Sir Walter Scott**, **Percy Bysshe Shelley**, **Matthew Arnold**, **Alfred (Lord) Tennyson**, **Thomas Carlyle**, **George Eliot**, **Charlotte Brontë**, **Ralph Waldo Emerson** and **Nathaniel Hawthorne** all spent various periods in the Lake District. **Charles Dickens** and **Wilkie Collins** came together and climbed Carrock Fell, a trip recounted in Dickens' *Lazy Tour of Two Idle Apprentices* (1857).

The twentieth century: protecting the park

Some of those who made a career of boosting the Lake District were also among the first to notice that two thousand years of farming and two hundred years of industrialization were taking their toll. Ruskin's unsuccessful campaign to prevent the damming of Thirlmere was just one example of an increased **environmental awareness** which manifested itself most obviously in the **creation of the National Trust** in 1895. Ruskin's disciple, Octavia Hill, and a Keswick clergyman, Canon Rawnsley, were the Trust's co-founders (with Rawnsley its first Secretary) – Brandlehow Woods on Derwent Water's western shore was the Trust's first purchase in the Lakes (1902). The Trust is now the largest landholder in the Lake District, gaining early impetus from the generous bequests of **Beatrix Potter**, who has probably done more than anyone – after Wordsworth – to popularize the region through her children's stories.

The **formation of the Forestry Commission** in 1919 presented another threat to the natural landscape as afforestation gathered pace, turning previously bare valleys and fellsides into thick conifer plantations. Successful environmental battles in the 1930s limited the scope of the plantations, but afforestation is still an emotive subject today.

Similarly, **water extraction** has long fuelled fears for the landscape. The Lake District has been used as a water source for northwestern England since Thirlmere was dammed in 1892. Construction at Haweswater in the 1930s raised the water level there by ninety feet (and drowned a village in the process). Ennerdale Water still supplies the coastal towns and as late as 1980 there were serious proposals to raise levels there and at Wast Water in an attempt to drain more water for industrial use. Meanwhile, on the coast near Ravenglass, lurks **Sellafield nuclear-reprocessing plant**, symbol of all that threatens the local environment.

Legal protection of the Lake District was, therefore, long overdue by the time of the establishment in 1951 of the **Lake District National Park** now one of thirteen in England and Wales), spreading over 880 square miles, or half a million acres. For the first time, there was to be direct control over planning, building and development within the Lake District, as well as systematic maintenance of the footpaths, bridle ways, drystone walls, open land and historic monuments. The visitor centre at **Brockhole**, near Windermere, was the country's first National Park Visitor Centre.

In 1974, centuries of tradition were abandoned when local government reorganization resulted in the scrapping of the old counties of Cumberland, Westmorland and Lancashire: the Lake District became part of the new **county of Cumbria**.

The Lakes today

In many ways, the **continuing story of the Lakes** is that of the rest of modern rural England. Hill-farming is in crisis, with sheep farmers unable to turn a profit on their sheep and no amount of diversification – from farmhouse B&Bs to activity centres – addresses the deep-rooted problems of British farming. In a region where hunting with hounds dates back to Norman times, local concern about the fate of agriculture manifests itself in solid support for the pro-hunting "Countryside Alliance" cause. Others rail at the necessary development restrictions imposed by the National Park Authority, the National Trust (which owns a quarter of the land) and the district councils, which – to many locals – seem only to conspire against people from making a living on "their" land. At the same time, second-homers from the towns and cities ("off-comers" in the local parlance) push up housing prices, thus forcing the lakeland youth away from home and from the land. The mining and quarrying industries have largely collapsed and while tourism brings in jobs and money, much of the work is only seasonal and is poorly paid.

The **National Park** itself faces its own pressures since it's simply too successful for its own good. A local population of just 42,000 is swamped by annual visitor numbers topping sixteen million, with all the traffic and environmental pressure which that entails. Expanded bus services, the promotion of cycling and an integrated transport strategy are starting to have some effect, but it's a long haul to persuade people to leave their cars at home. Over three hundred **voluntary wardens** help manage the environment (patrolling lakeshores, maintaining footpaths, planting trees, restoring hedgerows and rebuilding stone walls) but they are faced with an exponential increase in leisure activities which impinge directly upon the Park's habitats –

such as mountain-biking, 4WD safaris and power-boating. Hikers, meanwhile, have seriously eroded the fellsides and turned trailheads and country lanes into car parks.

Happily, it's not all bad news. A new statutory "right to roam" across open countryside provides new rights for the public while safeguarding the landscape and wildlife. Over two thousand miles of paths and bridle ways are virtually all clear of obstructions and some have been made suitable for wheelchair users. Projects designed to preserve some of the Lake District's most threatened species (such as the red squirrel) are under

way, and new native woodlands are being established. **The Lake District Environmentally Sensitive Area** (ESA), set up in 1993, covers almost one thousand square miles of land in which traditional farm buildings are being restored, hedges and orchards re-planted, and moorland and riverbanks protected. **Sites of Special Scientific Interest** (SSIs) cover another seventeen percent of the Park. Conservation, at last, is being made fundamental to the National Park's well-being; the future challenge is to extend the same protection to lakeland traditions and the way of life.

Books

We've highlighted a selection of books below which will give you a flavour of Lake District life, past and present, as well as the impressions of the visitors, writers and poets who have toured and settled in the region. As a glance in any bookshop will show you, there are hundreds of lakeland titles available. We've concentrated on titles of interest to the general reader (which discounts most of the academic literary criticism of the Lake Poets) and those most useful to the non-specialist visitor – for rare historical monographs, mountain-climbing guides, lavish limited-edition pop-up Beatrix Potter books and other arcana, consult a specialist bookshop or the comprehensive Web site of the Internet bookseller Amazon (*www.amazon.co.uk* in the UK, *www.amazon.com* in the US).

Publishers are detailed with the UK publisher first, separated by an oblique slash from the US publisher, in cases where both exist. Where books are published in only one of these countries, UK or US follows the publisher's name; where the book is published by the same company in both countries, the name of the company appears just once. UP designates University Press. If a book is out of print, the year of its original publication is given followed by "o/p".

Lakeland life, travel and topography

Melvyn Bragg *Land of the Lakes* (Hodder & Stoughton, UK). Scholarly yet highly readable large-format introduction to lakeland history, society and culture. See overleaf for Bragg's novels.

Hunter Davies *A Walk Around the Lakes* (1978; o/p); *Good Guide to the Lakes* (Forster Davies, UK). The journalist and author Davies was born in Carlisle and takes every opportunity to plug the Lakes in print. His account of a walk around the region is an entertaining mix of anecdote, history and reportage; while the *Good Guide* is an idiosyncratic round-up of what he considers to be the "best" of the Lakes.

A.H. Griffin *Inside the Real Lakeland* (1961); *In Mountain Lakeland* (1963); *Pageant of Lakeland* (1966); *The Roof of England* (1968); *Still the Real Lakeland* (1970); and others; *The Coniston Tigers* (Sigma Press, UK). The lakelander climber, writer and former *Guardian* newspaper country diarist Harry Griffin produced a dozen volumes which ranged around the fells with a keen eye for nature and tradition. The early books are mostly out of print; *The Coniston Tigers*, his last book, is a climbing and walking memoir.

Norman Nicholson *The Lakers* (Cicerone Press, UK); *Portrait of the Lakes* (1965; o/p); *The Lake*

SECOND-HAND AND ANTIQUARIAN BOOKSHOPS

Those listed below are all recommended, especially if you're searching for out-of-print or interesting lakeland titles.

Ambleside: The Little Bookshop, 1 Cheapside (☎015394/32094).

Cartmel: Peter Bain Smith, Bank Court, Market Square (☎015395/36369).

Gosforth: Archie Miles, Beck Place, Main St (☎019467/25792).

Whitehaven: Michael Moon, 19 Lowther St (☎01946/599 010).

Windermere: Bookfare, 21 Victoria St (☎015394/45855).

District: An Anthology (o/p). Cumbria's best-known poet turns to prose with his informed, sympathetic studies of lakeland life, history, geology and people. The comprehensive *Anthology* is a joy, with extracts from writings of every period since the first visitors, and incorporating dialect verse, legends, letters and journals.

Nikolaus Pevsner *Cumberland and Westmorland* (Penguin, UK). The regional edition of Pevsner's classic architectural guide to the old counties of England. First published in 1967 (when there was still a Cumberland and Westmorland, rather than Cumbria) and detailing every church, hall, house and cross worth looking at.

William Wordsworth *Guide to the Lakes* (Oxford UP). The old curmudgeon's guide to the Lakes went through five editions between 1810 and 1835. This facsimile of the last, and definitive, edition is full of his prejudices (on the "colouring" of buildings, the shape of chimneys, forestation, the railway, the great unwashed) and timeless scenic observations.

Walking and cycling guides

Bill Birkett *Complete Lakeland Fells* (HarperCollins); *Lakeland Fells Almanac* (Neil Wilson Publishing, UK). The *Complete* edition is the definitive, modern fell-walking reference

guide from a leading Cumbrian mountain writer and photographer; classic walks to the top of 541 separate fells for all levels of walker. The *Almanac* distils the *Complete* fells into 129 circular walks taking in the tops, with maps, times and route details.

Anthony Burton *The Cumbria Way* (Aurum Press, UK). This is the guide to pack for the 72-mile Cumbria Way (Ulverston to Carlisle), which cuts right through the heart of the Lakes. Clear walking instructions, Ordnance Survey map extracts, plus history and anecdotes.

Nick Cotton *Cycle Tours* (Ordnance Survey). The trusted choice for cyclists – 24 one-day bike routes in Cumbria and the Lakes, ring-bound, with clear maps and detailed directions.

Pathfinder Guide *Lake District Walks; More Lake District Walks* (both Jarrold, UK). The best walking guides for the back pack: slim volumes of walks, graded from short-and-easy to challenging, with accompanying text and Ordnance Survey map extracts.

Walt Unsworth *Classic Walks in the Lake District* (Haynes, UK). Coffee-table format, detailing forty great hikes, from afternoon strolls to the classic horseshoe routes and famous ascents.

A. Wainwright *A Pictorial Guide to the Lakeland Fells* (7 vols); *In the Valleys of Lakeland; On the*

HISTORIC GUIDEBOOKS

The first guidebook to the Lake District was written in the late-eighteenth century and dozens more followed as the region opened up to people of leisure. Most of the earliest guides are long out of print but a trawl through the stock in any local second-hand/antiquarian bookshop throws up old copies of other classic publications. They make interesting souvenirs, while you'll often find that the landscapes described have hardly changed in more than a century.

The earliest lakeland writings were contained in the journal of the poet **Thomas Gray**, first published as part of **Thomas West's** *Guide to the Lakes in Cumberland, Westmorland and Lancashire* (1778). In 1810, **William Wordsworth** wrote down his own observations, appearing in the most complete form as his *Guide to the Lakes* (1835) which, alone of all the historic guides, is still in print (see above).

His friend in later life, the writer and political observer **Harriet Martineau** of Ambleside, produced her own *Complete Guide to the English Lakes* (1855). Fifty years later, **W.G. Collingwood**'s *The Lake Counties* (1902) set new standards of erudition, while **Canon H.D. Rawnsley** (founder of the National Trust) also found time to produce a multitude of lakeland volumes: *Round the Lake Country* (1909) is typical. Between 1904 and 1925, in the days before cheaply available colour photography, landscape watercolourist **Alfred Heaton Cooper** illustrated guidebooks for A. & C. Black; the Lake District titles are fairly easy to come by, as are the four lakeland books illustrated by his son **William Heaton Cooper**, starting with *The Hills of Lakeland* (1938). *The Lake Counties* (1937) volume in **Arthur Mee**'s classic "King's England" series is widely available too.

Lakeland Mountain Passes; Favourite Lakeland Mountains; Fellwalking with Wainwright (all Michael Joseph, UK). Wainwright's Pictorial Guide is his masterpiece: seven beautifully produced small-format volumes of handwritten notes and sketches (written between 1952 and 1966) guiding generations of walkers up the mountains of the Lake District. Later spin-off publications (most with superb photography by Derry Brabbs) include Wainwright in elegiac mood, holding forth on the majesty of lakeland mountains, passes and valleys.

Lakeland books, novels and journals

Melvyn Bragg The Maid of Buttermere (Sceptre/Putnam); Without A City Wall (Sceptre, UK); The Silken Net (Sceptre, UK); The Second Inheritance (Sceptre, UK); For Want of a Nail (Sceptre, UK); The Soldier's Return (Hodder & Stoughton). The writer, broadcaster, professional Cumbrian (born in Wigton) and butt of Dame Edna Everage – "don't write any more, Melvyn dear, or we'll never catch up" – Bragg is at his best in The Maid of Buttermere, a fictionalized romantic tragedy involving one of the Lakes' most enduring heroines, and in The Soldier's Return, a Cumbrian tale drawing heavily on the experiences of his own family. Other novels all lovingly explore the Cumbrian past and present.

Beatrix Potter The Tale of Peter Rabbit; The Tale of Jemima Puddle-duck; The Tale of Squirrel Nutkin; and many more (all Frederick Warne). Rabbits, pigs, hedgehogs, mice and ducks in lakeland stories of valour, betrayal, adventure and romance. The original twenty-odd titles have metamorphosed into literally hundreds of different formats at varying prices – colouring books, pop-up books, foam-filled fabric books . . .

Arthur Ransome Swallows and Amazons; Swallowdale; Winter Holiday; Pigeon Post; The Picts and the Martyrs (Red Fox, UK). Ransome's innocent childhood stories of pirates and treasure, secret harbours and outdoor camps, summer holidays and winter freezes still possess the power to entrance. The series starts with Swallows and Amazons (first published 1930), and there's no better evocation of the drawn-out halcyon days of childhood.

Hugh Walpole Rogue Herries; Judith Paris; The Fortress; Vanessa (all Sutton, UK). Largely forgotten now, Walpole was a successful writer by the time he moved to the Lake District in 1923. He immersed himself in the local history to produce four volumes covering two hundred years of the rip-roaring lives and loves of the Herries clan – too flowery for today's tastes but full of lakeland lore and life.

Dorothy Wordsworth The Grasmere Journals (Oxford UP/Clarendon Press); Home at Grasmere (Penguin). Was she a poet in her own right? Judge for yourself from the sharply observed descriptions of nature and day-to-day Grasmere life contained in the Journals. Home at Grasmere lets you see the debt Wordsworth owed his sister by placing journal entries and completed poetry side by side.

People

Hugh Brogan The Life of Arthur Ransome (Jonathan Cape, UK); Signalling From Mars (Pimlico, UK); The Letters of Arthur Ransome (Pimlico, UK). Ransome's biographer adds flesh and bones to a fascinating man – Ransome was a journalist and Russian political expert before he was a childrens' writer – and gets to the bottom of the books' influences. The edited letters chart Ransome's life, marriages, sailing and writing career – a useful counterweight to Ransome's own (now out-of-print) Autobiography (1976).

A.S. Byatt Unruly Times (Vintage/Random House). Authoritative, insightful study of Wordsworth and Coleridge "in their times", which charts their relationship, ideas, work and family situation against a lively backdrop of contemporary politics, society and culture.

Hunter Davies Wainwright: The Biography (Penguin); William Wordsworth (Sutton, UK). Davies turns his informal, chatty style upon two of the Lake District's biggest enigmas. Hard biographical detail aside, there's not much to learn about the character of either man that a close reading of their respective works won't tell you already – but then that's not Davies's fault.

Stephen Gill William Wordsworth: A Life (Oxford UP/Clarendon Press). The standard academic biography (published 1989), relying on close readings of the manuscripts and contemporary records to build up a cradle-to-grave account of a poet's single-minded dedication to his work at the expense of friends, relationships and politics.

Richard Holmes Coleridge: Early Visions (Harper-Collins/Pantheon); Coleridge: Darker Reflections

(HarperCollins/Pantheon). The supreme account of the troubled genius of Coleridge, who emerges from Holmes's acclaimed two-volume biography as an animated intellectual and creative poet in his own right as well as the catalyst for Wordsworth's poetic development.

Kenneth R. Johnston *The Hidden Wordsworth: Poet, Lover, Rebel, Spy* (W.W. Norton). Tries to inject some controversy into Wordsworthian circles but the conclusions are hardly earth-shattering: illegitimate child – yes, and his sister knew; was he excited by the French Revolution – yes; was he a spy – not really.

Kathleen Jones *A Passionate Sisterhood* (Virago, UK). Welcome feminist take on the lives of the sisters, wives and daughters of the Lake Poets, whose letters and journals reveal not quite the rustic idyll we've been led to expect by the poetry.

Margaret Lane *The Tale of Beatrix Potter* (Penguin). The standard biography (written in 1946, shortly after her death) of the tale-writing, sheep-farming Mrs Heelis. No reason to disagree with the author's assessment that this is a "modest and unsensational" account of Potter's life and work.

Thomas De Quincey *Confessions of an English Opium-Eater* (Penguin/Oxford UP); *Recollections of the Lakes and the Lake Poets* (Penguin). Tripping out with the best-known literary drugtaker after Coleridge – "Fear and Loathing in Grasmere" it isn't, but neither is the *Confessions* a simple cautionary tale. The famous *Recollections* collected together magazine features De Quincey wrote in the 1830s, providing a highly readable, often catty, account of life in the Lakes with the Wordsworths, the Coleridges and Southey.

Mark Storey *Robert Southey: A Life* (Oxford UP). Generally eclipsed by the shining lights of Coleridge and Wordsworth, Southey's reputation is somewhat rehabilitated by this biography – although he's little known now, in his day Southey was a major man of letters, expert on Brazil, and Poet Laureate (not to mention surrogate father and husband to the Coleridge brood).

Poetry

Samuel Taylor Coleridge *Selected Poems* (Penguin); *The Complete Poems* (Penguin); *Critical Edition of the Major Works* (Oxford UP). Final texts of all the poems in varying editions: the Penguin *Selected* (edited by his biographer Richard Holmes) also includes extracts from Coleridge's verse plays and prefaces; the *Complete* edition includes unfinished verses.

Norman Nicholson *Collected Poems* (Faber & Faber, UK). The bard of Cumbria – who lived all his life in Millom, on the coast – produced five books of verse by the time of his death in 1987, collected here. He writes beautifully and movingly of his country, its trades, its past and its people.

William Wordsworth *The Prelude* (Penguin); *Lyrical Ballads* (Penguin); *Poetical Works* (Oxford UP); *Selected Poems* (Penguin). There are dozens of editions of the works of Wordsworth on the market, but these are the current pick. The major poems, sonnets and odes are all collected in *Selected Poems*, which has the advantage of being a cheap, pocket-sized edition. For the full text of major works, you'll need *Lyrical Ballads* and *The Prelude* – the latter presenting the four separate texts of 1798, 1799, 1805 and 1850 (Wordsworth revised his original, 1798, text three times, the last published after his death). *Poetical Works* contains every piece of verse ever published by Wordsworth.

Climbing in the Lake District

Two centuries ago, no one climbed rocks for fun. That's not to say that people didn't go up mountains, but they would never have thought of themselves as climbers or what they were doing as a sport. Shepherds, soldiers and traders ventured onto high ground, but only with good reason. Mountains were the stuff of myth and legend – useless to farmers, dangerous to travellers, largely unknown and often feared. Daniel Defoe, writing of the Lake District in the 1720s, thought the region's mountains "had a kind of inhospitable terror in them"; and Dr Johnson, some fifty years later, was "astonished and repelled by this wide extent of hopeless sterility". But revolution was afoot in the late-eighteenth century, as much in man's perception of the natural world as in politics, and two new influences were making themselves felt upon the landscapes of Europe: Romanticism and the urge for scientific discovery.

Early steps

In August 1786, Mont Blanc in the French Alps (the highest summit in Western Europe) was climbed for the first time by a young Chamonix doctor, **Michel-Gabriel Paccard**, and his porter **Jacques Balmat**. The pair made notes, and collected botanical and geological specimens as they went – and picked up a substantial prize in addition, offered by the Swiss scientist and explorer Horace-Benedict de Saussure for the first successful ascent. Given that only eighty years previ-

ously a serious attempt had been made to seek out and classify "alpine dragons", Paccard's climb was both a mountaineering *tour de force* and a triumph of scientific rationalism over superstition.

In England it was the artistic, rather than the scientific, community which began to influence the general attitude towards the Lake District's own, lesser, mountain range. **The Picturesque Movement**, precursor of Romanticism, had made the depiction of landscape fashionable and, by the 1760s, various English artists were making good money out of the developing public taste for mountainous scenery. Idealized prints of Derwent Water by Thomas Smith and William Bellers proved both popular and profitable; while in 1783, the renowned artist Thomas Gainsborough visited the Lakes and produced three well-received works (including one of the Langdale Pikes).

Capturing the prevailing Romantic spirit, other visitors published successful accounts of their lakeland expeditions, and in the writings of **William Gilpin**, **Thomas West** and novelist **Mrs Ann Radcliffe** are found the first descriptions of mountains as objects to be climbed (primarily for the "picturesque" views from the top). But the relatively easy ascent of Skiddaw aside (which could be conquered on horseback), most Lake District mountain-tops were still well off-limits. It took the energy and vision of an opium-riddled, rheumatic poet to transform the way people regarded lakeland crags and cliffs.

Coleridge and the birth of rock climbing

If Wordsworth was the great walker in the Lake District, then **Samuel Taylor Coleridge** was the pioneer of rock-climbing. In August 1802, setting off from his home in Keswick, he made a nine-day solo tour – which he dubbed his "circumcursion" – taking in the peaks and valleys of the central and western Lakes in a hundred-mile circuit. Coleridge was escaping a troubled marriage and an ebbing literary career and, recording his travels in his journal and in a series of letters to his beloved "Asra" (Wordsworth's sister-in-law, Sara Hutchinson), he became the sport's first great writer.

Coleridge had no time for most contemporary visitors to the Lakes, who tended to follow the same routes set down by early guidebook writers, viewing picturesque beauty spots from pre-determined stations and idling in boats. Coleridge's was a wilder spirit and it was with a real sense of exhilaration that he found himself on the top of **Scafell** on the fifth day of his tour. In a famous passage from his journal he records his hair-raising descent, dropping down the successive ledges of **Broad Stand** by hanging over them from his finger-tips. In this manner, he soon found himself in a position where: ". . . every Drop increased the Palsy of my Limbs . . . and now I had only two more to drop down, to return was impossible – but of these two the first was tremendous, it was twice my own height, and the Ledge at the bottom was so exceedingly narrow, that if I dropt down upon it I must of necessity have fallen backwards and of course killed myself." A moment's reflection brought respite: "I know not how to proceed, how to return, but I am calm and fearless and confident."

This ability to overcome the body's response to fear is a quality all climbers must possess and Coleridge's breathless account marks him out as a true mountaineer. His descent of Broad Stand may have been accidental but his reasons for being on the fells, and his response to them, would be understood by any modern climber. He revelled in the activity for its own sake and in his "stretched and anxious state of mind" he discovered calm and an escape from the cares of home.

Others followed Coleridge onto the fells. The description of Ennerdale's **Pillar Rock** as "unclimbable" by a guidebook writer, John Otley, in 1825, led to a competition among local dalesmen to ascend the only sizeable summit in the area that could not be gained by walking alone. It was duly scaled in 1826 by a shepherd, **John Atkinson**. By 1875, some fifty annual ascents were being recorded, amongst them that of the first woman, a Miss Barker of Gosforth, and a fourteen-year-old boy, Lawrence Pilkington, later a pioneering Alpine climber (and the founder of the famous glass company).

Wasdale and the Victorian climbers

For the most part, the Lake District crags were largely ignored by daring English gentlemen climbers and their professional guides.

Mountaineering meant Alpine glaciers and snow ridges, and most Alpinists regarded lakeland rock-climbers as mere "chimney sweeps" and "rock gymnasts". But change was in the air. A handful of more broad-minded climbers began to gather for winter practice at **Wasdale Head**, from where Coleridge had set off for Scafell in 1802. On the whole they were professional men from the industrial cities or academics, with the time and energy to indulge their passion for the mountains. From their ranks came the Cambridge classicist and unlikely sporting revolutionary **Walter Parry Haskett Smith**. Having been introduced to the high fells at Wasdale in 1881, Haskett Smith returned the following year and set out to discover challenging routes up the gullies and chimneys that cleave their way through the rocks. Climbing for the sheer thrill of it, Haskett Smith began to record his routes, guiding those who might choose to follow his footsteps and hand-holds. The visitor's book at the **Wastwater Hotel** (now the Wasdale Head Inn) became the lakeland climber's bible, and the hotel doubled as the rock climbers' clubhouse.

An almost chivalrous code developed amongst the climbers: comradeship tempered the excesses of competition, and bar-room bragging was not tolerated. These men found in climbing an escape from the demands of their professions, families and society, and a few days spent at Wasdale each year was an excuse for the sort of behaviour not usually associated with the staid lives of Victorian gentlemen. After a hard day on the crag, there were often evening gymnastic revelries: the "billiard room traverse" – circling and leaving the room without touching the floor – or the "passage of the billiard table leg", completed by climbing beneath the table and around a table leg. Boyish games, certainly, but by the end of the century these supple lakeland climbers were pioneering routes unmatched anywhere else in the country.

In 1886, Haskett Smith made the first ascent of **Napes Needle**, that slender pillar of rock that rises on the southern flank of Great Gable. This was no simple gully scramble, nor could it be rationalized as merely an alternative route to a fell-top. This was climbing pure and simple, and climbing for its own sake at that. If one climb set the standard for a new sport, this was it. The route is short, but exposed, and is still many a novice's first lakeland climb. Haskett Smith did it alone, unroped and in nailed boots, at the end of a full day in the hills. (He later repeated this pioneering climb on its 50th anniversary, when he was a sprightly 76-year-old.)

Haskett Smith's exploits didn't go unnoticed. **Owen Glynne Jones**, the son of a Welsh carpenter, was teaching at the City of London School when, in 1891, he saw a photograph of Napes Needle in a shop on the Strand, and within a fortnight had climbed it during his Easter holidays. He was a bold, brash man ("The Only Genuine Jones", as he called himself), who climbed ferociously well and pioneered several physically demanding routes, eagerly taking up the right of first ascenders to name new climbs (a tradition that remains to this day) – "Jones's Route Direct" on Scafell owes its name to him.

Jones came to dominate lakeland climbing in the 1890s, doing much to publicize the new sport in the process. In 1897, his book, *Rock Climbing in the English Lake District* was published, including thirty magnificent full-page photographs by Keswick brothers and photographers **George** and **Ashley Abraham** – examples of these pictures still hang in Keswick shops and pubs, and in the Wasdale Head Inn. Jones's accompanying descriptions of the routes included **grades** allocated according to the difficulty of the climb – from Easy to Severe. This was the first attempt to put some order into what had been, until now, a sport without classification and Jones's basic grading framework still stands, although there are now some twenty intermediate and additional grades (to accommodate the huge rise in standards over the last century).

Danger and progress on the fells

Jones was killed in a fall in the Alps in 1899 and his death highlighted the dangers facing the early climbers. Their **specialist equipment** was basically limited to nails arranged in varying patterns on the sole or around the edge of the boot to help grip the rock. Heavy hemp ropes (as used when crossing crevasse-strewn Alpine glaciers) were of dubious benefit on lakeland crags. Two or more climbers might rope themselves together but, as the rope itself was not attached to the rock (as it is today), the chances of surviving a fall were slim. Put bluntly, it was "one off, all off" and the tragic results can be seen in St Olaf's graveyard at Wasdale Head, where three headstones mark the graves of a roped party who fell together from the Pinnacle Face of Scafell in 1906.

Some measure of organization came to lakeland rock-climbing with the establishment in 1907 of the **Fell and Rock Climbing Club (FRCC)** of the English Lake District. Ashley Abraham became its president, with honorary memberships granted to Haskett Smith, Cecil Slingsby (a great lakeland climber on Scafell and Gable, and probably the first Englishman to learn the art of skiing) and Norman Collie (an experienced climber in Skye, the Alps, the Rockies and the Himalayas, who also found time to discover the gas neon and develop the first practical application of the X-ray). The Fell and Rock, as the club came to be known, not only promoted safer climbing techniques but helped usher the sport out of the Victorian age with its revolutionary acceptance of women members (something the more established Alpine Club didn't do until after World War II).

Meanwhile, lakeland climbers continued to push at the boundaries of possibility. **Siegfried Herford** (Welsh-born but with a German mother) began climbing in 1907 and his eventual ascent of **Central Buttress** on Scafell in the spring of 1914 was a landmark climb, requiring a new grade to be added to the grading framework – it was so tough, no one else repeated the climb for seven years.

A democratic sport

By the **mid-1930s**, climbing had become a popular, rather than a specialist, pastime. Partly, this was because it was now a safer sport than it had been: rubber-soled gym shoes were worn in dry weather rather than nailed boots, and rope techniques had improved markedly. But, more importantly, what had once been the preserve of daring gentlemen was now open to all – better road access, more holiday time, and the establishment of youth hostels and rambling clubs all brought new faces onto the crags.

Jim Birkett, a quarryman from Langdale, and **Bill Peascod**, a Workington coal-miner, were typical of the new breed of climber. Birkett was a reserved man and a traditionalist, who kept climbing in nailed boots long after his contemporaries had abandoned them. On May 1, 1938, he pioneered his first classic route on **Scafell East Buttress**, calling it "May Day". This was followed by "Gremlin's Groove" on the same face and two other classics on **Esk Buttress** ("Afterthought" and "Frustration"), before Birkett turned his attention to **Castle Rock** in Thirlmere, climbing what was then known as the Lakeland Everest in April 1939 by a route he called "Overhanging Bastion". Meanwhile, the more extrovert Peascod was making similar advances in **Buttermere**, with routes such as "Eagle Front", climbed in June 1940, followed by nine other new routes of a similarly severe standard in 1941.

Popularity and professionalism

By **the 1960s**, thanks to the conquest of Everest, climbing rode high in the public conscience. Men like **Joe Brown** and **Chris Bonington** became household names – although they were better known for their achievements in the Alps and Himalayas than for any of the notable lakeland routes they had also created. Other British climbers were also branching out from the Lakes, not only to Scotland and Wales but to the warmer rocks of France, Spain and Morocco. However, fashions come and go and the Lake District has always attracted climbers back, drawn by the huge variety of rock faces crammed into such a tightly packed mountain range.

By **the 1970s**, an increasing number of professional climbers were taking a new approach to their sport, training as hard as any top athlete in order to push the boundaries still further. Typical of this single-minded athleticism were the exploits of the Yorkshireman **Pete Livesey**, whose great lakeland season came in 1974. In **Borrowdale** alone he put up four routes of such a magnitude that many at first thought them impossible without using "aid" (pitons, ropes or other artificial help on the rock). But Livesey maintained the tradition of so-called "free climbing" (whereby equipment is used only to provide safety in the event of a fall), thus proving it was simply another psychological barrier that had to be broken. Soon others were climbing even more "impossible" routes than Livesey. **Bill Birkett** – son of the Langdale climber, Jim – undertook some audacious climbing in the Patterdale area, most notably on **Dove Crag**, in the 1970s and 1980s. And today, Bill's cousin, **Dave Birkett**, is creating a new standard right back in the heart of Langdale:

on Pavey Ark, his "Impact Day" (graded Extreme 9) is about as tough as it gets in the Lakes.

Modern equipment and challenges

Climbing equipment has developed alongside the athletic professionalism. Nailed boots and gym shoes have given way to specialized climbing shoes, first developed in the 1950s by the French climber Pierre Allain (and known by his initials as PAs). Where Haskett Smith would have climbed in tweeds, modern climbers don multicoloured Lycra leggings: chalk bags hang from belts, ready to dry sweat-dampened fingers, along with a battery of safety chocks and slings, placed in the rock to give the nylon rope a secure anchor point in the event of a fall. Despite the severity of today's climbing, accidents are few and far between, since a securely placed sling or "runner" (through which the rope is clipped) holds anyone whose ambition out-runs their ability. There was a move towards "**aid climbing**" in the Lakes in the 1960s, when pitons and screws were used to assist an ascent, but it was largely frowned upon and today nearly all lakeland climbers climb "**free**"; that is by their own efforts alone.

The number of climbers on the Lake District's crags has increased to such an extent that queues now form on popular routes in the summer. But there are still **challenging routes** to be discovered alongside the classics on Gable and Scafell. Hikers, meanwhile, have the history of climbing all around them. Take a walk up from the Wasdale Head Inn, and the very names of the features around the Great Napes on Great Gable – Sphinx Ridge, Needle Gulley and Napes Needle itself – are all attributable to the pioneer climbers. You may not know it, and it will not be listed by the Ordnance Survey, but on Scafell Crag you could pass by "Botterill's Slab" (1903, F.W. Botterill), "Pegasus" (1952, A. Dolphin & P. Greenwood) or "The White Wizard" (1976, C.J.S. Bonington & N. Estcourt), and find climbers on each. All are finding something different in the challenge of hand and foot on rock, and all are, in their own way, conquering the impossible. In that, nothing has changed.

William Wordsworth: A Life

"Wordsworth was of a good height, just five feet ten, and not a slender man . . . Meantime his face . . . was certainly the noblest for intellectual effects that, in actual life, I have seen."

Thomas De Quincey,
Recollections of the Lake and Lake Poets

William Wordsworth and the Lake District are inextricably linked, and in the streets of Grasmere, Hawkshead and Cockermouth, and the fells surrounding Ullswater, Borrowdale and the Duddon Valley you're never very far away from a house or a sight associated with the poet and his circle. His birthplace, houses, favourite spots and final resting-place are all covered in the Guide, together with anecdotes about, and analysis of, his day-to-day life, his poetry and personal relationships. Below, a general biographical account of Wordsworth's life is provided to place the various sites and accounts in context.

Childhood, school and university

William Wordsworth was **born in Cockermouth** (April 7, 1770), the second-eldest of four brothers and a sister, Dorothy. His father, John, was agent and lawyer for a local landowner, Sir James Lowther, and the family was comfortably off, as the surviving Wordsworth home in Cockermouth attests. The children spent much time with their grandparents in Penrith – William even attended a school there – and when their mother Ann died (she was only thirty) in 1778, the family was split up: Dorothy was sent to live with relations in Halifax in Yorkshire, while William and his older brother Richard began life at the respected **grammar school in Hawkshead**, lodging with **Ann Tyson** and going back to Penrith or Cockermouth in the holidays. On his father's death in 1783, William and the other children were left in relative poverty as the Lowthers refused to pay John Wordsworth's long-owed salary (indeed, it was almost twenty years before the debt was honoured).

At school in Hawkshead, Wordsworth (now supported by his uncles) flourished, storing up childhood experiences of ice-skating, climbing, fishing and dancing that would later emerge in his most celebrated poetry. In 1787, finished with school and clutching new clothes made for him by Ann Tyson and the already devoted Dorothy, Wordsworth went up to **St John's College, Cambridge**, where his uncles intended that he should study to become a clergyman. His academic promise soon fizzled out. Despite a bright start – to his evident amusement, De Quincey later recalled that Wordsworth briefly became a "dandy", sporting silk stockings and powdered hair – he abandoned his formal studies and left in 1790 without distinction and with no prospect of being ordained. His uncles were furious, but Wordsworth had other plans for his future.

In France

A walking tour through **France and the Alps** in the summer of 1790 excited the young, idealistic Wordsworth who had grand thoughts of being a poet. His interest was fired by the contemporary revolutionary movements of Europe. The Bastille had fallen the previous year and Wordsworth's early republicanism flowered ("Bliss was it in that dawn to be alive, but to be young was very Heaven!"). He returned to France in 1791 where he met one **Annette Vallon**, with whom he fell in love – she became pregnant, giving birth to their child, Caroline, in December 1792. But by this time, Wordsworth had returned to England, to oversee the publication, in 1793, of his first works, *Descriptive Sketches* (inspired by his revolutionary travels) and the lakeland reverie *An Evening Walk*. When war broke out between England and France in 1793 Wordsworth was unable to return to France or to Annette; they didn't meet again until 1802.

Depressed by the events of the Terror in France, which rather dented his revolutionary enthusiasm, Wordsworth alternated between fretting and idling in London and making walking tours around England. He thought he might become a teacher and shared Dorothy's oft-expressed dream of setting up home together and devoting his life to poetry – something that at last seemed possible when a small, but unexpected, bequest from the dying **Raisley Calvert**, the brother of an old schoolfriend, gave him just enough to live on.

Becoming a poet: the Lyrical Ballads and Germany

William and Dorothy moved to **Dorset** in 1795 (where they'd been offered a house), and William became acquainted with a fiery, widely read, passionate young critic and writer. **Samuel Taylor Coleridge** had read and admired Wordsworth's two published works and, on meeting Wordsworth himself, was almost overcome with enthusiasm for his ideas and passions. There's no doubt that they inspired each other and the Wordsworths moved to **Somerset** to be near Coleridge – "three people, but one soul", as Coleridge later had it. Here they collaborated on what became the **Lyrical Ballads** (1798), a work which could be said to mark the onset of English Romantic poetry and which contained some of Wordsworth's finest early writing (quite apart from Coleridge's *The Rime of the Ancient Mariner*): not just the famous *Lines Written above Tintern Abbey*, but also snatches later incorporated into *The Prelude* (Wordsworth's great autobiographical work, unpublished during his lifetime – Wordsworth only ever knew it as the "Poem on my own Life"). It's hard to see today quite how unusual the *Lyrical Ballads* were for their time: conceived as "experiments", the mixture of simple poems with a rustic, natural content and longer narrative works flew right in the face of contemporary classicism. Sales and reviews were universally poor.

Wordsworth, Dorothy and Coleridge went to **Germany** in 1798, during which time their joint idea for a long autobiographical, philosophical work began to gel in Wordsworth's mind. He produced a first version of *The Prelude* in Germany, along with the affecting "Lucy" poems (including "Strange fits of passion have I known"), which some say pointed to an unnatural passion for his sister. It was certainly an unusual relationship: Dorothy devoted herself entirely to William (her favourite brother since childhood) and his work; she kept house for him, walked with him, listened to his poems, transcribed and made copies of them, and he wrote passionate poems about nameless women who could be no one else but Dorothy. But there's no evidence – to be blunt – that she slept with him, despite the claims of some critics.

Grasmere

In 1799 William and Dorothy moved to **Grasmere** (and Coleridge followed), in the search both for conducive natural surroundings in which Wordsworth's work could flourish and for somewhere they could survive on a restricted budget. William was to spend the last two-thirds of his life in and around the village.

Brother and sister first moved into **Dove Cottage** where they remained until 1808, a period in which Wordsworth established himself as a major poet. A new edition of the *Lyrical Ballads* (1801) appeared, including some of the poems he'd written in Germany together with his first major Grasmere poems, such as *The Brothers* and *Michael*, based on local stories and characters. This edition also included its famous **preface** expounding his theories of poetry (against "inane phraseology"; for simple, natural, emotive language), which many critics found arrogant. Wordsworth was at his most productive in the years to 1805, resulting in the publication of *Poems in Two Volumes* (1807), containing the celebrated odes to "Duty" and "Immortality", the Westminster Bridge sonnet, the "Daffodils" poem (untitled when first published) and a hundred other new poems and sonnets. A third edition of *Lyrical Ballads* appeared, and he had also found time to expand and complete a second version of *The Prelude*. All this early work set new standards in poetry: questioning the nature of perception, challenging contemporary prejudices and orchestrating a highly original vision of the human soul within nature.

Dorothy, meanwhile, kept a **journal** recording life at Dove Cottage which has become a classic in its own right. Her skilled observations of the local people and landscape prompted some of William's best-known work, most famously the "Daffodils" stanzas – Wordsworth relied heavily on her journal for the famous images of the flowers dancing and reeling in the breeze.

Marriage and money

Wordsworth's dire financial position slowly improved. His sales and reviews weren't getting any better (Byron trashed most of *Poems in Two Volumes*) but the Lowthers finally stumped up the debt owed to William's long-dead father. This allowed him to marry an old childhood friend from Penrith, **Mary Hutchinson**, in 1802, having first travelled with Dorothy to France to make amends with his first love Annette; Wordsworth later provided an annuity for Annette and their young daughter. Outwardly, the **marriage to Mary** seemed precipitous and passionless and scholars have speculated about Wordsworth's motives, though letters between William and his wife (discovered in the 1970s) tend to scotch the myth that he was marrying out of duty. **Children** followed – John, Dorothy (always known as Dora), Thomas, Catherine and William – though Catherine and then Thomas, both infants, succumbed to mortal illnesses in the same tragic year of 1812.

Dove Cottage became too small for comfort as the family grew. His wife's sister, Sara Hutchinson, was a permanent fixture, as was Coleridge (by now separated from his wife) and his visiting children. The Wordsworths moved to other houses in Grasmere (Allan Bank and the Old Rectory), and then in 1813 finally settled on **Rydal Mount**, a gracious house two miles south of the village. Here William lived out the rest of his life, supported for some years by his salaried position as **Distributor of Stamps for Westmorland** (good fortune, caused as De Quincey noted, by the current incumbent distributing "himself and his office into two different places"). It was hardly a sinecure – he had to travel through the county, collecting dues and granting licences, work which he undertook assiduously – but it brought him in £200 a year.

The Rydal years

Wordsworth may have already written his finest poetry, but after the move to Rydal he was at the peak of his fame. Over the years, the literary world made its way to his door, a procession recorded in detail by the critic and essayist **Thomas De Quincey** who first made the pilgrimage to Grasmere to meet his hero in 1807. After a long friendship interrupted by disagreements, De Quincey's frank series of articles on Wordsworth and his family in 1839 (later published as *Recollections of the Lakes and the Lake Poets*) caused an irreparable rift. **Coleridge**, too, was *persona non grata* after a falling-out in 1810, though the two old friends did come to some kind of an accommodation in later life, and *The Prelude* remained dedicated to him.

There were family setbacks. The death of William's brother, John, in 1805 had affected him deeply (and led later to a burgeoning religious faith); after 1828, his beloved sister Dorothy suffered a series of depressive illnesses, which incapacitated her mind for most of the rest of her long life; and his wife's sister, Sara Hutchinson – who had so besotted Coleridge and who had lived with them for thirty years – died of the flu in 1835.

Wordsworth continued to be productive, at least in the early Rydal years. *The Excursion* (1814), long enough in itself, was conceived as part of an even longer philosophical work to be called "The Recluse", which he never completed. His first *Collected Poems* appeared the following year, together with *The White Doe of Rylstone*; but it wasn't until *Peter Bell* (1819) and *The River Duddon* sonnets (1820) that sales and reviews finally flourished. His *Vaudracour and Julia* (1819) also had deep significance: a tale of seduction, it was a fictionalized account of his affair with Annette.

As Wordsworth grew older he lost the radicalism of his youth, becoming a loud opponent of democracy, liberalism and progress. Political developments in France and the threat of the mob and the Reform Bill at home appalled him. His views on nature and the picturesque had led him to produce his own descriptive **Guide to the Lakes** ("for the minds of persons of taste"), at first published anonymously (1810) to accompany a book of drawings; its later popularity (a final, fifth edition, appeared in 1835) did much to advertise the very charms of the region he was keen to preserve. In the end, fulminating against the whitewashed houses and fir plantations he thought were disfiguring the Lakes, Wordsworth retreated to his beloved garden at Rydal Mount.

Apart from the rare crafted sonnet or couplet, Wordsworth's later work was largely undistinguished. The third major revision of *The Prelude* had been completed in 1838; the poem didn't see the light of day until after his death, when Mary gave it a name and handed it over for publication. But in 1843, on the death of Robert Southey and at the age of 73, Wordsworth's position as Grand Old Man of the literary establishment was confirmed by his appointment as **Poet Laureate**.

After his **death in 1850**, William's body was interred in St Oswald's churchyard in Grasmere, to be later joined by Dorothy (1885) and by his wife Mary (1889).

Index

Stay in touch with us!

ROUGH*NEWS* **is Rough Guides' free newsletter. In four issues a year we give you news, travel issues, music reviews, readers' letters and the latest dispatches from authors on the road.**

I would like to receive ROUGH*NEWS*: please put me on your free mailing list.

NAME . . . .

ADDRESS . . . .

Please clip or photocopy and send to: Rough Guides, 62–70 Shorts Gardens, London WC2H 9AB, England or Rough Guides, 375 Hudson Street, New York, NY 10014, USA.

ROUGH GUIDES: Travel

AVAILABLE AT ALL GOOD BOOKSHOPS

ROUGH GUIDES: Mini Guides, Travel Specials and Phrasebooks

MINI GUIDES

Antigua
Bangkok
Barbados
Big Island of
  Hawaii
Boston
Brussels
Budapest

Sydney
Tokyo
Toronto

Dublin
Edinburgh
Florence
Honolulu
Jerusalem
Lisbon
London
  Restaurants
Madrid
Maui
Melbourne
New Orleans
Rome
Seattle
St Lucia

TRAVEL SPECIALS

First-Time Asia
First-Time
  Europe
Women Travel

PHRASEBOOKS

Czech
Dutch

Egyptian Arabic
European
French
German
Greek
Hindi & Urdu
Hungarian
Indonesian
Italian
Japanese

Mandarin
  Chinese
Mexican
  Spanish
Polish
Portuguese
Russian
Spanish
Swahili
Thai
Turkish
Vietnamese

AVAILABLE AT ALL GOOD BOOKSHOPS

NORTH SOUTH TRAVEL

DISCOUNT FARES

PROFITS TO CHARITIES

- North South Travel is a friendly, competitive travel agency, offering discou l-wide.
- North South Travel's profits contribute to community projects in the d
- We have special experience of booking destinations in Africa, Asia an.
- Clients who book through North South Travel include exchangets and independent travellers, as well as charities, church organisation businesses.

To discuss your booking requirements: contact Brenda Skinner between 9am and 5pm, Monday to Friday, on (01245) 492 882: Fax (01245) 356 612, any time. Or write to: North South Travel Limited, Moulsham Mill Centre, Parkway, Chelmsford, Essex CM2 7PX, UK

Help us to help others – Your travel can make a difference